The German Operation at Anzio

A STUDY OF THE
GERMAN OPERATIONS
AT ANZIO BEACHHEAD
FROM 22 JAN 44 TO 31 MAY 44

Produced at
GMDS
by a combined
British, Canadian, and U.S.
Staff
APR 9 1946

Published by Books Express Publishing
Copyright © Books Express, 2011
ISBN 978-1-78039-562-3

Books Express publications are available from all good retail and online booksellers. For
publishing proposals and direct ordering please contact us at: info@books-express.com

TABLE OF CONTENTS

PREFACE   PAGE   1

INTRODUCTION   PAGES   2- 9

DAILY ACCOUNTS OF THE BATTLE OF ANZIO
     22 JANUARY TO 31 MAY 1944   PAGES 10-119

SUMMARY   PAGES 120-122

ANNEX I:
          ORDER OF BATTLE OF GERMAN, AND
          ALLIED DIVISIONS   PAGES 123-124

ANNEX II:
          GERMAN TACTICAL SYMBOLS   PAGES 125-126

ANNEX III:
          DESCRIPTION OF GERMAN UNITS   PAGE 127

ANNEX IV:
          DESCRIPTION OF GERMAN ARMOR   PAGE 128

THE GERMAN OPERATION AT ANZIO

Page 5, line 45 should read:

preparations. Detailed orders, determined which troops the armies and the

Page 15, line 25 should read:

command in the sector Cecina (south of Livorno)-Terracina. At this

Page 17, line 30 and 31 should read:

with the first Artillery Battalion and the reinforced 955th Infantry
Regiment. As the staff of the 4th Parachute Division

Page 18, line 2 should read:

LI Mountain Corps took over the coastal sector north of the

Page 21, line 20 should read:

defensive front from Isola Bella to bench mark 45 (3 km southeast) –

Page 28, line 9 should read:

Estimate of the Situation Sent by Fourteenth Army to the

Page 29, last line should read:

the enemy should be rolled up in a northerly direction.

Page 33, line 14 should read:

Therefore, our 85 batteries are opposed by 59 Allied batteries.

Page 35, line 21 and 22 should read:

battalion, Panzer Company "Schwelbach" (Tiger tanks) currently
with the 3d Panzer Grenadier Division, and one Panzer company

Page 36, line 30 should read:

line along the road 1 km east of Cantoniera (F 880353). Divisionary
    attempts

Page 36, line 33 should read:

In spite of heavy defensive fire by artillery and naval guns, the attack–

Page 37, line 2, 3, and 4 should read:

Army Reserves with the I Parachute Corps are: three battalions of the
4th Parachute Division; with the LXXVI Panzer Corps are 2d Battalion
of the 194th Grenadier Regiment, and the

Page 38, line 25 should read:

The alleged mission of this unit is an attack against Littoria (G 0818).

Page 40, line 15 should read:

The I Parachute Corps was organized as follows:

Page 88, line 6 should read:

Orvieto. The 103d Reconnaissance Battalion has been dispatched

Page 90, lines 16 – 17 should read:

The coastal defense sector north of Castiglione (west of Grosseto) up to Cecina was separated from the Fourteenth Army.

Page 108, line 32 should read:

company; one Tiger Company; Regiment Staff 145th Grenadier Regiment

Page 112, line 14 – 16 should read:

lery bombardments: All guns except 6 Field Howitzers 15 cm of 671st Artillery Regiment 715th Infantry Division and the 3d Battalion Artillery Demonstration Regiment were lost,

Page 119, line 10 should read:

4th Moroccan Mountain Division (FF)

Page 127, line 23 should read:

infantry battalions, except that it has more mobility through

Page 41, line 41 should read:

Genzano (towns excluded). Raids by this division will be

Page 44, line 21 should read:

An enemy attack on Aprilia was expected, and therefore, the

Page 49, line 51 should read:

3 to 4 km northeast of Cle Buon Riposo (F 853310) has been reconfirmed.

Page 52, line 43 should read:

The 65th Infantry Division and the 4th Parachute Division

Page 54, line 16 should read:

Division and the 114th Jäger Division. The initial objective

Page 58, line 43 should read:

of Hill 67, 2km west of Cle Buon Riposo (F 853310), was

Page 59, line 8 should read:

A line, just north of Highway 82 (at F 875284) was reached

Page 61, line 21 should read:

The 362d Division which has been transferred from the coast defense sector

Page 61, line 55 should read:

and Le Ferriere (F 963242) , is expected. Increased counterattacks,

Page 62, line 13 should read:

the Gorge Campo di Carne (F 853300), the southwest edge

Page 67, line 30 should read:

the 10th and 11th Parachute Regiments began an attack to

Page 71, line 15 should read:

Division (US) was confirmed to be in the area of the Leschione

Page 75, line 18 should read:

"Today's (29 February) successes did not meet our

Page 78, line 49 should read:

the road crossing Campo di Carne (F 863286). Prisoners

Page 82, line 33 should read:

antiaircraft regiment and Panzer regiment, were sent to the new

Page 85, line 48 should read:

1st Infantry Division (Br)

ITALY   1:100,000.

For use by
War and Navy Department Agencies only
Not for sale or distribution

LITTORIA

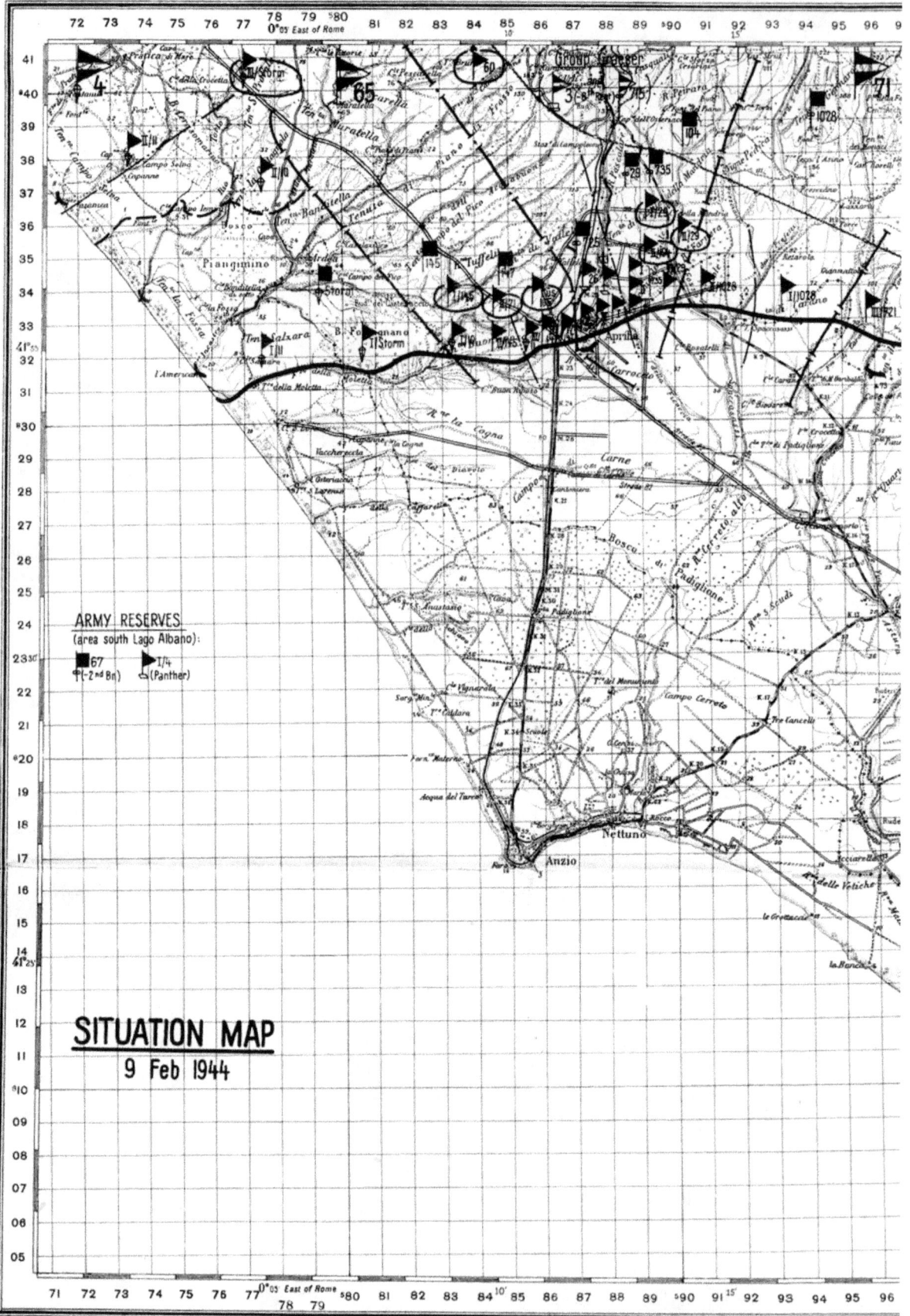

SITUATION MAP
9 Feb 1944

ARMY RESERVES
(area south Lago Albano):

■67   ▷I/4
(-2nd Bn)   (Panther)

Group Graeser

Anzio

Nettuno

Aprilia

GSGS 4164.
First GSGS Edition (AMS 1), 1941.
Second GSGS Edition (AMS 2), 1943.

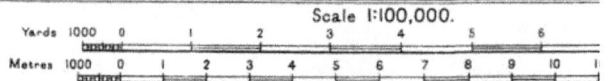

Scale 1:100,000.

Yards 1000 0   1   2   3   4   5   6

Metres 1000 0 1 2 3 4 5 6 7 8 9 10

PREFACE

The following study of German operations against the Allied beachhead at Anzio, from 22 January to 31 May 1944, is based on the available journals and records of the German Tenth and Fourteenth Armies. It should be noted that the facts and opinions expressed in the text reflect the German point of view, all statements on Allied troop strength, are German estimates.

Records of the German Air Force were not available, therefore the details of air action against the beachhead has not been included.

The expressions, tanks, armored, (Panzer), light motorized infantry, (Jäger), and armored infantry, (Panzer Grenadier), have been left in the German for purposes of clarification. German tactical symbols, for German units, have been used on all maps; a brief glossary of symbols will be found at the end of this publication.

The enclosed maps of the Anzio area are old editions, and do not include newly constructed habitations and roads. Grid coordinates in the text refer to Map of Italy, sheet 158 (Littoria), GSGS 4164 second edition, 1943, scale 1: 100,000.

Italy's capitulation on 9 September 1943, and the resulting surrender of the Italian Armed Forces gave rise to many problems for the German High Command. Chief among these was the question of how much territory the German High Command should strive to hold, i.e., at what point the Allied offensive would have to be halted. The surprise landings on the "toe" of Italy and at Salerno, coupled with rapid advances, led to the fall of the large airbases, such as Foggia. This left the High Command with the twofold task of securing the Po Basin with its great political, economic, and military significance, as well as the politically important region of Rome. A line of defense had to be established in the mountains of central Italy. How far to the south it could be established would depend upon the availability of troops. However, due to the number, condition, and distribution of German troops, at the time, an advantageous realization of this task was not possible.

In southern Italy, Marshal Kesselring, the Commander in Chief South, commanded eight divisions, mostly motorized or armored, which were fighting opposite seventeen Allied divisions. A portion of these German units had come from Africa and had not yet been brought back to full strength; the other part consisted of reactivated divisions from the eastern front. These forces had also been weakened during their retreat through southern Italy. Therefore, they could not be expected to establish a firm defense line, if the Allies should continue their concentrated offensive to the North.

Northern Italy was occupied by Army Group B under the command of Marshal Rommel. This Army Group comprised thirteen divisions, which had arrived in Italy shortly before or during the capitulation. These units were, for the most part, reorganized or reactivated divisions from the Eastern front. Due to the immobility of these units, and the lack of equipment, they were not suitable for combat duty in the south, as long as the front had not become stabilized.

The Commander in Chief South was directed to fight an initial delaying action with the forces available to him. Army Group B was left in northern Italy to secure the coast, and to devote itself to the fortification of the northern Apennines in case of a rapid loss of central Italy. In the beginning of October, the Commander in Chief South succeeded in establishing a thin line of resistance from Naples to Termoli. On 10 October 1943, the German High Command ordered the Commander in Chief South to continue these tactics up to the line, Gaeta to Ortona, and to make a stand in this advantageous mountain position (Bernhard or Gustav position). To bolster his forces, two infantry divisions of Army Group B were transferred to the Commander in Chief South. Simultaneously, he was charged with the task of securing the coast in the region of Rome. Army Group B was ordered to pacify its zone against partisan activities, especially the Istrian peninsula, and to set up strongpoints for coastal security. For these tasks, nine divisions were left at the disposal of Army Group B; two of its divisions having been transferred to the Commander in Chief South, and two to the Eastern Front. There were constant threats of an Allied invasion in central Italy, which would bring the front in southern Italy to a state of collapse. Therefore, Army Group B was ordered to consolidate an Apennine defensive line, south of Bologna, and to

NORTHWESTERN ALPS

ALPINE APPROACHES

CG OPER ZONE

188 REPL

CG OPER ZONE

14

○MILANO

BRESLIA   14

PLENIPOT. REPRES.

○VERONA

90

VENICE

GORZIZA

162

TRIESTE

ADRIATIC

COASTAL

FIUM   71

POLA

REGION

LXXXVII

○PARMA

356   334

GENOA

○BOLOGNA

RAVENNA

LA SPEZIA   LI

WITHOUT   CESENA

162

APENNINE LINE

RIMINI

PESARO

PISTOIA

371   FLORENCE

○LIVORNO

ANCONA

○CIVITANOVA

○PERUGIA

PIOMBINO

14 TH ARMY

○TODI

10 TH ARMY

ORBETELLO

C in C SOUTH WEST
ARMY GP "C"

PESCARA

ORTONA

LXXVI   65

16

10

○AVEZZANO

78(BR)

8(IND)

51(BR)

1(CAN)

5(BR)

ROME   XI

3

HG

XIV   305

26

29

15

94

ANZIO

1

34(AM)

45(AM)

3(AM)

56(BR)

7(BR)

46(BR)

GAETA

1

ORDER OF BATTLE IN ITALY
AS OF 21 NOV 1943

NAPLES

1(BR)

6(BR)

50(BR)

82(AM)

1(AM)S

36(AM)

make preperations for its occupation.

Until the end of November, the situation was further stabilized. On 21 November 1943, Marshal Kesselring acquired the title Commander in Chief Southwest, and took over command of the entire Italian theater. The Commander in Chief Southwest was responsible for all military action in Italy. The High Command of Army Group C, was activated to assume charge over all the Army units remaining in Italy, and constituted the staff for the Commander in Chief Southwest. It did not command the Navy and Air Force, but controlled units of the Air Force fighting on land, and was charged with administration in the zone of operations. Rommel and the High Command of Army Group B was shifted to France.

At the time of the appointment of the Commander in Chief Southwest, two armies were formed under Army Group C the Chief of Staff being Brigadier General Westphal. The distribution of these forces is shown in map number 1.

Tenth Army

Commander:	General von Vietinghoff
Chief of Staff:	Colonel Wentzell, GSC
Area:	Central Italy
Units:	14th Armored Corps
	76th Armored Corps
	Ten divisions

To the rear, the army boundary followed the line Piombino to Porto Civitanova. The area of Terracina-Rome-Orbetello, was not part of this zone; it was administered by the XI Air Force Corps which was directly under the Army Group.

Fourteenth Army*

Commander:	General von Mackensen
Chief of Staff:	Colonel Hauser, GSC
Area:	Northern Italy
Units:	87th Army Corps
	51st Mountain Corps
	Nine divisions (only two qualified for combat)
Operational Zones:	
	Adriatic Coastal Region under Lieutenant General Kübler
	Alpine Approaches under Lieutenant General Witthöft, who also commanded the sector, Ancona-Venice on the east coast

* Its staff had been formed in part, from Rommel's Army Group B headquarters.

The following is a translation of a teletype understanding reached between the Armed Forces High Command (OKW) and Marshal Graziani, showing Germany's relationship with the new Italian Republican Government:

1. It is essential that Italy will continue to make extensive contributions in the continuation of the war. For that, it is necessary that:

    a. the German occupied part of Italy shall not be treated as enemy territory, but as a friendly country;

- 3 -

b. and, the authority and independence of the Italian (Republican) government shall be established and maintained.

2. In this spirit, the zone of operations shall be confined to an area of 35 miles, behind the front in central Italy, and to the frontier regions in the North where the lines of communication to France and Germany must be protected.

The remainder of the country will be administered by the Italian Government. Zones of operations at the coast have been designated, but only at the time of an enemy landing will the German Armed Forces take over the administration from the Italians.

A Plenipotentiary Representative for the German Armed Forces in Italy (General of the Infantry Toussaint) is appointed for the territory administered by the Italian government. He is directly subordinate to the German Armed Forces High Command. His main tasks are:

a. to represent the interests of the German Armed Forces with the Italian government, and insure that their demands are carried through by the Italian government or its subordinate authorities;

b. and to lend support to the Italian government and its authorities, as far as necessary, in the execution of governmental measures and in their relations with the German troops.

3. The defense of the line Gaeta-Ortona has a decisive significance in the continuation of the common struggle. With the loss of Rome, Italy would cease to be a belligerent country on the side of the Axis. Consequently, all auxiliary forces of the country have to be mobilized to protect the deep flanks and long shorelines, in order to free the German forces as much as possible for employment at the front. Units of the Army, the Navy, and the Air Force are to utilize Italian volunteers without restrictions.

4. The reactivation of large Italian formations is to be carried out in Army Training Centers outside of Italy.

The outstanding consideration was the apparent small number of German troops in Italy, and the relative equality in strength between the Tenth and the Fourteenth Armies. Tactically, this was not to be expected, but there were several reasons for such distribution. Because of events in the East, and the necessity to prepare against an invasion in the West, the German High Command was in no position to substantially strengthen the forces in Italy. The uncertainty regarding new Allied landings, the political unrest, and the resistance movement in northern Italy, forced the High Command to leave a large number of available forces in northern Italy. Therefore, until the Allied invasion of Normandy, only two divisions were assigned to the Fourteenth Army. Its other components were made-up from divisions in rest or reactivated divisions, from training and replacement units, and numerous smaller formations, namely, fortress battalions, security battalions, etc. As soon as a division of the Fourteenth Army reached full combat strength, it was assigned to the Tenth Army and exchanged for a battle-weary division. This lead to a constant exchange of units between the two armies, and enabled the Germans to continue the defense at the front with

relatively few divisions. On the other hand, this procedure put
a heavy load on the communications system in Italy, which had
been greatly incapacitated by Allied air attacks as well as slow-
ing up the defense preparations along the coasts. Under these
circumstances, the Fourteenth Army was forced to act as a reser-
voir of forces for the front. It also had to carry out its
mission of fortifying the coast and pacifying the country with
weak and untrained units.

Until the landing at Anzio, and even up to the time of the
Normandy invasion, the preparations for the coastal defense of
Italy had primary importance. By means of small and poorly
equipped air reconnaissance units, and other intelligence sources,
an estimate of the available Allied reserves and shipping could
be made. Nevertheless, the German command was not informed as
to the actual preparations and target areas for a landing. Landings were possible on a tactical scale in support of the existing Italian front, or on a strategical scale with the aim to
cut-off the entire Army Group. Thus, the entire Italian coast
was under constant threat. Five defense sectors, centered
around Genoa, Livorno, Rome, Rimini-Ravenna, and Istria, were
formed because various coastal sectors were suitable as possible
landing points. These defense sectors were fortified and reinforced with the available forces. The shoreline between these
sectors was guarded by small units and obstacles. In October,
the Fourteenth Army began to consolidate, the Gothic Line, a
land defense line across the Apennines between La Spezia and
Pesaro, and the Voralpen Line, in the Alps from the Swiss frontier to Istria. In the case of a successful Allied landing, these
lines would provide prepared defensive positions in the rear of
the central Italian front.

The number of German troops in Italy was barely sufficient
to hold the southern front, as well as to strengthen the rear
areas. In the case of an enemy landing, reinforcements would
have to be dispatched from adjacent theaters, and from Germany
proper, in order to prevent a collapse of the Army Group. In
preparation for this the German High Command, at the end of
December 1943, issued orders to the Commander in Chief West
(France and Lowlands), the Commander in Chief Southeast
(Balkans), and the Commander of the Replacement Army, specifying the units that were to be transferred to Italy in the event
of a landing. Thus, the prompt arrival of reinforcements was
assured to the Commander in Chief Southwest. Until their arrival,
the Commander in Chief Southwest was directed to throw his own
forces into the struggle. The Army Group had made extensive
preparations. Detailed orders, which troops the armies and the
independent corps were to dispatch to the endangered defense
sector, in the case of an Allied landing; in this regrouping,
only the combat units and the essential service troops for these
units were to be transferred. The rest would remain in situ and
secure their sectors. For deceptive purposes, the various defense
sectors used code designations. (See Map No. 2.) The Army Group
assigned a timetable for alerting and redeploying specific units;
it issued directives to alerted units, specifying the march and
convoy routes, and the location of dumps for gasoline, munitions,
and rations. It also assigned troops to road and bridge repair,
and provided for communications during the march. Emergency units
were formed by all rear area troops to combat possible airborne
attacks.

Units were to be ready to march or load within eight to twelve
hours after the alert had been received. With the alert the code
name of the landing place was to be issued, so that each unit could

proceed according to the prescribed schedule and along the proper route.

Army Group C was fully aware of the inadequate shore fortifications, and of the paucity of occupation forces at the coast. The Army Group considered it unlikely that it would be able to repulse a major enemy landing, since reinforcements would not immediately be available. This was also realized by the German High Command, and constant efforts were made to strengthen endangered coastal sectors; additional coastal artillery was set up, obstacles were constructed, and specific areas were mined and inundated.

The extent to which the coast was defended relied on the military situation on the Tenth Army front. If an Allied offensive caused an emergency on the southern front, new units were dispatched from northern Italy. They were replaced by a battle-weary unit, and this tended to weaken the coastal defenses. Since this played a decisive role in the success of the Anzio landing, a review of the situation at the Tenth Army front in the months preceding the landing follows.

November and December 1943, were characterized by extremely bitter defensive action by the Tenth Army. By tenacious defense and by repeated local counterattacks the front was held, and the retreat to the prepared Gaeta-Ortona position was delayed. Thus, valuable time was gained to consolidate this line (Bernhard or Gustav position), and later proved extremely advantageous.

Allied tactics along the front were partly responsible for the success of the relatively weak Tenth Army. Since the attacks by the American Fifth Army alternated with the attacks by the British Eighth, the German Command was able to move divisions from the quiet sectors and commit them to the endangered sectors. Thus, a breakthrough was avoided. The Germans yielded territory to the British Eighth Army, so as to concentrate on the Fifth Army front. An American breakthrough would mean the loss of Rome, and a German withdrawal from central Italy. In these two months, serious emergencies developed whenever an offensive was started by one of the Allies, prior to the completion of the preceding attack by the other. German mobile operations achieved an initial success, so that at the end of 1943, the battle was still being waged in front of the line, Gaeta-Ortona. The motorized and armored divisions of the Tenth Army underwent terrific strain, since they were continually engaged in active sectors and had little time for rest and repair. During November and December, strong materiel and personnel reinforcements had to be injected to prevent a disintegration of the Tenth Army. To keep the strength of the Army at its former level, it became necessary to increase the number of divisions. The serious situation in Russia did not permit a transfer of divisions to a secondary theater. Army Group C was forced to release some of its own troops for the front, and thereby weaken its forces in northern Italy.

The only three divisions of the Fourteenth Army fit for combat, the 44th Infantry Division, the 90th Panzer Grenadier Division, and the 334th Infantry Division were transferred to the Tenth Army. To counteract this loss in the north, the battle-weary 65th Infantry Division was taken out of the front at Ortona, and assigned to northern Italy. In addition, the activation of the 278th Infantry Division, and the 16 SS Panzer Grenadier Division was ordered. The German High Command directed the Fourteenth Army to release the 371st Infantry Division for use in Russia, so that eight divisions were left with this Army. Since none of these divisions had full combat strength, the coastal defenses in

ALPINE APPROACHES

NORTHWESTERN ALPS

MILANO

C6 OPER ZONE

PLENIPOT. REPRES.

14

OVERONA

REPL

REPL

REPL

188 REPL

SECURITY

C6 OPER ZONE

16 SS in ACTIVATION

REPL

U62

ADRIATIC

TRIESTE

COASTAL

FIUME

114 FROM CinC

SOUTH EAST TO 14th ARMY

POLA

REGION

OPADUR

VENICE 52 Mi

LXXXVII

356

65

65th ARRIVING FROM 10th ARMY

GENOA

13 Mi

58

FORTRESS BRIG

LA SPEZIA

LI

53 Mi

LUCCA

FLORENCE

LIVORNO

110 Mi

PIOMBINO

ELBA

278 in ACTIVATION

BOLOGNA

362

ARENNA

CESENA

RIMINI

APENNINE LINE

130 Mi

ANCONA 39 Mi

PORTO CIVITANOVA

71

TO 10 ARMY

73 Mi

AREZZO

PERUGIA

FOLIGNO

TODI

ORVIETO

ORBETELLO

78 Mi

CinC SOUTH WEST ARMY GP "C"

BRACCIANO

3rd PZ GREN DIV

ROME

1

SGM PZ GREN DIV

TO ROME

10

(REMAINDER)

LXXVI

334

51

26

GRUPP HRUK

305

VELLETRI

29th PZ GREN DIV

29th PZ GREN DIV

XIV

ANZIO

29th

62 Mi

15

GAETA

NAPLES

3

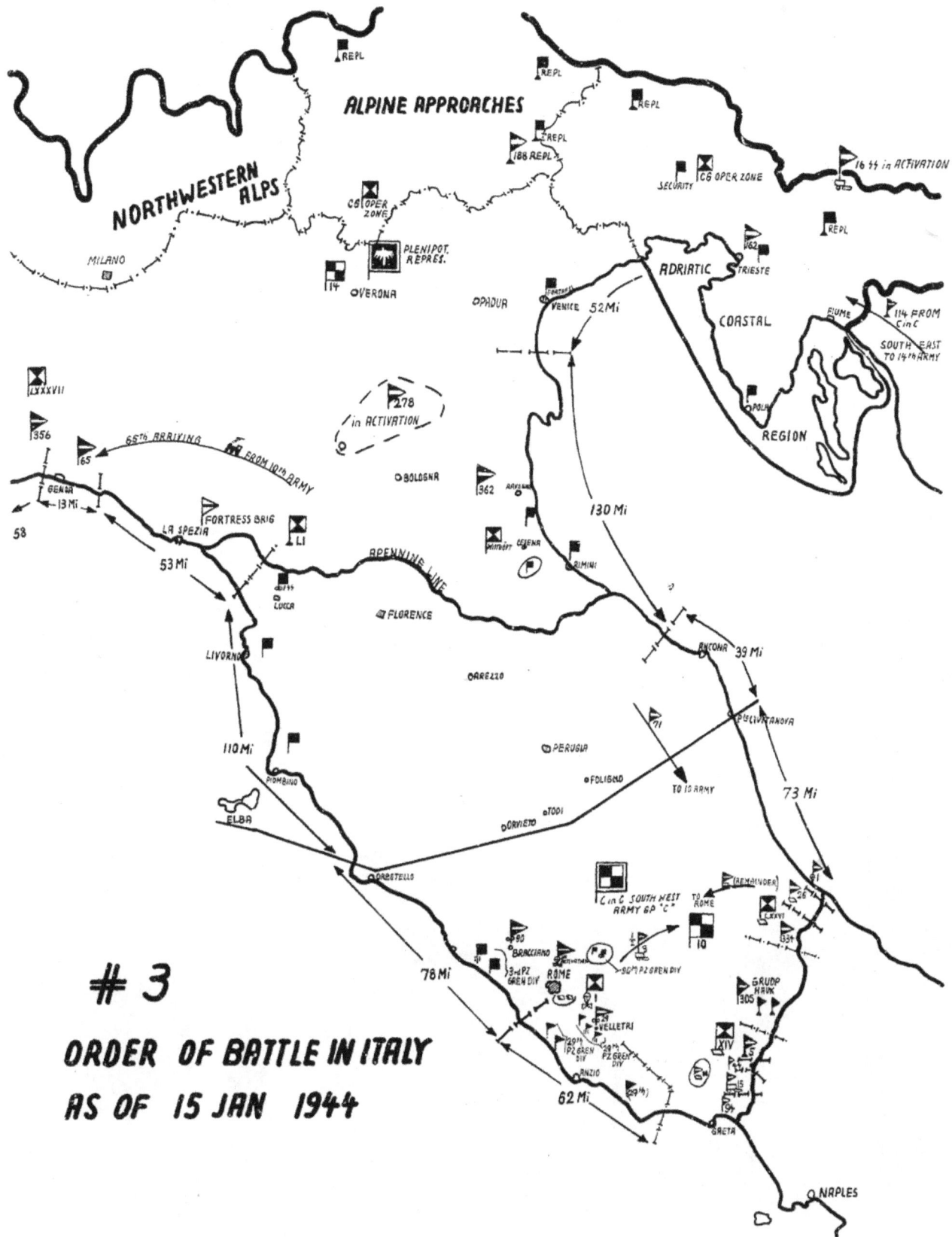

ORDER OF BATTLE IN ITALY
AS OF 15 JAN 1944

northern Italy were decidedly weakened.

The unfavorable results of continuous emergencies at the front were plainly revealed by the situation in the sector west of Rome. A landing in the rear of the Tenth Army in support of the offensive at the front, had always been considered a possibility. Therefore, the task of securing the coast near Rome had a special significance. The Fourteenth Army could not assume this additional assignment. A further weakening of northern Italy was not dared, inasmuch as the German High Command was uncertain about the intentions of the Allies, such as landings at Rome, Gulf of Genoa, and Istria. As a result, troops from the Tenth Army were used to secure the coastal sector near Rome. This area was commanded by the 1st Parachute Corps operating directly under the Army Group.

Existing documents, of the Army Group and of the Tenth Army, revealed the constant conflict between the demands of the Army for reinforcements at the front and the necessity of maintaining a strong occupation force along the coast in the Rome sector.

Since no division, fit for combat, could be spared from the front, only battle-weakened units were employed in the Rome sector. At the beginning of November, with the aggravation of the situation at the front, merely one division could be released at a time. After a short rest period near Rome, the division would be sent back to the front. The continual flow of units that ensued, caused defensive preparations along the coast to be neglected, at the time of the Anzio landings.

The offensive activities of the Allies slackened. At the beginning of the new year, the Tenth Army planned a regrouping, in order to rest exhausted divisions and to strengthen coastal defenses in its area. It was planned to retire the Panzer Division "Hermann Göring" (HG) and the 29th Panzer Grenadier Division from the Cassino front. The 29th Panzer Grenadier Division was to be assigned to the coastal sector at Rome, to replace the 3d Panzer Grenadier Division. The latter was to be transferred to the Adriatic sector on the left flank of the Tenth Army, where the 90th Panzer Grenadier Division was to be relieved for employment in the coastal sector, Pescara-Ancona, and the 26th Panzer Division as a reserve behind the front. The requirements of this scheme could not be met because new attacks by the Allies at Cassino and on the Adriatic coast tied-up the German forces, so that only the Panzer Division "Hermann Göring" and the 90th Panzer Grenadier Division could be removed from their respective sectors. Consequently, a large part of the 3d Panzer Grenadier Division remained in the region of Rome, pending relief by the 29th Panzer Grenadier Division.

At the beginning of January, a new tenseness arose, when various signs pointed to an impending Allied landing. Air and ground reconnaissance revealed troops and ships assembling in the region of Naples. Another indication was the fact that the offensive actions of the Allies against the Tenth Army changed to strong holding attacks. Since intelligence as to the date and place of an Allied landing was lacking, preparations for the defense of all the threatened coastal sectors, were speeded up. Consequently, the Army Group modified its plan for regrouping, but ordered the transfer of the 90th Panzer Grenadier Division from the east coast to the region of Rome. The transfer of this division was delayed by continued British Eighth Army attacks west of Ortona and by transportation difficulties in the mountains due to the weather. By 15 January, only half the division had arrived in the vicinity of Rome. Numerous difficulties were encountered in relieving the 29th Panzer Grenadier Division from

Cassino. The distribution of the German forces in Italy on 15 January 1943 is shown on Map No. 3.

At this critical stage, the preparations of the American Fifth Army for the offensive at the Garigliano River became manifest. Since 13 January, the Allies had been observed regrouping troops south of Cassino. At first, the intentions of these moves were not apparent. However, during the following days, up until 17 January, Allied air attacks at the Garigliano sector increased, and the registration fire of newly emplaced batteries was observed. The German command was now convinced that a major Allied attack at the Garigliano was imminent.

According to reconnaissance reports at Army Group, the Allies had enough forces at their disposal to simultaneously launch a landing and a new offensive. This assumption, coupled with the observation of increased naval activity in the region of Naples, excluded the advisability of removing reserves from the region of Rome, in order to oppose the coming offensive at the Garigliano. Therefore, the Army Group resolved to denude all sectors of the front not immediately threatened, especially the Adriatic sector, and hastily to transfer the 3d Panzer Grenadier Division to the south. The bulk of the Panzer Division "Hermann Göring" was still available as a reserve, and thus a weakening of the Rome sector could be avoided. Originally the German High Command had ordered the latter division to be transferred to France on 20 January. As its replacement, the 71st Division was on the way from Istria. This would further strengthen the southern flank of the Tenth Army, which until the arrival of all these units considered itself able to bridge the crisis by committing all available local reserves.

On 18 January 1944, the expected offensive of the American Fifth Army against the Garigliano started. The attacker gained initial successes by a surprise landing of strong forces west of the mouth of this river. In heavy fighting on February 18 and 19, the Allies crossed the lower Garigliano on a wide front. It appeared that the German front in the south would collapse. The bulk of the Panzer Division "Hermann Göring" and all local reserves had already been committed in action, and the arrival of the 3d Panzer Grenadier Division and 71st Infantry Division could not be expected before 22 January. New measures had to be taken in order to prevent an Allied breakthrough.

In spite of the threat of an Allied invasion in central or northern Italy, the Army Group now decided to deplete the coast west of Rome except for small security units. Thus, two divisions, the 29th and 90th Panzer Grenadier Divisions, were designated to conduct a counterattack at the Garigliano under the command of the 1st Parachute Corps. The Army Group foresaw a quick success in this action. This would release at the earliest possible moment the forces required to secure the coast near Rome. It was also estimated that a successful counterattack at the Garigliano might interrupt preparations and delay a possible Allied landing. However, an Allied breakthrough south of Cassino was regarded as dangerous as a successful landing near Rome. The issue was to settle the immediate crisis first. For this purpose, the German High Command gave the go-ahead signal to launch the counterattack, thereby committing reserves of the Rome area.

In execution of this order, a redeployment of troops began on the evening of 19 January. Forty-eight hours later, on the eve of the landings at Anzio, the 29th and 90th Panzer Grenadier Divisions, under the command of the 1st Parachute Corps, were in position for a counterattack at the Garigliano. At this time, there were only small contingents of the 29th and 90th Panzer Grenadier Divisions left to secure the coast west of Rome, a sector nearly 100 miles long, stretching from Terracina through Anzio to Civitavecchia. A little further to the rear laid the newly activated 4th Parachute Division, which had not been brought up to strength, and a few tank and antitank companies. All these units were under the direct control of the Army Group, after the 1st Parachute Corps had been placed under the command of the Tenth Army.

The coastal sector west of Rome was greatly weakened and was believed unable to effectively resist an amphibious operation. According to estimates, an Allied landing in this sector would bring the southern front to a state of collapse, since there were no reserves available to oppose such an operation. However, since the start of the Allied offensive at the Garigliano, no further intelligence about preparations for a landing had been obtained, and the German Command believed that the crisis had been averted.

I. 22 JANUARY 1944 to 25 JANUARY 1944

Allied landings at Anzio in the morning of 22 January came as a surprise to the German High Command, and confronted the German defense at its weakest point, in respect to time and place. Army Group C had believed in the possibility of an Allied landing because concentrations of troops, and ships had been reported between Naples and Sicily since 13 January. However, pending the outcome of the operations on the Garigliano river, the execution of an amphibious landing seemed improbable. This opinion was further supported by the belief that the German counterattack from the right flank of the Tenth Army would create a crisis. This would delay a planned landing. Heavy air raids on the railways and roads in central and northern Italy could not be interpreted as preparations for a landing, since it was also possible that these raids were intended to cut the Tenth Army supply lines.

In view of the threatening Allied breakthrough at the Garigliano river, Army Group C had withdrawn combat forces from the Rome area and transferred them to the south for the counterattack. The only units remaining in the Rome area were battle-fatigued, and not prepared for offensive warfare. The strength of the troops remaining in the area west of Rome was so small that they could merely be employed for coastal observation in the Tarquinia-Terracina sector. Units were committed along the coast as follows:

Sector Tarquinia – Mouth of the Tiber: 46 miles long.

Two battalions of the 90th Panzer Grenadier Division were located on the coast, and one battalion in the rear, at Lake Bracciano. The following Italian coast artillery was available: two antiaircraft guns (7.6 cm), twelve light howitzers (10 cm), twelve heavy howitzers (15 cm), eight guns (7.5 cm), and six guns (10.5).

Sector Mouth of the Tiber – Anzio – Mouth of the Astura: 41 miles long.

The following units were located on the coast: two engineer companies of the 4th Parachute Division, one engineer company of the 29th Panzer Grenadier Division, and one Panzer Grenadier battalion, of the 29th Panzer Grenadier Division. The following coast artillery was available: one howitzer (7.5 cm), seven howitzers (10 cm), eleven howitzers (15 cm), three guns (7.5 cm), eight guns (10 cm), two guns (10.5 cm), three guns (15.5 cm), and six guns (17 cm).

Sector Mouth of the Astura – Terracina: 32 miles long.

The Reconnaissance Battalion of the 29th Panzer Grenadier Division was employed for coastal observation. The following coast artillery was available: four antiaircraft guns (7.5 cm), five antiaircraft guns (9 cm), two howitzers (10 cm), two guns (7.6 cm), four guns (10.5 cm), two guns (12.2 cm), and two guns (15.2 cm).

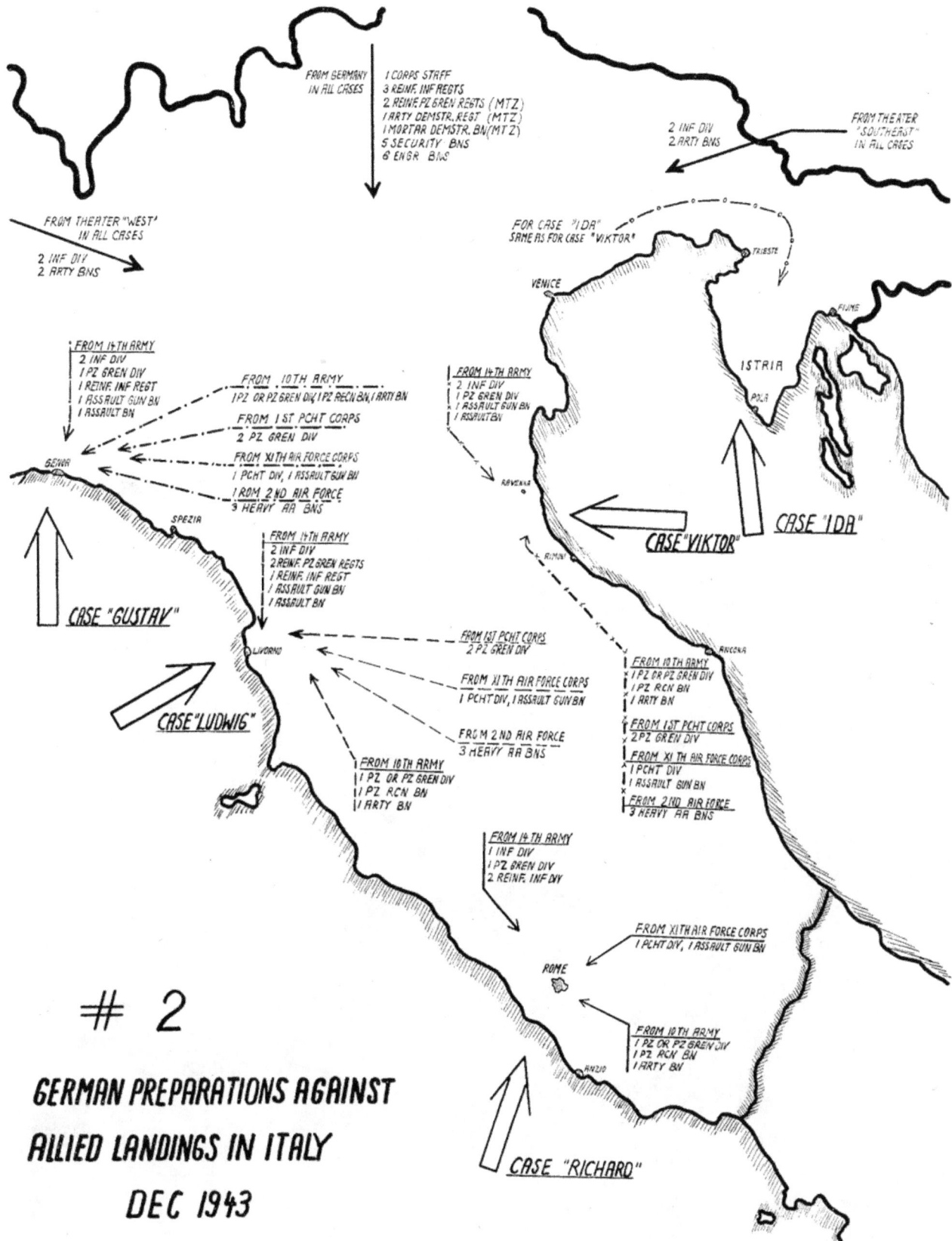

FROM GERMANY
IN ALL CASES
1 CORPS STAFF
3 REINF. INF. REGTS
2 REINF. PZ. GREN. REGTS (MTZ.)
1 ARTY. DEMSTR. REGT. (MTZ.)
1 MORTAR DEMSTR. BN. (MTZ.)
5 SECURITY BNS.
6 ENGR. BNS.

2 INF. DIV
2 ARTY. BNS

FROM THEATER "SOUTHEAST" IN ALL CASES

FOR CASE "IDA"
SAME AS FOR CASE "VIKTOR"

FROM THEATER "WEST" IN ALL CASES
2 INF. DIV
2 ARTY. BNS

TRIESTE

VENICE

ISTRIA

POLA

FIUME

FROM 14TH ARMY
2 INF. DIV
1 PZ. GREN. DIV
1 REINF. INF. REGT
1 ASSAULT GUN BN
1 ASSAULT BN

FROM 10TH ARMY
1 PZ. OR PZ. GREN. DIV, 1 PZ. RECN. BN, 1 ARTY. BN

FROM 1ST PCHT. CORPS
2 PZ. GREN. DIV

FROM XI TH AIR FORCE CORPS
1 PCHT. DIV, 1 ASSAULT GUN BN

FROM 2ND AIR FORCE
3 HEAVY AA BNS

FROM 14TH ARMY
2 INF. DIV
1 PZ. GREN. DIV
1 ASSAULT GUN BN
1 ASSAULT BN

RAVENNA

CASE "VIKTOR"

CASE "IDA"

GENOA

SPEZIA

CASE "GUSTAV"

FROM 14TH ARMY
2 INF. DIV
2 REINF. PZ. GREN. REGTS
1 REINF. INF. REGT
1 ASSAULT GUN BN
1 ASSAULT BN

LIVORNO

FROM 1ST PCHT. CORPS
2 PZ. GREN. DIV

FROM XI TH AIR FORCE CORPS
1 PCHT. DIV, 1 ASSAULT GUN BN

FROM 2ND AIR FORCE
3 HEAVY AA BNS

RIMINI

ANCONA

FROM 10TH ARMY
1 PZ. OR PZ. GREN. DIV
1 PZ. RCN. BN
1 ARTY. BN

FROM 1ST PCHT. CORPS
2 PZ. GREN. DIV

FROM XI TH AIR FORCE CORPS
1 PCHT. DIV
1 ASSAULT GUN BN

FROM 2ND AIR FORCE
3 HEAVY AA BNS

CASE "LUDWIG"

FROM 10TH ARMY
1 PZ. OR PZ. GREN. DIV
1 PZ. RCN. BN
1 ARTY. BN

FROM 14TH ARMY
1 INF. DIV
1 PZ. GREN. DIV
2 REINF. INF. DIV

FROM XI TH AIR FORCE CORPS
1 PCHT. DIV, 1 ASSAULT GUN BN

ROME

FROM 10TH ARMY
1 PZ. OR PZ. GREN. DIV
1 PZ. RCN. BN
1 ARTY. BN

ANZIO

CASE "RICHARD"

2

GERMAN PREPARATIONS AGAINST
ALLIED LANDINGS IN ITALY
DEC 1943

<u>The Rome - Albanese Mountains area:</u>

One Panzer company, one Italian assault gun company, one light antiaircraft battery, units of the 4th Parachute Division, and replacement units of the Panzer Division "Hermann Göring". Units of the 4th Parachute Division and the Panzer Division "Hermann Göring" were neither completely up to strength nor trained.

As a result, Allied landing forces met practically no resistance in the morning of 22 January, and no German forces were available for an immediate counterattack. The situation was rendered more serious for the German Army, because the only headquarter in the Rome area was Army Group C Headquarters. No other staff was available to organize an emergency defense.

German air reconnaissance had failed. Neither the embarkation of invasion forces nor their approach was observed. At about 0500 Headquarters Army Group C received the first report of the landing. The basic German documents, of Army Group C and of Headquarters I Parachute Corps, outlining the course of the landing and subsequent battle are not available at present. Therefore, information about the events until the evening of 25 January, was limited to records of telephone calls between Army Group C and its armies. These notes gave the following situation until 25 January 1944, when the Fourteenth Army took over the command at the beachhead.

The critical situation at the southern flank of the Tenth Army had necessitated the commitment of all trained German reserves available in the Italian Theater. The absence of immediate German countermeasures, in the face of Allied landings south of Rome, could cut-off positions of the Tenth Army. This would lead to the collapse of the entire southern Italian front. Army Group C, recognizing this dangerous situation, intended to establish a defensive line on the beachhead as quickly as possible. At that time, it had to be assumed that the disembarking Allied forces might seize the Albanese Mountains, i.e. the key position in the area south of Rome, before sufficient German troops could be brought up for a defense. These considerations determined the necessity for a German counterattack. For this purpose, reinforcements were to be transferred to Italy from other theaters.

After the Allied landing was reported, Army Group C initiated the following measures. First, it alerted the 4th Parachute Division, which was being activated pursuant to the provisions of operation "Richard", and the replacement units of the Panzer Division "Hermann Göring", both in the Rome area. Their mission was to block all roads leading to Rome and all roads leading from the south to the Albanese Mountains. The Commandant of Rome, Brigadier General Schlemmer, was assigned to the tactical command in the landing area. Second, at 0600, Army Group C sent a report to the Armed Forces High Command that a landing took place, and requested that the task forces provided for in operation "Richard" be sent to Italy. The Armed Forces High Command ordered the following troops from other theaters to Italy. The 715th Motorized Infantry Division, the 998th Artillery Battalion (GHQ troops), the 1st Battalion, 4th Panzer Regiment, and the 301st Panzer Battalion, with remote controlled demolition vehicles, were to be transferred from the West. The Commander Southeast was to furnish the 114th Light Division (Jäger-Division), and two artillery battalions (GHQ troops). Because neither the Commander West nor the Commander Southeast could provide a second division as was planned in operation "Richard" because of the transfer of troops to Russia, the immediate activation of the 92d Infantry Division, in Italy, was ordered. The following units, from the Replacement Army in Germany, were ordered to Italy: Headquarters LXXV Corps, the Infantry Demonstration Regiment, 1026th Grenadier Regiment, 1027th Panzer Grenadier Regiment, the Artillery Demonstration Regiment, the Rocket Demonstration Battalion, three battalions of security troops, two battalions of Russian volunteers, (Ost-Bataillone), six construction battalions, and the 508th Panzer Battalion with Tiger tanks. Third, at 0710, Headquarters Army Group ordered Headquarters Fourteenth Army to transfer, to the assault area, all forces provided for in operation "Richard". The Fourteenth Army ordered the 65th Infantry Division, from Genoa (less one regiment), 362d Infantry Division, from Rimini (less one regiment), and 16th SS Panzer Grenadier Division with two regiments (one from Livorno and one from Lubiana) to proceed immediately to the beachhead. These troops left for Rome on the evening of 22 January and during the course of 23 January. Fourth, at 0830, Army Group ordered Headquarters Tenth Army to transfer the Headquarters of I Parachute Corps and all combat troops that could be spared to the beachhead as quickly as possible. Units most suitable, for release by the Tenth Army, were the 71st Infantry Division and the bulk of the 3d Panzer Grenadier Division. Only parts of these divisions were employed at the Tenth Army front, while the remainder was still on the march from the north. In addition, local reserves were also withdrawn from the southern front. Since tanks were landed at the very beginning of the Allied landing at Anzio, it was important to release antitank forces and artillery for employment at Anzio. The following troops of the Tenth Army were moved to the beachhead on 22 January and during the night of 23 January. From the area of Cassino came the 3d Panzer Grenadier Division, (less one regiment, one artillery battalion, and one engineer company); the Staff, Reconnaissance Battalion, one artillery battalion, and one antiaircraft artillery battalion of Panzer Division "Hermann Göring"; Reconnaissance Battalion of the 26th Panzer Division; Antitank Battalion (Panzerjäger) of the 71st Infantry Division; 525th Heavy Antitank Battalion (GHQ troops); 450th and 451st Light Artillery Battalions (GHQ troops); and 764th Heavy Artillery Battalion (GHQ troops). The Adriatic sector lost the 3d Battalion, 1st Regiment of the 1st Parachute Division; the Machine Gun Battalion of the 1st Parachute Division; one battalion of the tank regiment, 26th Panzer Division; and 590th Heavy Antitank Battalion (GHQ troops). Headquarters 71st Infantry Division and all elements of the 71st Infantry Division now enroute from the north to the Tenth Army were thrown into the Anzio positions. At 1700, Headquarters I Parachute Corps assumed command in the sector Tarquinia - Terracina and established a defensive line around the Allied beachhead with all available and arriving forces as they were allotted by Tenth Army.

Tenth Army units moved to the beachhead rapidly, despite enemy air raids. This was made possible by employing staff officers, available at Headquarters Army Group, Tenth Army, and Corps, to reroute the traffic. These officers had to divert troops, arriving from northern Italy and originally destined for the southern front of Tenth Army, in the direction of the beachhead. Units with no organic transportation were brought-up quickly, by the use of available supply columns. Available rear area troops were employed to clear the icy, snow-covered mountain passes.

The Allied advance on the beachhead on the first day of the landing did not conform to the German High Command's expectations. Instead of moving northward with the first wave to seize the Albanese Mountains and north-eastward with Mount Lepini as the target, the landing forces limited their objective. Their initial action was to occupy a small beachhead. This measure fully corresponded with the Allied landing plan, a copy of which had fallen into

German hands at the beginning of the operation, but German defenses and troops were insufficient to prevent further advances, had they been made. Consequently, during 22 and 23 January, the German Command had time to reinforce the defenses, so that by 24 January the beachhead was encircled, and the Allied reconnaissance patrols met German resistance.

Initially, the only available forces for the construction of a defensive line were, except for the minor detachments alerted in the Rome area, the units allocated by Tenth Army. Under the command of the I Parachute Corps, three divisional sectors were set up. Reinforcements were assigned to these sectors as they arrived. The 4th Parachute Division was in command of the Western Sector. The six infantry and two artillery battalions in this sector were hastily assembled. Their mission was, in addition to the occupation of defensive positions, to protect the coast up to the Tiber river. The 3d Panzer Grenadier Division commanded the Center Sector. This sector was to be the center of resistance, since the first objective of an Allied attack was assumed to be the Albanese Mountains. Therefore, its front was less broad and more strongly manned. The Eastern Sector, considered unsuitable for an enemy attack, was under the command of Headquarters, Panzer Division "Hermann Göring", which had only incomplete units at its disposal. In addition, these units were responsible for the protection of the coast as far as Terracina.

The 71st Infantry Division was moved to the coastal sector above the line, Tiber - Tarquinia, because the German Command expected another Allied landing north of the Tiber. Previously, only three battalions of the 90th Panzer Grenadier Division were employed in this sector.

When it became clear on 22 January that the Allied landing at Anzio was a major operation, Headquarters Army Group C decided in the evening to discontinue the counterattack at the Garigliano river. Thus, additional troops would be made available for commitment against the beachhead. In the evening of 22 January, Army Group ordered the Tenth Army to send three Grenadier battalions and one artillery battalion from the Panzer Division "Hermann Göring", one Panzer Grenadier regiment and two artillery battalions from the 15th Panzer Grenadier Division, one battalion from Regiment "Brandenburg", 60th Engineer Battalion (GHQ troops), and one antiaircraft artillery battalion (GHQ troops), to the beachhead. In addition, the 26th Panzer Division, which was employed on the left flank of the Tenth Army, was relieved and transferred to Avezzano. This division was to participate in the intended counterattack at Anzio.

On 22 January, the situation on the beachhead had improved considerably for the Germans. From signal intelligence and prisoner of war statements, it was learned that the Allied landing forces were under the command of the VI Corps (US). The Allied forces identified on the beachhead were the 3d Infantry Division(US), 1st Infantry Division (Br), 751st Tank Battalion (US), and 504th Parachute Regiment (US). It was believed that the 45th Infantry Division (US) and the 601st Tank Destroyer Battalion (US) would be landed as reinforcements. As the Allied forces made no preparations for a large-scale attack on the first day of the landings, the German Command estimated that the Allies would improve their positions, and bring up more troops during the following day. During this time, sufficient German troops would arrive to prevent an Allied breakthrough. The previously prepared plans, to move troops quickly to a threatened area, as well as preparations for designating specific units as reinforcements if landings were made, now benefited the German Command. While the transfer of troops from the Tenth Army had to be improvised, the disposition and departure of the detachments from the Fourteenth Army, the West, the Southeast, and from the Replacement Army, proceeded according to plan without requiring special orders. At 1900 on 22 January, the troops of the Fourteenth Army began to leave their areas in northern Italy. On 23 and 24 January, the transportation of troops from France, Germany, and the Balkans began. These forces arrived in Italy by 31 January, despite constant enemy air attacks on roads and railroads. By this time, the advanced detachments of these units were already employed at the beachhead.

No major actions occurred on the beachhead during 23 January. On the Tenth Army front, the enemy continued his attacks south of Cassino with undiminished ferocity. The crisis arising, from the combined attacks of the 34th and 36th Infantry Divisions (US), delayed the dispatch of reinforcements to Anzio. Telephone calls between Field Marshal Kesselring and the Commanding General, Tenth Army in the evening of 23 January, clearly indicated that the Army Group Commander believed that the danger of a large-scale expansion of the beachhead was no longer imminent.

On 22 and 23 January, the German Air Force repeatedly struck at the landing fleet and disembarkation points on the beachhead, and frequent reconnaissance missions were flown over the Ligurian and Adriatic Seas, as the German Command expected further Allied landings, because of the unusual lack of enemy activity. Allied preparations for a major attack were not observed on the beachhead. However, movements of troops and tanks north of Anzio, on the Aprilia road, were reported. Stronger enemy reconnaissance patrols were expected there during the next day.

24 January was generally uneventful. As was anticipated, the Allied landing forces limited themselves to reconnaissance and patrolling towards the north, as well as adjusting their artillery fire on German positions. By this time, the German defenses had been strongly reinforced, and the German Command considered the danger of an Allied breakthrough to be removed. A telephone call made by Army Group indicates, that on 24 January, a total of 70 batteries, including antiaircraft, were available for German defenses. This estimate of the situation was supported by the belief that the enemy did not have sufficient troops available on the beachhead for a large-scale attack. It was learned that the 2d Armored Division (US) and a British tank brigade were newly employed on the beachhead. This would, at the most, give the enemy a total of three infantry divisions, one armored division, and two to three armored battalions or brigades. The strength of these troops was considered insufficient for an attack, on a strategic objective such as the Albanese Mountains, as such an operation would require effective flank protection. Therefore, it was expected, that for the next few days the enemy would only attempt to expand and consolidate his beachhead for a full-scale attack. Army Group C concluded that the enemy would make only local attacks. These raids would not begin before 26 January, since the enemy had just adjusted his artillery in the afternoon of 24 January.

With these assumptions in mind, Army Group C decided to launch a counterattack, to destroy the Allied landing forces, or drive them back into the sea. The time for such an attack depended on the arrival of reinforcements. Every effort was to be made to deliver this blow before the Allied forces had completed their initial consolidation. In preparation for a German assault, Army Group C ordered Headquarters Fourteenth Army, on 24 January, to take over the command at the beachhead. In addition, Fourteenth Army was ordered to hasten the consolidation of forces to be used in the counterattacks. The 26th Panzer Division and 56th Rocket Regiment (at Cassino) were ordered to the beachhead, and were designated as further reinforcement for the attack. The attack was not to be started before 28 January, as the initial regrouping could not be completed sooner. However, in the event the Allies should start their assault, prior to this date, the German counterattack was to begin immediately, from defensive positions.

The first major action on the beachhead occurred on 25 January. After a raid on Aprilia (F 875333) before noon had been repelled, the Allied troops succeeded in capturing the town at 1600, after a desperate struggle. The Allies also gained some ground in the northeast, but were thrown back at Borgo Piave (G 053203) by a German counterattack. More Allied troops disembarked on the beachhead during the day, while forces of the German Air Force in Italy frequently raided troop transports and disembarkation points. The movement of German reinforcements from the south, to the beachhead, was facilitated as Allied attacks in the area of Cassino had slackened, and bad weather limited Allied Air Force operations. Bad weather was considered to be most favorable for the execution of a German counterattack. Success or failure depended on the activity of the Allied Air Forces, and on naval artillery support, as was demonstrated at Salerno. Under bad weather conditions both factors would be reduced to a minimum. However, destruction of railroads by Allied air attacks, caused a delay in the arrival of ammunition and reserves from the north.

At 1800, on 25 January, the Fourteenth Army took over the command in the Cicina sector, south of Livorno - Terracina. At this time the following German troops were employed in the area of Rome.

Sector north of the Tiber river - Tarquinia

Elements of the 90th Panzer Grenadier Division and the 71st Infantry Division.

Sector south of the Tiber river - Terracina

Headquarters I Parachute Corps; numerous GHQ troops; and, elements of the 4th Parachute Division, 3d Panzer Grenadier Division, Panzer Division "Hermann Göring", 16th SS Panzer Grenadier Division, 29th Panzer Grenadier Division, 26th Panzer Grenadier Division, 90th Panzer Grenadier Division, 1st Parachute Division, and 356th Infantry Division, and 15th Panzer Grenadier Division.

All these units were employed in the defense line on the beachhead, with the exception of elements of the 4th Parachute Division and the 29th Panzer Grenadier Division. These excepted units were employed along the coast on both sides of the beachhead. Moving towards Anzio were the following German Divisions: 26th Panzer Division, from the left flank of Tenth Army; 65th Infantry Division, (less one Grenadier regiment, and one artillery battalion,) from Genoa; 114th Light Infantry Division (Jäger Division) from the Balkans; two regiments of the 362d Infantry Division from the coastal sector Rimini, and 715th Infantry Division from southern France.

After 26 January 1944, the Journal of the Fourteenth Army gives an account of the battle on the Anzio beachhead in chronological order. The following daily reports, outlining these events, are translations of this Journal.

A. Operations Report

On the right flank, a successful ~~Allied~~ raid was carried out by an assault detachment. An enemy counterattack, in company strength, was repulsed. The 29th Panzer Grenadier Regiment, supported by tanks, attacked Aprilia (F 875333), and pushed forward from the west to the center of the town. 58 prisoners were taken, 3 antitank guns destroyed, 4 Sherman tanks destroyed, and 3 put out of commission. In the evening our forces in Aprilia were withdrawn from the town.

In the sector of the Panzer Division "Hermann Göring", at Cisterna (G 0232), the enemy attacked in battalion strength, at 1545, but was repelled. At 1700, the attack was resumed with one to two battalions. The battle was still on at 2000, and during the night small penetrations were sealed-off.

West of this sector, an attack by two to three enemy infantry battalions with 20 tanks was broken up by effective artillery fire.

B. Intelligence Report

The 24th Grenadier Brigade (Br) is confirmed at Aprilia. The 1st Irish Guards, and 5th Grenadier Guards are stationed west of Aprilia. The 751st Armored Battalion (US) has been identified 8 km south of Cisterna. The 1st Battalion of the 504th Parachute Regiment (82d Airborne Division, US) is confirmed along the Mussolini Canal. At 1730, 100 vessels were observed at sea in the sector 8 km southwest of Anzio.

Estimate of enemy situation: Attacks are likely against our positions north of Aprilia, and reconnaissance raids are expected against Cisterna and Borgo Piave (G 053203).

C. Statistics

German losses: no reports

Allied losses: 90 prisoners, 7 tanks destroyed, 3 tanks put out of commission, and 4 antitank guns destroyed.

III. 27 JANUARY 1944

A. Operations Report

Sector of the 3d Panzer Grenadier Division: Two combat patrols of the enemy were repelled on right flank. No action at Aprilia (F 875333). In the morning, attacks by one to two companies were repelled east of Aprilia. In the afternoon, a heavy enemy attack inflicted casualties on our outposts, forcing them to withdraw about 1 km to the northeast.

Sector of the Panzer Division "Hermann Göring": An attack on the right flank was repulsed. In the center of the sector, the enemy attacked in regimental strength, supported by 10 tanks, and infiltrated south of Isola Bella (G 006294) and 2.5 km northwest of Borgo Podgora

ITALY 1:100,000.
For use by
War and Navy Department Agencies only
Not for sale or distribution
LITTORIA

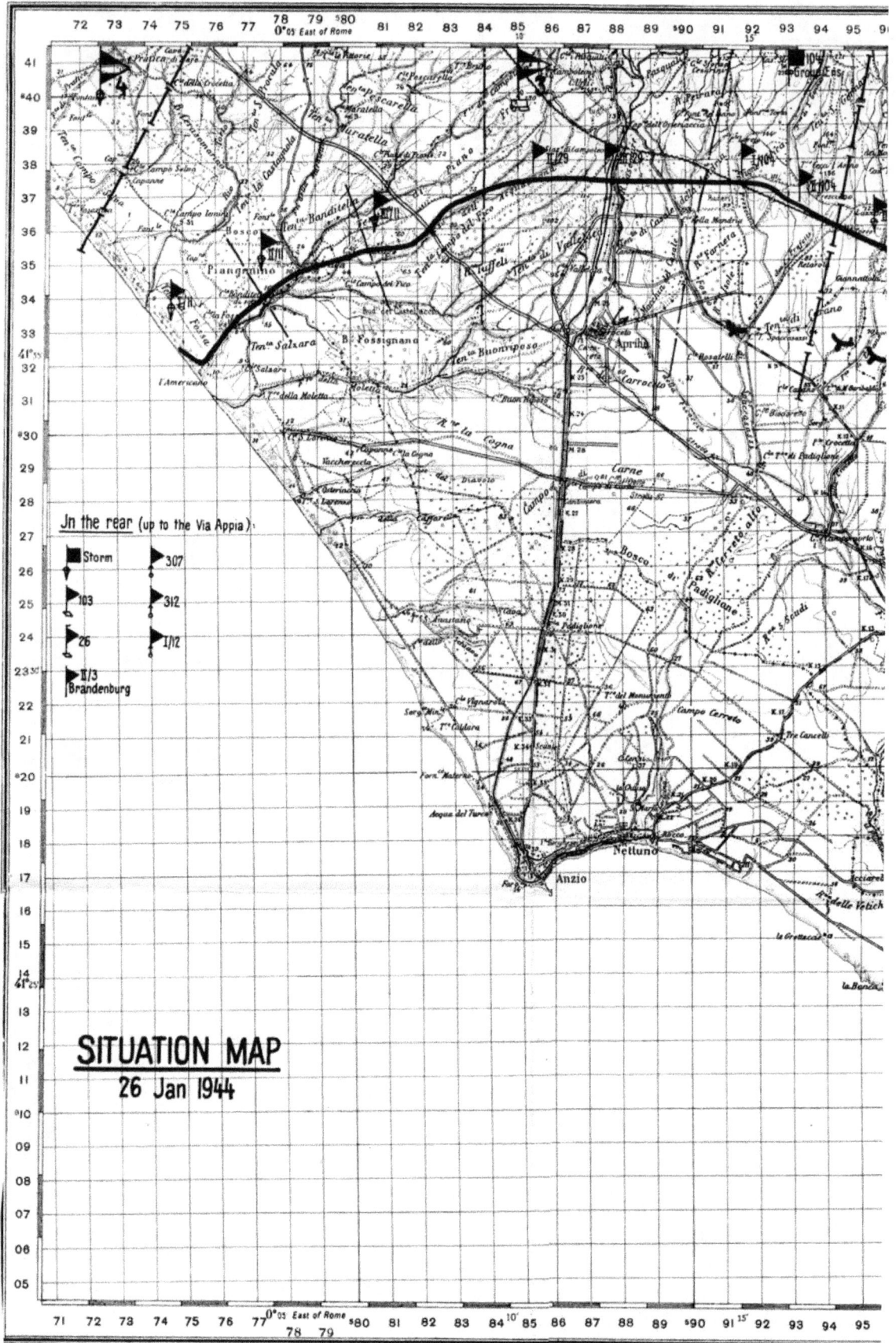

Jn the rear (up to the Via Appia):

Storm   307

103   312

26   1/12

II/3
Brandenburg

SITUATION MAP
26 Jan 1944

GSGS 4164.
First GSGS Edition (AMS 1), 1941.
Second GSGS Edition (AMS 2), 1943.

Scale 1:100,000.

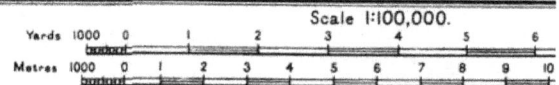

Yards 1000 0   1   2   3   4   5   6

Metres 1000 0 1 2 3 4 5 6 7 8 9 10

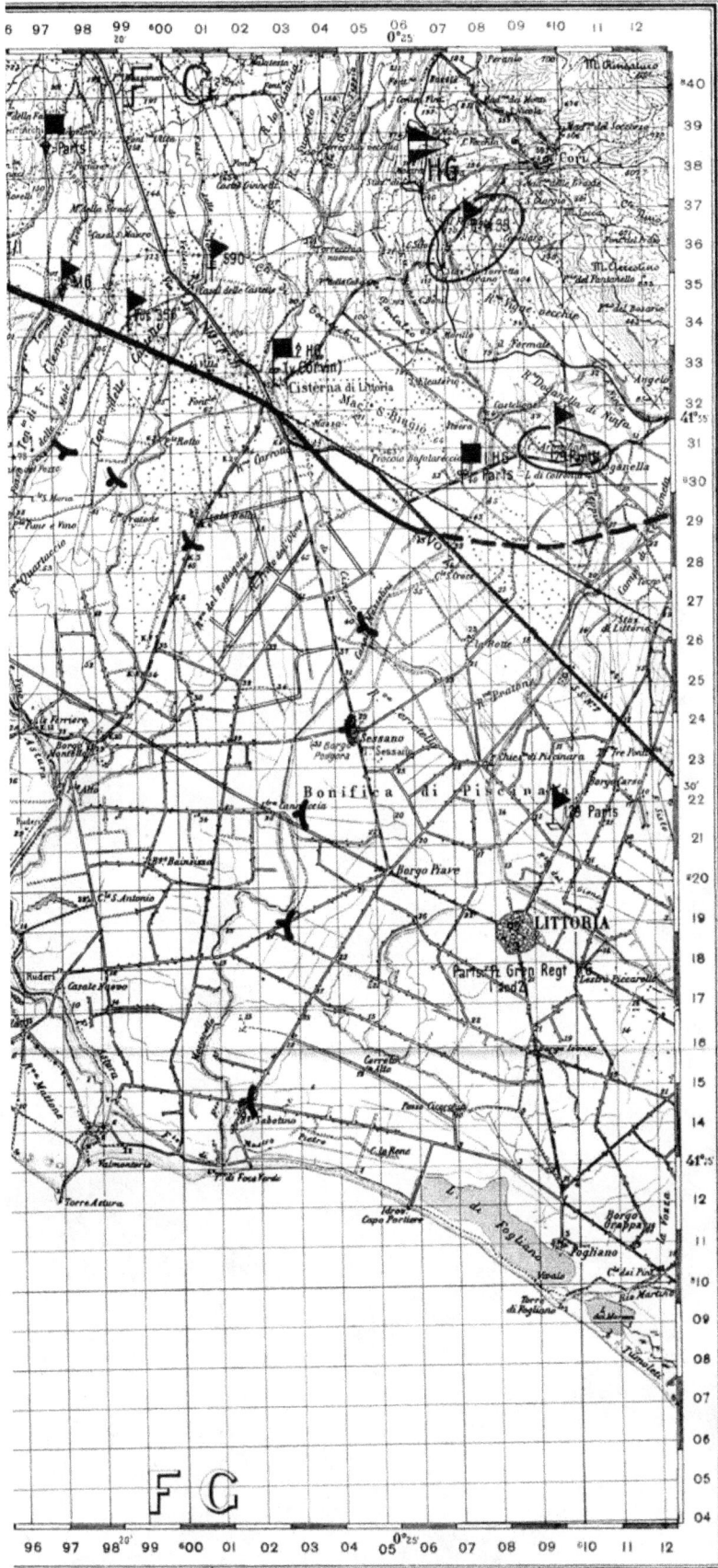

SOUTH ITALY GRID (BLUE)

TO GIVE A GRID REFERENCE ON THIS SHEET

Pay no attention to the smaller co-ordinate figures at the corners and in margins.
They are for finding full co-ordinates.

PAY ATTENTION TO LARGER MARGINAL FIGURES AND TO
THOSE PRINTED ON THE FACE OF THE MAP

POINT	Cava	F 844247

East		North	
Take west edge of square in which point lies and read the figures printed opposite this line on north or south margin or on the line itself (on the face of the map)	84	Take south edge of square in which point lies and read the figures printed opposite this line on east or west margin or on the line itself (on the face of the map)	24
Estimate tenths eastwards	4	Estimate tenths northwards	7
East	844	North	247

Nearest similar reference on this grid 500 Km. distant

GRID DATA
Southern Italy Grid

Colour	Blue
Projection	Lambert Conical Orthomorphic
Spheroid	Bessel
Origin	39° 30' N. 14° E of Greenwich
False Co-ordinates of origin	700.000 metres E / 600.000 metres N

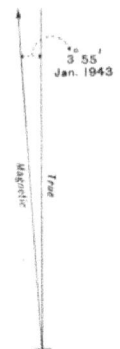

3° 55'
Jan. 1943

Magnetic   True

Annual change 8' East

CONVERGENCE

At the West Edge of this sheet Grid North is 0°59'West of True North
At the East Edge of this sheet Grid North is 0°40'West of True North

REFERENCE

Railway: two or more tracks with station	
single track and electrified	
narrow gauge or Tramway	
Tram lines on a road	
Cable railways	
National Highways (Autostrade) 8 Metres wide, metalled	(2-way M.T.)
Main Roads (Strade Statali with route numbers) 6 Metres wide or over, metalled	No 7
Other Main Roads (Strade di grande comunicazione) 5 Metres wide or over, metalled	(Mostly 2-way M.T.)
Secondary Roads 3-5 Metres wide, generally metalled	(1-way M.T.)
Other Roads and Cart Tracks, generally unmetalled	
Mule Tracks	
Paths	
Boundaries: state	
province	
Canal	
Aqueducts, over and underground	
Wells, perennial, non-perennial	
Marsh and Swamp	
Church, Chapel, Cemetery	
Names of physical features	Moncova
Trigonometrical points	△ 170
Heights in metres	· 160
Cliffs	
Embankment or Dyke	
Woods	

Contours at 50 metres interval

ADJOINING SHEETS

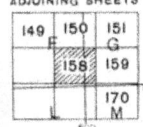

149	150	151
F	G	
	158	159
	170	
	M	

COMPARATIVE INDEX

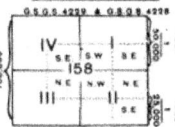

G.S.G.S. 4229 & G.S.G.S. 4228

	IV	
SE	SW	SE
	158	
	III	II
NE	NW	NE
		SE

AREA REVISED
FROM AIR PHOTOS

AUTHORITIES
Copied from Carta Topografica
1/100.000 Sheet 158. 1933.
1/25.000 Sheets IV S.E., I S.W., I S.E.
III N.E., II N.W., N.E., S.E., 1936.
Instituto Geografico Militare
Partially revised for communications, 1943.

Reproduced under the direction of the Chief of Engineers by the Army Map Service,
U. S. Army, Washington, D. C., 1944 from GSGS
Second Edition 1943 Kodalines.

ARMY MAP SERVICE, U. S. ARMY, WASHINGTON, D. C. 113496
LITTORIA
N4120-E1227/20x30
1944

7   8 Miles

11   12   13 Kilometres

Longitudes are based on the meridian of Rome, which is 12°27'7·1" East of Greenwich.

LITTORIA

Bonifica di Piscinara

Cisterna di Litoria

Borgo Piave

(G 045240)*. A continuation of attacks was expected, especially
northward, in the direction of the railroad, as well as from Aprilia.

B. Intelligence Report

Captured documents confirm previous information that these
units are on the beachhead: 1st Infantry Division (Br), composed
of the 24th Guards Brigade, 2d and 3d Brigades, and the 504th Parachute Regiment (US). 21 enemy batteries have been observed in the
area l'Americano (F 755315) to Spaccasassi (F 917330).

Air situation: Active patrol activity.

Sea situation: Heavy disembarkations east of Anzio. Aerial
photographs taken at 1100 showed the following vessels: 5 destroyers
and escort vessels, 5 small auxiliary vessels, 39 LST, 59 LCT, 1 LCF,
1 LCG, 17 LCJ, 16 LCM, LCA, LCP, 9 freighters with 53,000 tons
(Register), 1 special ship 3,000 tons (Register), and 1 auxiliary
cruiser 3,500 tons (Register). At 1330, 1 light cruiser and 2
destroyers were shelled by our coast artillery northwest of Anzio.

C. Statistics

German losses: 29 killed, 49 wounded, and 41 missing.

Allied losses: 16 prisoners, 1 tank destroyed and 1 rendered
immobile, 2 antitank guns destroyed, 3 planes shot down by antiaircraft, 1 mortar, 2 machine guns, and a number of small arms.

IV. 28 JANUARY 1944

A. Operations Report

A message from Berlin states, that according to reliable sources
the enemy is planning an attack against Civitavecchia. Consequently,
the motorized Combat Group "von Behr" (part of the 90th Panzer Grenadier Division) will be transferred from the coastal defense sector
north of the Tiber, to a concentration area near Vetralla. The
sector will be taken over by the staff of the 362d Infantry Division
with the 1st Artillery Battalion and a reinforced Regiment of the
955th Infantry Division. As the staff of the 4th Parachute Division
is still in the process of being activated, the staff of the 65th
Infantry Division, commanded by Brigadier General Pfeiffer, will
take over the sector of the 4th Parachute Division and the right
flank of the 3d Panzer Grenadier Division, the sector of the 11th
Parachute Infantry Regiment. This new command is named Battle Group
"Pfeiffer". On the right flank of the sector, the enemy pushed
closer to the Moletta creek (F 7631 to 8332).

An attack by motorized infantry, with 20 scout cars, 1.3 km
northwest of Aprilia (F 875333) was repulsed, and 3 scout cars were
put out of action.

In the sector, Isola Bella (G 006294), our front line was
practically restored. Later, an enemy attack, in battalion strength,

----

* Borgo Podgora may also be known as Sessano

3 km west of Isola Bella was repulsed after a two hour battle. Around noon, the enemy temporarily penetrated our front line, 2 km southwest of Isola Bella, during a new attack in battalion strength. At hill 32, 4 km southeast of Isola Bella, the former front line was regained.

In the morning, our artillery fired at 9 invasion barges at Anzio. Two enemy ammunition dumps exploded from direct hits by our artillery. Combat Group "Ens" (104 Panzer Grenadier Regiment of the 15th Panzer Grenadier Division), which has been on the left flank of the 3d Panzer Grenadier Division, west of Aprilia, was relieved during the night by the 71st Infantry Division (less the 211th and 191st Regiments).

B. Intelligence Report

2d Company 7th Middlesex Battalion (element of the 24th Guard Brigade) is located in area northeast of Aprilia. According to captured documents, the Reconnaissance Battalion of the 1st Infantry Division (Br) is in the vicinity of Canale S. Lorenzo (G 780300). The boundary between British and American troops runs along route Cas. Torre Spaccasassi (F 917330) Cas. Tre di Padiglione (F 921289).

Sea and Air situation: Continued heavy landings were made at Anzio; and air activity over the front line remained steady.

C. Statistics

German losses: 31 killed, 100 wounded, and 18 missing.

Allied losses: 1 prisoner from 1st Reconnaissance Battalion (Br), 2 prisoners from 3d Battalion, 504 Parachute Regiment (US), 6 heavy machine guns captured, and 4 planes, including 1 Mustang, shot down by antiaircraft.

V. 29 JANUARY 1944

A. Operations Report

51st Mountain Corps took over the coastal sector north of the mouth of the Tiber to the army border at Cecina.

There was less enemy activity than usual on the beachhead. An enemy attack, in battalion strength, on hill 61 (F 980297), 3 km west of Isola Bella was halted by artillery fire. Enemy reconnaissance, in company strength, partially with tanks and armored scout cars, was turned back. North of Aprilia (F 875333), a stalled tank was destroyed by a magnetic antitank charge, and other vehicles were destroyed by fire. The enemy was thrown back, west of Borgo Piave (G 053203), to Moscarello creek (G 0220). Thirteen prisoners were taken. One heavy machine gun and several bazookas were captured. In the evening a concentration of approximately 30 tanks and 70 to 80 trucks loaded with troops was observed in the vicinity of Aprilia.

Harassing artillery fire from the entire beachhead and the sea, was primarily directed on the right flank and on the Panzer Division "Hermann Göring". Two cruisers and several PT boats withdrew under coast artillery fire.

B. Intelligence Report

From prisoner of war interrogation it was learned that the 3d Battalion, 504th Parachute Regiment is still at Borgo Piave (G 053203); 1st Scots Guards at Macchia del Casale (F 8934); 5th Grenadier Guards at Cle Vallelata (F 863347). Disembarkation of troops continues at Anzio-Nettuno. In the evening a large convoy of approximately 100 ships was reported as approaching.

C. Statistics

German losses: 17 killed, 63 wounded, and 24 missing.

Allied losses: 20 prisoners (13 US and 7 British), 2 fighters shot down (1 US and 1 British), 1 tank, 1 machine gun carrier, and several vehicles destroyed.

D. The German Plan of Attack

The main mission of the Fourteenth Army is to annihilate the beachhead, which the enemy is reinforcing. The attack must be made as soon as possible; the date depends on the arrival of the necessary forces, which is being delayed, as the railroad system in Italy has been crippled by enemy air raids.

The attack will be launched from north to south along the Albano-Anzio road, with the main concentration on either side of Aprilia. The date of attack was to be 28 January, but in a meeting between Army and Army Group Commanders on 26 January, D-Day was postponed to 1 February, so that reinforcements would be available. These reinforcements were: 1027th and 1028th Infantry Regiments, the Special Artillery Demonstration Regiment, the Special Rocket Projector Demonstration Battalion, and the 1st Battalion of the 4th Panzer Regiment. These units left by train from Germany, and are expected to pass through the Brenner Pass on 26 and 27 January. The plan of attack as proposed by the 1st Parachute Corps follows.

Combat Group "Pfeiffer"

Consists of nine infantry battalions of the 65th Infantry Division and the 4th Parachute Division. Its objective in the attack was to penetrate towards the south and link up with the main group. In addition to the artillery assigned to coastal defense, the group will have 9 light field howitzers (10.5 cm).

Combat Group "Gräser"

Located in the sector previously held by the 3d Panzer Grenadier Division. This group will be employed for the main effort. On the right flank of the main effort are the 3d Panzer Grenadier Division and the 26th Panzer Division, the latter supported by the 1st Battalion of the 4th Panzer Regiment. On the left flank will be the 715th Infantry Division, making a total of seventeen infantry battalions. This unit will have 11 long-range artillery guns (17 cm); assault artillery: 29 heavy field howitzers (15 cm), 34 light field howitzers (10.5 cm), 8 guns (10 cm), 36 rocket launchers (each with six 15 cm tubes), 18 rocket launchers (each with five 21 cm tubes), and 8 rocket launchers (each with ten 15 cm tubes).

Combat Group "Konrad"

This group is composed of elements of the Panzer Division "Hermann Göring" and elements of the 114th Infantry Division, giving it a total of four infantry battalions. Its mission is to penetrate to the Astura creek from the area west of Cisterna (G 0232). It will be furnished with 32 heavy field howitzer (15 cm), 42 light field howitzers (10.5 cm), and 3 guns (10 cm).

Corps Reserve

Located in the region south of Albano. It will consist of elements of the 71st Infantry Division and the 16th SS Panzer Grenadier Division, with a total of six infantry battalions.

The following antiaircraft artillery is to be employed in ground action and air defense at the discretion of the divisional staffs.

	Antiaircraft guns		
	8.8 cm	3.7 cm	2 cm
Combat Group "Peiffer"	12	9	42
Combat Group "Gräser"	43	18	108
Combat Group "Konrad"	11	9	31

Contrary to previous instructions, the attacks will begin simultaneously in the morning of D-Day after a coordinated ten minute artillery barrage. Only on the southern flank of the beachhead in the area of Borgo Piave (G 053203) a local diversionary attack will be executed on D minus 1.

VI. 30 JANUARY 1944

A. Operations Report

During the night, 29 to 30 January 1944, the enemy began the anticipated large-scale attack, on either side of the Anzio-Albano road. The attack was preceded by heavy artillery fire, which lasted for two hours. In the sector of the Panzer Division "Hermann Göring", the enemy made a penetration at dawn, on both sides of the Nettuno-Cisterna road (G 0232). Later, the attacks expanded to other sectors of the beachhead. By late afternoon, the enemy renewed his attacks after reserves were brought in. Heavy fighting occurred, with the positions changing hands frequently. The attacks were generally repulsed. Operation reports by units follow.

Combat Group "Pfeiffer": The right flank was infiltrated by Allied forces, which were eliminated, and 60 men captured. During early morning, an enemy attack, with tanks, against the center section was stopped. In the afternoon, a heavy tank formation, of at least 70 tanks attacked the left flank (at Vallelata Heights, 3 km northwest of Aprilia; F 875333). The main line of resistance, within the entire sector, generally remained in our hands, except for partial withdrawals at Vallelata Heights.

3d Panzer Grenadier Division: After heavy artillery fire, the enemy attacked, at about 0100, with two infantry battalions supported by armor. The attack made a negligible penetration, along both sides of the Aprilia-Albano road. In the afternoon, our own counterattack met a second enemy attack, which was halted. At 1700, a unit supported by armor, penetrated our defense line and by sunset had advanced to the railroad crossing about 6 km north of Aprilia. A new defensive line was established there. However, contact was not reestablished with Combat Group "Pfeiffer", and a 2 to 3 km gap between units remained.

71st Infantry Division: No unusual activity.

Panzer Division "Hermann Göring": In the early morning, enemy infantry, supported by tanks, attacked in the area Tba. di M Garibaldi (F 940313) - Canale Mussolini. The first attack force made several penetrations, which were repulsed by local counterattacks. Enemy units which advanced to Cisterna (G 0232) were destroyed. During the morning, the enemy began a new counterattack, with a strong infantry force, northeast of Tba. di M Garibaldi - Isola Bella (G 006294). Our forces counterattacked, and fought heavily until darkness. A defensive front from Isola Bella to bench mark 45, 3 km southeast along the Canale Mussolini to north of bench mark 31, 6 km southeast of Isola Bella, was restored.

An enemy breakthrough from the beachhead, had to be prevented and a closed main line of resistance, in the sector of the 3d Panzer Grenadier Division had to be restored. In the sector of the Panzer Division "Hermann Göring", the 26th Panzer Division was to counterattack the 3d American Infantry Division, which had penetrated south of Cisterna. The 26th Panzer Division was concentrated in the area north of Cisterna, and units of the 114th Jäger Division, which have arrived in the region south of Velletri, were attached, as Regimental Group "Berger" to the Panzer Division "Hermann Göring".

B. Intelligence Report

Prisoners of war stated that the 7th and 30th Regiment, of the 3d Infantry Division (US) are still on the line, the 601st American Tank Destroyer Battalion is attached to the 30th Regiment, and that the 1st Irish Guards were committed west of Aprilia.

C. Statistics

German losses:* 94 men killed, 260 men wounded, and 231 men missing.

* These losses do not include those of the Panzer Division "Hermann Göring", which will be included in the statistics report of 31 January.

Allied losses: Enemy suffered heavy losses, especially in the area of the Panzer Division "Hermann Göring". 786 men, including 29 officers, were taken prisoner ; 680 of them by Panzer Division "Hermann Göring". 3 enemy tanks were destroyed.

A. Operations Report

The enemy attacked, in battalion strength, supported by armor, at several points along the front. The attacks were repulsed despite heavy, continuous barrages of all calibres, including naval gunfire. Small penetrations were repulsed or cut off. Only west of Cisterna (G 0232) was a penetration achieved, but it stopped just south of the railroad line. In the evening, the Commander in Chief Southwest reported to the Armed Forces High Command, that the enemy began to attack, on 30 January, with about 3 divisions; the bulk of our own forces, including those which had been withheld for our planned offensive, were now committed in the defense of the front. Consequently, the offensive for the annihilation of the enemy had been postponed. Now our mission is to prevent an expansion of the beachhead, and to inflict heavy losses on the enemy. The enemy has suffered heavily, but our own losses have also been high. We are not certain whether the forces, at our disposal, will be sufficient to drive the enemy into the sea, if an extensive defensive battle has to be fought. Because of the difficult rail situation, we also doubt whether an ammunition issue can be assured for the Fourteenth Army, especially since the Tenth Army requires a great deal of ammunition at Cassino.

The Fourteenth Army is to start a counteroffensive, if, in the course of the defense, a good opportunity presents itself. Assault groups are to be held in readiness, in order that such a possibility can be exploited at any given time. The entire Army coast artillery south of the Tiber has been put under the I Parachute Corps, so as to achieve a greater concentration of forces. The artillery is to be emplaced near the coast, so that as many pieces as possible will be able to fire, from the flank, at enemy shipping at the beachhead. Since additional enemy landings appear likely, the Fourteenth Army ordered the thorough demolition of the harbor of Civitavecchia.

B. Eyewitness Report

An infantry battalion located near Campoleone (F 860406) repulsed, with machine gun and mortar fire, 10 light and medium tanks. This battalion did not possess any antitank weapons, since it had taken position only the preceding night. The fact that the enemy tanks retreated from the fire of infantry weapons, gave the men a feeling of confidence. However, they are impressed by the enemy's superiority in materiel, especially his artillery and planes. It is not understood why the enemy tanks halted their attacks, when they had advanced at several points, within 50 yards of our main line of resistance and were not subjected to any antitank fire. A breakthrough of tanks could not have been stopped, as neither antitank weapons nor suitable reserves were available.

C. Intelligence Report

3d American Infantry Division (US): 2 Ranger battalions (1st and 2d) in the area between the Mussolini canal and the road from Borgo Montello (F 976236) to Isola Bella (G 006299). With them are the 30th, the 7th, and the 15th Infantry Regiments of the Division. The 15th Infantry Regiment is in the region of Cle Carano (F 940309).

1st Infantry Division (Br): The division is in the bulge, north of Aprilia (F 875333). East of the highway is the 3d Brigade. On the west side is the 24th Guard Brigade, which according to a prisoner's report, will be removed. The 2d Brigade is in the rear of the 24th.

The deployment of enemy forces in the sector between the Moletta valley and the coast (F 7631 to F 8332), is not clear. Our reconnaissance is trying to ascertain the enemy order of battle.

On the right flank of the 30th Infantry Regiment (US) is the 751st Tank Battalion. English prisoners report that American tanks of an unknown unit are attached to the 1st Infantry Division (Br).

The continuation of enemy attacks with the main effort on the bulge north of Aprilia is expected.

D. Statistics

German losses: 94 killed, 205 wounded, and 212 missing.

Allied losses: 4 tanks destroyed, one rendered immobile.

VIII. 1 FEBRUARY 1944

A. Operations Report

At dawn, the 71st Infantry Division and the Panzer Division "Hermann Göring" counterattacked west of Cisterna (G 0232), where the enemy had made a penetration on 31 January. Despite stubborn resistance, the former main line of resistance was restored. In the course of the day, enemy attacks, in company to battalion strength, were made near Aprilia (F 875333), south of Cisterna, and at the Mussolini canal; they were repulsed.

It is intended to eliminate the bulge north of Aprilia on 3 February. Heavy fighting is expected, due to the presence of strong enemy infantry forces, and the constant reports of the movement of enemy armor. But a concentric attack against the flanks with co-ordinated artillery fire, should bring about the desired result.

Army Group C points out that at the present moment great stress is placed on intelligence since further enemy landings are expected. Army Group also states that the situation is so serious on the Tenth Army front, especially at Cassino, that new reserves will soon be required. These can only be drawn from units, which are now employed by the Fourteenth Army. It is exceptionally well equipped with artillery and antiaircraft; consequently it is to eliminate the beachhead.

The Commanding General of the Fourteenth Army indicates that although this numerical superiority in artillery doubtlessly exists, operations can be only conducted after thorough preparations. This is due to the weakness in number and training of the infantry troops. If this fails it will be impossible to repeat the undertaking, due to the lack of forces.

<u>Order of the Fourteenth Army to subordinate units:</u>

In the sectors where we are not able to attack for the time being, an intensive consolidation of positions must be started, such as the laying of mines, construction of trip wire entanglements, etc. Not a foot of soil will be given up. Enemy penetrations or breakthroughs must be prevented by a consolidation of the assigned main line of resistance and of the battle positions behind it. In addition, forces from the defensive sectors will be employed at the points of concentration in attacks. Foxholes will be converted into individual points of resistance and will be connected by trenches, and connecting wire entanglements will be set up. The next priority is the construction of a secondary connecting trench system along the artillery entrenchments. The battle position will consist of a system of mutually supporting points of resistance, machine gun nests, antitank gun and infantry howitzer positions, observation posts, artillery and mortar positions, shelters for reserves, distributing points, etc. They will all be consolidated as strong points, as soon as possible. The strong points assigned to the local reserves will be kept as near to the main line of resistance as the terrain and the missions will permit.

In front of the main line of resistance as many anti-tank and anti-personnel mines as possible will be laid. Natural and artificial tank obstacles and antitank weapons of all kinds are to be supplemented by barriers of anti-personnel mines.

Only a battle position, based on the system of strong points and supplemented by a system of tank defense is capable of breaking up a large-scale attack by the enemy. Penetrations cannot be avoided, but a breakthrough must be prevented.

These constructions must not lower the offensive spirit of the troops. Entrenchment is a means of maintaining power for the offensive. Positions must be consolidated, even though the commanding officer is aware that he will no more than start this construction. Whatever he can do will be profitable for the reserves which follow. It is the task of all commanders, especially company commanders, to fight against indifference, and to force the men to entrench themselves.

C. <u>Intelligence Report</u>

From the interrogation of prisoners of war the following units have been identified.

<u>1st Infantry Division</u> (Br):

Irish Guards, located near Cle Vallelata (F 863347)
5th Grenadier Guards on the left flank of the Irish Guards (5 km northwest of Aprilia).
C Company of the 2d Foresters (1 km south of Cap Dell' Osteriaccia — F 883390) was inserted between the 1st Irish and the 1st Scots Guards on 31 January.

<u>3d Infantry Division</u> (US):

Reconnaissance Company located north of Cle Carano (F 940309)

1st and 3d Ranger Battalions, east of highway at
Borgo Montello (F 976236)
4th Ranger Battalion is behind the 1st and 3d Ranger
Battalions.

45th Division (US):

On the beachhead.

36th Engineer Battalion:

On the beachhead, as indicated on a captured map.

83d Chemical Battalion:

On the beachhead, as indicated on a captured map.

6th Armored Infantry Regiment:

Part of the 1st Armored Division (US)
Located 2 km northwest of Aprilia.

D. Statistics

German losses: 38 killed, 107 wounded, and 49 missing. This
does not include Combat Group "Gräser" and the 71st Infantry Division.

Allied losses: 39 prisoners, 11 Sherman tanks destroyed, 1
tank rendered immobile, and 6 vehicles destroyed.

IX. 2 FEBRUARY 1944

A. Operations Report

An enemy attack of more than two companies has been repulsed
4 km north of Aprilia. Our counterattack to straighten the line 4
km west of Cisterna (G 0232) is stopped, because an American battalion with a few tanks, is putting up a stubborn defense in an
olive grove. The right flank of the Panzer Division "Hermann Göring"
advanced about 1 km but was later forced to withdraw to the original
line in a costly fight. The enemy advance against the main line of
resistance 6 km east of Borgo Montello (F 976236) in company strength
was repulsed.

The I Parachute Corps requested Army Headquarters to move back
the main line of resistance of the 71st Infantry Division and of the
right wing of the Panzer Division "Hermann Göring". These units,
especially the 71st Infantry Division, have been greatly weakened,
and since pressure from the enemy has not abated, it is necessary
to form reserves, which can be done only by shortening the front.
The Commanding General of the Fourteenth Army replied that only under
the most compelling circumstances could he permit withdrawal of the
frontline on the beachhead. In this case the withdrawal is approved,
in view of the critical situation of the 71st Infantry Division.
The 1028th Panzer Grenadier Regiment is transferred to Velletri,
in order to place reserves in the rear of the 71st Infantry Division.
Strong activity by assault detachments is ordered during the night
of 2 - 3 February, in order to reduce the enemy bulge into our
lines as much as possible.

Counterbattery fire was effectively maintained by our artillery. It also fired at a concentration of tanks, which was sighted by air reconnaissance 1 km south of Aprilia (F 875333). Enemy area bombing in area of Combat Group "Gräser", destroyed the artillery communications net, and all fire direction charts for the action, planned to reduce the bulge north of Aprilia, were lost. This bombing of communications minimizes the supply of ammunition. The attack has been postponed for 24 hours as it needs the total support of artillery.

In the evening the Commanding General of the Fourteenth Army reported to the Commander in Chief Southwest and described his personal impressions gained in his tour of units fighting west of Cisterna. He observed that the partial failure of these units to push forward, viz, Panzer Division "Hermann Göring", was due to the magnitude of enemy artillery bombardments. They demoralize many young soldiers, and the older men often lose their courage. However, he believed that these men will regain their composure.

Army Group C declared that an invasion in the region of Civitavecchia was probable. An enemy air reconnaissance unit, which always has only been encoutered where invasions occurred, has made its appearance there. The following countermeasures were taken: first, one battalion was made available for the Viterbo region; second, air reconnaissance was stepped up in the Civitavecchia region; third, our heavy airforce units were alerted; and fourth, an anti-aircraft battalion of the Tenth Army was made available for the region of the Tiber bridges.

Army Group C intends to transfer troops from the Fourteenth Army to the Tenth Army, which is having difficulties at Cassino. The machine gun battalion of the 1st Parachute Division is contemplated for this transfer. The Commanding General of the Fourteenth Army has noted, that this battalion is employed, in the sector of the Allied penetration, west of Cisterna, and can be removed only by placing reserves in its place. The staff of LXXVI Panzer Corps, formerly with Tenth Army opposite the British Eighth Army, is transferred to the Fourteenth Army. It assumes command of the former left sector of the I Parachute Corps. The following regrouping is ordered by Fourteenth Army.

LXXVI Panzer Corps at present will defend the main line of resistance. The command post of the LXXVI Panzer Corps, will open at 1200, 4 February in the region of Giulianello (8 km east of Velletri). Its chief mission will be to prevent an enemy breakthrough, where the heaviest attacks are made, i.e. north of Aprilia and southwest of Cisterna. Apart from the defense, it is the task of the Panzer Corps to make preparations for the decisive attack, which will annihilate the beachhead. It assumes command of Combat Group "Gräser" (3d Panzer Grenadier Division, 715th motorized Infantry Division, Combat Group "Raapke" (reinforced 71st Infantry Division), and Combat Group "Konrad" (reinforced Panzer-Division "Hermann Göring", 26th Panzer Division).

I Parachute Corps, with command post at Grotta Ferrata, retains command of the 4th Parachute Division and the 65th Infantry Division. Group "Pfeiffer" is to be dissolved. The current mission of I Parachute Corps is to defend the main line of resistance between the sector of the LXXVI Panzer Corps (north of Aprilia) and the coast, and also the coastline up to the mouth of the Tiber. Apart from the defensive preparations, plans will be made for an early attack conforming to the mission given to the former Group "Pfeiffer". For this attack, the front of the 4th Parachute Division is to be extended to reduce the sector of the 65th Infantry Division, so that this Division will be available for this attack. It is responsible for the construction of a rear defense line in the Campagna from the Tiber to Lake Albano. The Commandant of Rome is placed under the command of the I Parachute Corps, but will retain his present duties. The boundary between the I Parachute Corps and the "Coastal Defense Sector Cecina – mouth of the Tiber", runs along the Tiber up to the junction of the Maglianella, and then skirts the western and northern outskirts of Rome.

Army reserves consist of: 114th Jäger Division (less Regimental Group "Berger") in the region of Lago Albano, 1st Battalion of the 4th Panzer Regiment (Panther tanks) in the region of Torrenova – Torre Gaia southeast of Rome, 301st Panzer Battalion (remote control tanks) on the march from Peronne, France, and a Battery of Assault Howitzers on the march from St. Poelten, Austria.

Among the newly arrived units of the Fourteenth Army are the railroad battery "Erhardt" 8 km west of Lake Albano, and the antitank battalion of the 114th Jäger Division at Regimental Group "Berger". Parts of the 1027th Panzer Grenadier Regiment have arrived near Lake Albano. The 56th Projector Regiment, with Combat Group "Gräser" is ready for action.

B. Intelligence Report

Prisoners of war identified the Reconnaissance Battalion of the 1st Division (Br), 1 km southeast of Cle della Mandria (F 898365); the 2d Battalion of the 7th Infantry Regiment (US), at F 994322; confirmed the 45th Infantry Division (US) on the beachhead, and located the 39th Engineer Battalion, attached to the VI Corps, at G 32260.

C. Statistics

German losses minus Combat Group "Gräser": 70 killed, 191 wounded, and 423 missing.

Allied losses: 35 prisoners, and 1 Sherman tank destroyed.

X. 3 FEBRUARY 1944

A. Operations Report

One of our assault detachments inflicted heavy losses on the enemy by attacking a bridge under construction 6.5 km northeast of Borgo Montello (F 976236). By counterattacks with superior forces, the enemy prevented the destruction of the bridge. Our forces had to withdraw.

In the enemy bulge north of Aprilia (F 875333) our assault detachments advanced their outpost positions. An enemy infantry attack, supported by 12 tanks and 2 assault detachments was repulsed. New enemy intentions in the area northwest of Aprilia are indicated by the extreme calm that prevails in that area, except for artillery adjustment fire.

The Commanding General of the I Parachute Corps reported to Fourteenth Army that preparations for the night of 3 to 4 February are adequate, and that a further delay because of enemy air attacks is unlikely. Fourteenth Army ordered Combat Group "Gräser" to attack without further orders, in case the expected enemy attack in the sector of the 71st Infantry Division occurred. General Gräser was advised that a successful night attack should be exploited to the point, where a push past Aprilia towards the south would be feasible. The 3d Heavy Company of the 764th Artillery Regiment and the 1st Parachute Machine Gun Battalion were withdrawn from the beachhead, and transferred to the Tenth Army, for use at Cassino.

B. Estimate of the Situation Sent by Fourteenth Army to the Commander in Chief Southwest.

So far two enemy infantry divisions have appeared in the forward lines. In the west, opposite the northern flank of the 65th Infantry Division and opposite Group Gräser is the 1st Infantry Division (Br); in the east, opposite the eastern flank of the 71st Infantry Division and the western flank and center of the Panzer Division "Hermann Göring" lies the 3d Infantry Division (US). Each division is supported by a tank brigade. On the eastern flank the enemy has two to three ranger battalions and 1 parachute regiment of the 82d Airborne Division. On the western flank, opposite the southern flank of the 65th Infantry Division and the 4th Parachute Division, unknown enemy units are operating, but the 65th Infantry Division brought in a prisoner from the 1st Armored Division (US). In addition to units in the forward lines, we assume that the 1st Armored Division (US) and the 45th Infantry Division (US) are in the rear areas of the beachhead. The presence of the following units is questionable: units of the 2d Armored Division (US), one Corps Headquarters (Br), and another British division. The intense naval traffic indicates the arrival of reinforcements.

In the battle to enlarge the beachhead the enemy has suffered heavy losses in men and tanks, which was confirmed by prisoners. However, neither his will to attack nor his endurance to resist has been broken. The enemy strength is based in his accurate and strong artillery, which is abundantly supplied with ammunition, and on the supporting naval artillery, as well as his superior air force. The mental and physical strain is great on our fresh troops. Enemy movements and order of battle, indicate an attack with one assault group from the region northeast of Aprilia, and with another group, from the region west and southwest of Cisterna (G 0232), in the general direction of Velletri. Holding attacks in the other sectors are probable. The forces now in the rear of the beachhead will probably be committed at the center of the attack. The objective of the attack will be to occupy the heights near Velletri; to reach Valmontone, by advancing through the valley east of Velletri and, to break into the rear of the Tenth Army. An attack in the direction of Rome is not likely, unless it be executed in connection with a new landing north of the mouth of the Tiber.

Fourteenth Army intends to prevent the enlarging of the beachhead, and to prepare an attack to eliminate this area.

A number of army units are remnants from various organizations and are not able to mount an attack at this time; during the last days, they had to be used in the front lines to prevent an enemy breakthrough. With these forces a strong assault group to conduct the attack on the beachhead cannot be organized. Therefore, Fourteenth Army has planned attacks with limited objectives, to suit various situations as they arise. When the enemy is weakened by these attacks, an all-out counteroffensive will be launched.

The first attack will be launched during the night of 3 to 4 February, by one reinforced regiment, with tanks, in the bulge north of Aprilia. The I Parachute Corps will exploit the situation, by advancing south beyond the present objective, which is the line running 1.5 km northwest of Cle. Vallelata (F 863347) to Cle. della Mandria (F 898365). If successful, the attack will be continued, during the night of 4 to 5 February, by the 65th Infantry Division and Combat Group "Gräser". The objective will be to recover ground on both sides of Aprilia.

As yet, no further attacks have been planned. However, similar attacks will have to be executed in rapid succession, in order to prevent effective countermeasures by the enemy. Due to the enemy's strong artillery, superior air support, and stubborn determination, substantial losses are to be expected. It appears doubtful whether the Fourteenth Army will eliminate the beachhead, with the forces available at this time. In order to accomplish its mission, the Army requested Army Group to attach additional troops. Should this deplete coastal defenses in other areas it should be considered as a calculated risk.

The Commanding General, Fourteenth Army, issued these orders to subordinate Corps Headquarters:

An attack is imperative. Under all circumstances constant blows against the enemy, at least with strong assault detachments, must be delivered along the entire front. This will give us intelligence of the enemy situation, and the enemy, expecting an attack, will be forced to disperse his troops. Partial blows in preparation for the decisive offensive aiming to wipe out the beachhead should be delivered, with all available forces, in order to weaken the enemy.

Therefore, I order: First, the elimination of the enemy in the penetrated sector north of Aprilia, as planned by the I Parachute Corps Headquarters for the night of 3 to 4 February 1944. Second, that the present main line of resistance be held in the sectors which are not in active combat at the moment. Assault detachments will attack the enemy continuously. Our forces will be shifted in accordance with enemy moves. Forces will be reduced rapidly in sectors where the enemy is inactive.

In order to destroy the enemy near Aprilia this detailed plan will take effect: "Western Group" will push forward in an easterly direction from the area north and south of Hill 102 (F 858362) The "Eastern Group" will fight in a westerly direction toward the railroad from the area 1 km south of Cle. della Mandria (F 898365). Then, after establishing a defense line in the south, the enemy should be up in a northern direction.

"Western Group" will consist of a reinforced 145th Grenadier Regiment, of the 65th
Infantry Division, three infantry battalions,
two light artillery battalions, and two combat
companies. It will be equipped with ten 88 mm
self propelled guns (Hornets), and three heavy
antitank guns.

The "Eastern Group", will comprise a reinforced 104th Panzer Grenadier Regiment, two light
artillery battalions, three infantry battalions,
and two combat engineer companies. It will be
equipped with 8 (Hornets) and 4 heavy antitank
guns. There is a reserve of 12 assault guns, in
addition to the detached "Artillery Group"; with
three light artillery battalions, nine heavy
artillery battalions, including mortars and 170
mm guns, and rocket projectors.

Should the outcome of this attack be favorable, strong assault detachments will push southward past the planned main line of resistance,
to seize the enemy stronghold at the road
junction (F 878354), 1.5 km north of Aprilia.
Outposts will be established there.

The artillery, the antiaircraft artillery,
and the combat engineers, assigned to support
Combat Group "Gräser", will be brought forward
immediately, after the completion of the operation. This will enable us to follow up our
attack, during the night of 4 to 5 February 1944,
and to capture Aprilia. For the attack the 1st
Battalion of the 4th Panzer Regiment, equipped
with Panther tanks will be attached to the LXXVI
Panzer Corps. However, tanks and assault guns
will attack with the infantry; they will not
precede the infantry.

All officers are expected to understand the
urgency of the situation. Our grand strategy demands
that the beachhead be wiped out promptly.

After a telephone call with Field Marshal Kesselring
the Commanding General of Fourteenth Army issued the
following order:

Compared with other fronts, we have particularly
strong artillery forces, and an adequate supply of
ammunition. Enemy attacks must be repelled before they
reach our main line of resistance. Artillery officers
will be held responsible, if this task should fail, because of a lack of coordination between infantry and
artillery, faulty liaison, or bad leadership. Continuous artillery fire will support the infantry.
Single bursts of fire are not adequate for the support
of infantry. A barrage will be placed in front of our
lines. Long-range guns will engage enemy naval artillery, preventing it from interfering in our operations.
Sectors of the main line of resistance, where no attack
is planned, will be held and fortified by use of construction battalions. Tactical command posts will be
moved from communication centers and villages, for
protection against air-raids, which might cause a delay

For use by
War and Navy Department Agencies only
Not for sale or distribution

MLR 3 FEB.
MLR 5 FEB.

ARMY RESERVES (IN THE AREA OF LAGO ALBANO):

THE ALLIED BULGE
AND ITS ELIMINATION
3 FEB 44 – 5 FEB 44

GSGS 4164.
First GSGS Edition (AMS 1), 1941.
Second GSGS Edition (AMS 2), 1943.

Scale 1:100,000.

Yards 1000 0   1   2   3   4   5   6

Metres 1000 0   1   2   3   4   5   6   7   8   9   10

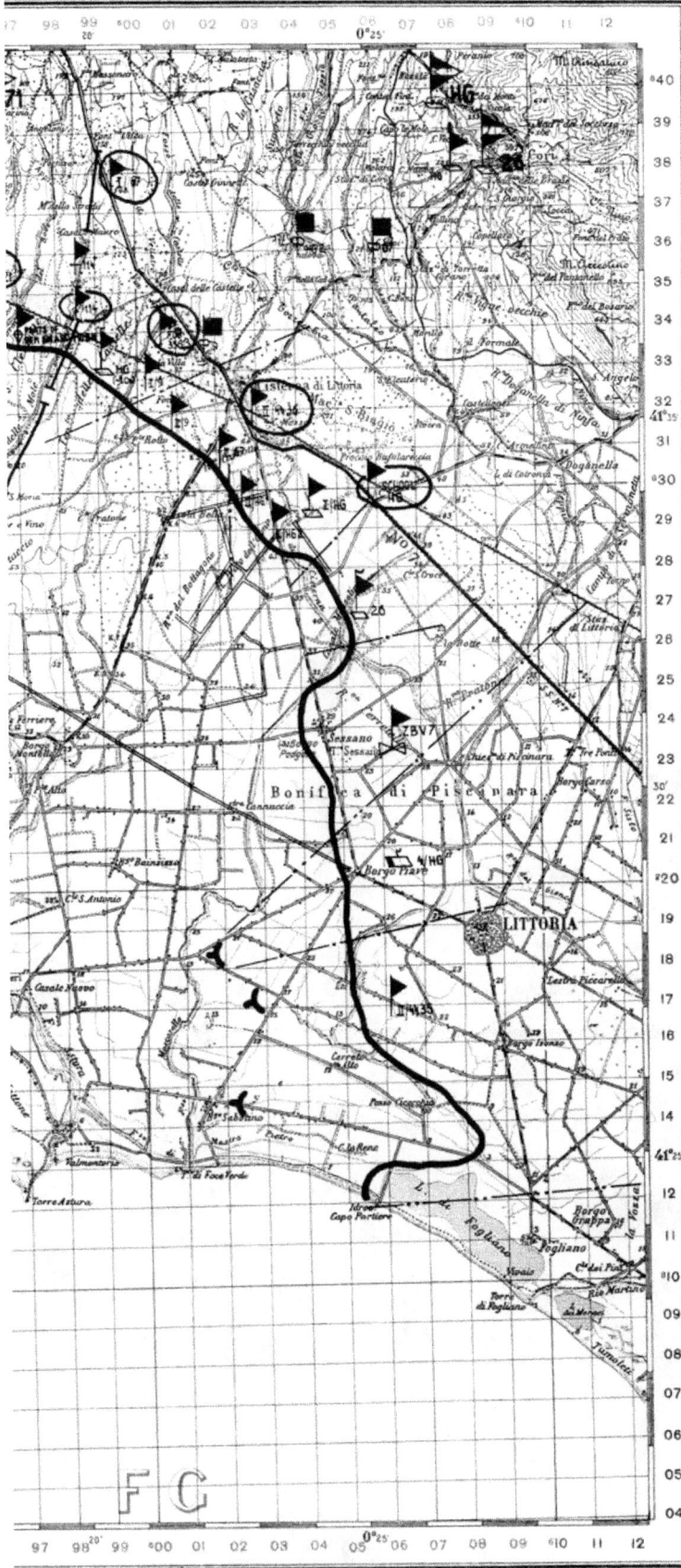

SOUTH ITALY GRID (BLUE)

TO GIVE A GRID REFERENCE ON THIS SHEET
Pay no attention to the smaller co-ordinate figures at the corners and in margins.
They are for finding full co-ordinates.

PAY ATTENTION TO LARGER MARGINAL FIGURES AND TO
THOSE PRINTED ON THE FACE OF THE MAP.

POINT	Cava	F 844247

East		North	
Take west edge of square in which point lies and read the figures printed opposite this line on north or south margin or on the line itself (on the face of the map)	84	Take south edge of square in which point lies and read the figures printed opposite this line on east or west margin or on the line itself (on the face of the map)	24
Estimate tenths eastwards	4	Estimate tenths northwards	7
East	844	North	247

Nearest similar reference on this grid 500 Km. distant

GRID DATA
Southern Italy Grid

Colour .... Blue
Projection .... Lambert Conical Orthomorphic
Spheroid .... Bessel
Origin .... 39°30' N. 14° E. of Greenwich
False Co-ordinates of origin .... 700,000 metres E.
                                        600,000 metres N.

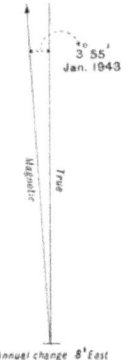

3°55'
Jan. 1943

Magnetic   True

Annual change 8' East

CONVERGENCE
At the West Edge of this sheet Grid North is 0°59' West of True North
At the East Edge of this sheet Grid North is 0°40' West of True North

REFERENCE

Railway, two or more tracks with station
single track and electrified
narrow gauge or Tramway
Tram lines on a road
Cable railway
National Highways (Autostrade)   } 2-way
     8 Metres wide, metalled   } M.T.
Main Roads (Strade Statali with route numbers)   } 2-way No 7
     6 Metres wide or over, metalled   } M.T.
Other Main Roads (Strade di grande comunicazione) } Mostly
     5 Metres wide or over, metalled   } 2-way M.T.
Secondary Roads   } 1-way
     3-5 Metres wide, generally metalled } M.T.
Other Roads and Cart Tracks, generally unmetalled
Mule Tracks
Paths
Boundaries, state
    ,, province
Canal
Aqueducts, over and underground   Undergd.
Wells, perennial, non-perennial
Marsh and Swamp
Church, Chapel, Cemetery
Names of physical features   M. Moncour
Trigonometrical points   Δ 170
Heights in metres   . 160
Cliffs
Embankment or Dyke
Woods

Contours at 50 metres interval

ADJOINING SHEETS

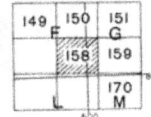

149	150	151
F	158	159
	G	
	170	
L	M	

COMPARATIVE INDEX

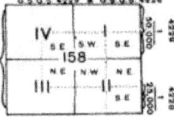

G.S.G.S. 4229 & G.S.G.S. 4026

IV		I
SE	SW	SE
	158	
NE	NW	NE
III		II

AUTHORITIES
Copied from Carta Topografica
1/100,000 Sheet 158. 1933.
1/25,000 Sheets IV S.E., I S.W., I S.E.,
III N.E., II N.W., N.E., S.E., 1936.
Instituto Geografico Militare
Partially revised for communications, 1943.

LITTORIA
N4120-E1227/20x30

AREA REVISED
FROM AIR PHOTOS

STORIA di Littoria
LITTORIA
Bonifica di Piscinara

Reproduced under the direction of the Chief of Engineers by the Army Map Service,
U.S. Army, Washington, D.C., 1944 from GSGS
Second Edition 1943 Kodalines.

ARMY MAP SERVICE, U.S. ARMY, WASHINGTON, D.C. 113496
1944

7   8 Miles
11   12   13 Kilometres

Longitudes are based on the meridian of Rome, which is 12°27'7.1" East of Greenwich.

in the attack, or the loss of staff personnel. As a countermeasure against possible further amphibious or airborne operations against Rome, the 1027th Panzer Grenadier Regiment is held as a motorized reserve. The 1027th Panzer Grenadier Regiment, 450th Artillery Battalion, 3d Company of 525 Antitank Battalion, with 88 mm self propelled guns, and the 1st Company of 60th Combat Engineer Battalion (motorized), are available to counterattack the expected enemy landing in the area of Civitavecchia.

The Commander of Artillery Group 317 is placed under the command of Army. He will command the long-range artillery group of the unattached 619th Regiment, and the 56th Projector Regiment, reinforced by the Projector Demonstration Battalion. He will coordinate the artillery of both Corps, in order to assure effectiveness of the artillery, particularly along the Corps boundaries.

B. Intelligence Report

Prisoners of war have confirmed the 1st Duke of Wellington, of the 3d Brigade/1st Infantry Division (Br) at Hill 115 (F 869369). Units of the 1st Armored Division (US) are employed in area north of Aprilia.

C. Statistics

German losses: 87 killed, 259 wounded, and 194 missing.

Allied losses: 2 prisoners (American), 2 trucks destroyed, and 3 aircraft downed.

XI. 4 FEBRUARY 1944

A. Operations Report

Our attack north of Aprilia (F 875333) began at 2300 last night. Combat Group "Pfeiffer" (65th Infantry Division) reached the road 3.2km southwest of Cie. Vallelata (F 863347), and defended this newly won position with artillery fire. Combat Group "Gräser" penetrated the main line of resistance 2.5 km north of Aprilia and contacted Combat Group "Peiffer". After setting up a defensive front toward the south, the cut-off enemy groups were attacked. Individual strongpoints were heavily fought over, and enemy attempts to relieve their encircled forces from the south, by attacks in battalion strength with tank support, were repulsed. Our artillery supported our attack by firing on Allied reserves, brought toward Aprilia. An enemy battalion north of Aprilia was destroyed. Heavy enemy artillery fire, partly supported by naval gunfire, interfered with our attacks. The main forces of the 29th Grenadier Regiment (motorized), were placed on the new main line of resistance during the night of 4/5 February.

B. Eyewitness Report

The terrain of our attack was difficult, because of the many deep cuts, running in a northeast to southwesterly direction. Supporting tanks were handicapped by the heavy rains and mud. Any success against the stubborn enemy was due to the efforts of our infantry. Our losses were light compared with those of the enemy. We captured 5 trucks, 2 armored reconnaissance cars, 1 Sherman tank, 3 ammunition carriers, and 2 motorcycles. With the exception of the 2 reconnaissance cars and 1 ammunition carrier damaged by artillery fire, all vehicles were intact. They were abandoned by their crews without attempting to destroy them.

C. Intelligence Report

The 1st Loyal Battalion of the 2d Brigade of the 1st Infantry Division(Br) is located 1.5 km northeast of Cle. Spaccasassi (F 917330), according to a British prisoner. He also said the 7th Infantry Regiment (US), with 3d Reconnaissance Battalion attached, was on the right of the 1st Loyal. This confirms our previous estimates of the boundary between the British and American forces. Captured papers confirmed previous information that the 1st Armored Division (US) was on the beachhead. The 6th Gordons Infantry Battalion (Br) was in the area 1.5 km south of Cle. della Mandria (F 898365), the 1st Duke of Wellington Infantry Regiment (Br) is 4 km northeast of Aprilia, and the 1st King's Shropshire Light Infantry Regiment (Br) is south of Stazione Campoleone (F 877386).

D. Statistics

German losses: 74 killed, 161 wounded, and 498 missing (probably 80 % killed).

Allied losses: 19 officers and about 900 enlisted men taken prisoner in pocket north of Aprilia, 12 tanks, 1 armored reconnaissance car destroyed, and 4 aircraft shot down.

XII. 5 FEBRUARY 1944

A. Operations Report

Only minor infantry activities took place during the day. The enemy artillery was active including naval guns. In the evening, the left flank of the 71st Infantry Division and the 26th Panzer Division attacked on Fourteenth Army orders with the objective to establish a new main line of resistance from Ponte Rotto (F 997314) to a crossing 3 km northeast of Cle. Carano (F 940309). Our armor crossed the railroad dam and penetrated the olive grove 1.6 km west of Ponte Rotto. An enemy attack, from the grove in battalion strength, was halted when it reached its own artillery impact area. Enemy losses were high. The Parachute Demonstration Battalion attacking the woods west of Ponte Rotto had to withdraw under enemy pressure. The left flank of the division reached its objective with armored support and occupied Ponte Rotto.

Our artillery fired on visual targets with good results. 1 cruiser and 1 destroyer 4 miles west of Anzio withdrew.

Army reserves included the 1st and 2d Battalions, 147th Grenadier Regiment (behind 1st Parachute Corps); two Battalions of 67th Panzer Grenadier Regiment; Panzer Grenadier Regiment 1028 (behind LXXVI Corps); Panzer Grenadier Regiment 1027 (former Army reserve) assigned to 4th Parachute Division.

By order of the Army High Command the reinforced Panzer Grenadier Regiment 1027 was assigned to the 3d Panzer Grenadier Division, and the reinforced Panzer Grenadier Regiment 1028 to the 26th Panzer Division. With the assignment of these regiments each of the two divisions now has three Panzer Grenadier Regiments.

Due to the possibility of new landings, particularly in the area between the Tiber river and Livorno, Fourteenth Army ordered the following units to be ready to move after a two hour warning: the 450th Artillery Battalion, 1st Company, 525th Antitank Battalion, 1st Company, 22d Engineer (Airforce), 1st Heavy Antiaircraft Battalion, 12th Regiment, and the newly arrived units of 114th Jäger Division.

Artillery situation: A total of 39 enemy batteries has been located. An additional 20 batteries are believed to be in the area. Therefore, our 85 batteries are opposed by 50 enemy batteries. Not included in this figure, are enemy heavy caliber naval guns, which give considerable support to the land forces, and armored self-propelled artillery. Unlike our own, the enemy's artillery has at its disposal an almost unlimited supply of ammunition. Due to the absence of enemy counterbattery fire, it is believed that he has no exact picture of our artillery positions.

The ensuing table depicts the artillery available to our own units.

Unit	Number of Batteries	Number of guns	Caliber
1st Parachute Corps	20	87	22, over 10.5 cm
LXXVI Panzer Corps	46	156	57, over 10.5 cm
Army coast artillery	10.5	43	19, over 10.5 cm
56th Rocket Projector Regiment	7	41	35 with 15 cm 6 with 21 cm
Panzer Projector Battery "Hermann Göring"		8	15 cm
Railroad artillery	2	4	
Army Reserve	9	33	None over 10.5
Total	94.5	372	
A projector demonstration battalion is expected			

The chart below indicates the tanks, assault guns, heavy antitank guns available in our area, less those employed in coastal defense.

Type tank	1 Feb 1944	4 Feb 1944
Panzer IV (Long)	11	20
Panzer V (Panther)	–	59
Flame-throwing Tanks	5	6
Panzer VI (Tiger)	4	–
Command Tanks German	7	7
Italian	3	3
Total	30	95

Assault guns	1 Feb 1944	4 Feb 1944
German	22	18
Italian	26	29
Total	48	47

Heavy Antitank Guns	169	193

B. Intelligence Report

Captured documents indicate that the 1st Irish Guards is supported by the 39th Battalion of the Field Artillery Regiment. The

81st Reconnaissance Battalion of the 1st Armored Division (US) has been established 1 km southeast of l' Osteriaccia (F 789283). The 2d Battalion of the 36th Engineer Battalion (US) is about 4 km southwest of Le Ferriere (F 963242). According to 4 prisoner's of war of F Company, the 30th Infantry Regiment of the 3d Infantry Division (US) is 1 km south of Padiglione (F 921289), and G Company 1 km east of that town. Most of the prisoners, taken in the pocket north of Aprilia (F 875333), are from the 6th Gordons and 1st Duke of Wellington Regiment. A prisoner of war says the 1st Battalion, 504 Parachute Regiment is near the bridge 1.5 km southwest Borgo Piave (G 053203). An enemy patrol had the mission to capture prisoners for interrogation as the enemy is preparing an attack from the Littoria (G 0818) area. Rumors are spreading, that the 509th Parachute Regiment will arrive in Anzio soon.

As the enemy is not committing his reserves, it is assumed that he is preparing a new attack. It is possible, that apart from continuing his efforts to break out of the beachhead, in the direction of Aprilia, the enemy will attempt to breakthrough towards Cisterna (G 0232). Another possibility is an attack in the direction of Ardea (F 787350), in coordination with a landing west of Ardea.

Enemy Strength on Anzio Beachhead as of 5 February 1944

At the front	Inf Bns	tanks	Anti-tank guns	arty pieces	AA guns	Armored scout cars
1st Infantry Division (Br)	6	—	59	72	48	39
46th Tank Battalion	—	45	—	—	—	9
3d Infantry Division (US)	8	—	36	48	32	8
751st Tank Battalion	—	16	3	—	—	—
601st Tank Destroyer Battalion	—	—	38	—	—	8
Tank Destroyers (Br)	—	—	36	—	—	—
1st Armored Division (US)	4	378	198	96	32	135
Rangers	2	—	—	—	—	—
504th Airborne Regiment	3	—	—	—	—	—
Corps Artillery (US)	—	—	—	54 (15 cm)	—	—
Corps Antiaircraft (US)	—	—	—	—	24	—
In Reserve						
45th Infantry Division (US)	9	—	64	48	32	10
Reported by reliable sources						
1 Infantry Division (Br)	1	—	64	72	48	—
Elements of 2d Armored Division (US)	—	158 (L)				
66th Armored Regiment	—	232 (M)				
Total	43	829	498	390	216	209

C. Statistics

German losses: 64 killed, 190 wounded, and 7 missing.

Allied losses: 63 prisoners and 102 dead.

Destroyed or captured : 3 howitzers (7.5 cm), 1 light gun, 4 bazookas, 4 light mortars, 1 machine gun, 2 antitank guns and numerous small arms, 7 planes shot down, and 34 vehicles destroyed.

A. Operations Report

With the exception of reconnaissance, artillery, and air activities by both sides, the day was quiet. During the night, an enemy attack, in company strength, against the right sector of the 26th Panzer Division was broken up, by concentrated fire of all weapons. Our artillery shelled enemy assembly areas, entrenchments, batteries, and ships at Nettuno and Anzio. Our antiaircraft guns (88 mm) shelled the airport 2,5 km southeast of Nettuno.

The 114th Jäger Division, less Combat Group "Berger", is assembling in the region of Frascati-Castel di Leva-Torre Chiesaccia. The 1st Battalion, 4th Panzer Regiment will be in the region 5 km west of Albano tonight. The 301st Panzer Battalion (remote controlled demolition vehicles), arrived in part in the region south of Stazione Agraria (5 km south of the outskirts of Rome).

By order of the Fourteenth Army the newly arrived staff of the 69th Panzer Regiment is attached to the LXXVI Panzer Corps. The staff and subordinate units will constitute Army reserves. They are: 1st Battalion, 4th Panzer Regiment (Panther tanks), 301st Panzer Battalion (remote controlled demolition vehicles), 1 assault howitzer battalion, Panzer Company "Schwelbach" (Tiger tanks) and currently with the 3d Panzer Grenadier Division, and First Panzer company (Ferdinand tanks). The units now in transit will assemble in the region south and southeast of Rome. All measures for a rapid drive to the south must be prepared.

The Army High Command has ordered the activation of the 92d Infantry Division, in the Civitavecchia area. The majority of the troops will be obtained from the reinforced 1026th Grenadier Regiment. It will consist of the 1059th Grenadier Regiment, 1060th Grenadier Regiment, and the 192d Artillery Battalion. Its activation will be completed by 1 March 1944, and the division will be ready for action by 15 April 1944.

The Commanding General of Fourteenth Army issued an order, setting forth the following directives: First, the aim of the next attack by the Army will be the capture of Aprilia (F 875333). This attack will be made during the night of 7 to 8 February. The approximate main line of resistance after the attack will be the line along the southern edge of the ridge Tenuta Buonriposo (F 8332) to 1 km southwest Casale Carroceto (F 869330) to the crossroads southeast of Aprilia to the roadfork, 5 km northeast of Aprilia. Second, diversions will be carried out along the entire front. Strong elements of I Parachute Corps will attack from the west. The main attack group consisting of the LXXVI Panzer Corps, reinforced by available elements of the 71st Infantry Division, will attack from the east. Third, the ground liaison officer of the 2d Air Force will be requested to provide strong fighter escort over the area of Aprilia, as early as possible on 8 February, and to have planes alerted for missions requested by the LXXVI Panzer Corps.

B. Intelligence Report

An undated paper captured in the sector of the 7th Infantry Regiment (US) indicated that the 45th American Infantry Division, supported by a second brigade (probably the 1st Infantry Division (Br)) will attack Ardea (F 787350).

The interrogation of two prisoners, captured north of Aprilia on 5 February 1944, indicated that the 169th Brigade (Br) was an element of the 56th Infantry Division (Br). The Brigade is on the beachhead, as well as the entire division.

It is possible that an attack toward Ardea will be made by the 45th Infantry Division (US), reinforced by the 1st Armored Division (US) and possibly parts of the 1st Infantry Division (Br). This attack may be coordinated with a landing in the region south of Rome.

C. Statistics

German losses: 46 killed, 132 wounded, and 5 missing.

XIV. 7 FEBRUARY 1944

A. Operations Report

The hill 1.5 km northeast of Cle S. Lorenzo (F 780300), captured last night by an assault detachment, was later taken by the enemy, as a result of counterfire which caused many casualties. An enemy attack, in battalion strength, on the right flank of the 26th Panzer Division was repulsed. Two assault detachments wiped out two enemy strongholds. Two hills 2,5 km northeast of Aprilia (F 875333) were seized by reconnaissance, in force.

In the evening, the attack to recapture Aprilia began as planned. The 4th Parachute Division, which occupies the edge of the woods south of the Moletta Creek (F 7631 to F 8332), made numerous feints with reconnaissance patrols and assault detachments. At 2100, the 65th Infantry Division penetrated the enemy's main line of resistance, after combating enemy forces which stubbornly defended their positions. After destroying points of resistance in the Buonriposo Valley (F 8431), we succeeded in seizing a hill 2 km southwest of Aprilia. At 2130, the LXXVI Panzer Corps attacked on the right flank (Combat Group "Gräser") and penetrated the enemy line along the road 1 km east of Cantoniera. Diversionary attempts were made by assault detachments of the 26th Panzer Division and the Panzer Division "Hermann Göring".

In spite of heavy defensive fire by naval guns, the attacking forces reached their designated objectives in all sectors. Our artillery supported the attack, with harassing and surprise fire on enemy troop concentrations and movements, shelters, and supply routes. In addition, the 280 mm railroad guns and 170 mm guns shelled enemy ships off Anzio and Nettuno. The attack on Aprilia is planned for 0600, 8 February.

After an air raid by the Luftwaffe on Nettuno, fires were observed.

After the completion of the attack on Aprilia, the Army Command has ordered the LXXVI Panzer Corps to reorganize its forces as follows: First, to withdraw the 26th Panzer Division, as soon as possible, to the vicinity of Cisterna (G 0233), where it is to act as a reserve. Second, to replace the 71st Infantry Division by the 715th (motorized) Infantry Division. Third, to prepare to place the 114th Jäger Division, less Regimental Group "Berger", in the sector currently held by Combat Group "Gräser". Fourth, to withdraw the 3d Panzer Grenadier Division from the front. This reorganization must be concluded no later than 14 February 1944.

Army Reserves are I Parachute Corps, with the 3d Battalion of the 4th Parachute Division as its components, and the LXXVI Panzer Corps, with the 2d Battalion of 194th Grenadier Regiment, and the 26th Panzer Reconnaissance Battalion, as its subordinate units.

B. Intelligence Report

Prisoners confirm the position of the 1st London Scots (169th Brigade of 56th Infantry Division) to be north of Aprilia, and the 1st Irish Rifles to be west of Spaccasassi (F 917330).

C. Statistics

German losses: (minus I Parachute Corps) 23 dead, 99 wounded, and 9 missing.

Allied losses: 8 British prisoners, 28 American prisoners, 4 tanks destroyed or captured, 1 tank rendered immobile, 1 scout car destroyed, 3 motor vehicles destroyed, and 5 fighter bombers downed. Captured material: 8 automatic rifles, 7 light machine guns, 1 bazooka, 13 mines, 1 radio set (tank), 2 ammunition carriers, and 2 motorcycles.

XV. 8 FEBRUARY 1944

A. Operations Report

Due to strong enemy resistance and our heavy losses, the main attack on Aprilia (F 875333), which had been planned for 0600, 8 February 1944, had to be postponed. The attack will take place during the night of 8 to 9 February after the troops regroup in the dark, due to increased enemy activity. The attack will begin at 0000.

Continued tank supported counterattacks during the whole day were repulsed. Tank supported enemy attacks recaptured the cemetery in the Combat Group "Gräser" sector, northeast of Aprilia. On the right flank of the 26th Panzer Division an advanced company was cut off about noon, but was relieved at 2300 by our tank attack. In the morning, an enemy attack against Ponte Rotto (F 997314) was smashed by artillery fire. Four enemy tanks, that were feeling their way forward towards our outposts were forced to turn back by our infantry gun fire. Our artillery laid harassing fire on important enemy supply routes, and engaged enemy artillery with counterbattery fire with observed results. The harbor of Nettuno and the airport east of it were shelled by 17 cm cannons and railway guns.

The Commander in Chief Southwest has ordered the Fourteenth Army to exchange elements of the 71st Infantry Division and of the 15th Panzer Grenadier Division for the 29th Panzer Grenadier Division, currently with the Tenth Army. The marchorder for the transferred units follows. During the night of 8 to 9 February, at least two infantry battalions and one artillery battalion will move to their new position; during the night of 9 to 10 February, two infantry battalions and two artillery battalions; and the remainder of 71st Infantry Division and 15th Panzer Grenadier Division, will move in the night of 10 to 11 February.

The 114th Jager Division previously employed in the sector north of Spalato, Yugoslavia, will soon arrive in the sector south of Rome.

It will be attached to the 76th Panzer Corps as of 0000, 9 February 1944. Fourteenth Army will determine the employment of this division.

B. Eyewitness Report

The attacking troops were weakened not so much by enemy infantry defense as by heavy artillery fire, which, supported by naval artillery, has increased to barrage strength. An infantry battalion attacking Aprilia, from the north, suffered heavy losses in a mine field 1 km north of Aprilia. A captured enemy situation map gave the extent of the mine field, so that a large number of mines could be removed during the day, and a new attack be prepared. The mines, British contact mines, are comparatively easy to find. Most of them have been laid openly without camouflage. The supply of rations and ammunition, for the attacking unit, was brought up regularly in spite of heavy fire by enemy artillery and air attacks on the supply routes.

C. Intelligence Report

Information from captured documents indicates that the 1st Regiment of the 1st Special Service Force (US) is near l' Osteriaccia (F 789283). According to statements made by prisoners, the 3d Regiment and parts of the 2d Regiment of this unit are also on the beachhead. The remainder of the 2d Regiment is expected to arrive. The alleged mission of this unit is an attack Littoria (G 0818).

According to our air reconnaissance, outside Nettuno harbor lie 1 aircraft carrier, 5 tankers, 1 large transport, 40 large and numerous small ships.

D. Statistics

German losses: (less Group Gräser and 65th Infantry Division) 29 killed, 98 wounded, and 26 missing.

Allied losses: 791 British prisoners. Most of the prisoners are from the 5th Grenadier Guards, 3d Staffords and Irish Guards. None from the 1st Scots Guards have appeared.

XVI. 9 FEBRUARY 1944

A. Operations Report

At midnight, the left flank of the I Parachute Corps and the right flank of the LXXVI Panzer Corps resumed the attack, according to plan. During the night, the 725th Grenadier Regiment of Combat Group "Graser" advanced toward the northeast town limits of Aprilia (F 875333), after by-passing an enemy mine field north of the town. Before noon, the southern part of the town was taken in heavy fighting; and a defensive front to the south was established. Several enemy counterattacks, with heavy tank support (20 to 30 tanks) and some by single tanks, were repulsed by artillery, assault guns, and "Hornets".

The 65th Infantry Division attacked Cle. Carroceto (F 869330) at 1400 hours. After heavy fighting during the day, the Germans succeeded in occupying the railway line southwest of Cle. Carroceto and south of Hill 80 (F 865325). The Allies put up a stubborn defense in strong points. Numerous counterattacks were launched by the Allies, with tank support. For the first time, bomber units supported the ground forces. It was difficult to bring forward artillery, since the streets leading to Cle. Carroceto, from the west and northwest, were heavily mined and subject to shelling. It is planned to attack again and take Cle. Carroceto, during the night of 9 to 10 February, in order to establish contact with Combat Group "Gräser" in Aprilia.

Even though enemy artillery activity was relatively light, due to the scarcity of ammunition, it was compensated for, by heavy bomber and fighter activity.

For political reasons, elements of the Italian Parachute Regiment "Nembo" will be attached to the 4th Parachute Division and employed at the front. Upon arrival at the beachhead, the following troops will be attached to the units designated: Artillery Demonstration Regiment and 56th Projector Regiment is attached to the 65th Infantry Division; the Infantry Demonstration Regiment to the 3d Panzer Grenadier Division; and the Staff of the 69th Tank Regiment with the 216th, 301st, and 508th Tank Battalion; as well as, the 1st Battalion of the 4th Tank Regiment to the LXXVI Panzer Corps. The following units now employed with the Fourteenth Army will be transferred to the Tenth Army. During the night of 9 to 10 February, the Staff of the 194th Grenadier Regiment, 1st Battalion of the 194th Grenadier Regiment, and one artillery battalion, all of the 71st Infantry Division will be transferred; in the night, 10 to 11 February, the Fusilier Battalion of the 356th Infantry Division, and the 104th Panzer Grenadier Regiment of the 15th Panzer Grenadier Division. By 14 February, the 2d Battalion of the 71st Grenadier Regiment (motorized) of the 29th Panzer Grenadier Division must be moved. Reserves of the LXXVI Panzer Corps include the 67th Panzer Grenadier Regiment (less the 1st Battalion) located in the sector 1 km south of Ariccia (near Lake Albano), and the 2d Battalion of the 194th Grenadier Regiment, in the woods 1 km northeast of Aprilia.

First order by the Fourteenth Army for the attack to wipe out the Nettuno beachhead (code name: "Fischfang").

During the last days the enemy has brought to and employed on the beachhead fresh reinforcements. The 56th Infantry Division (Br), has just been identified. More reinforcements can be counted on. After the seizure of Aprilia, heavy enemy attacks against that sector are expected.

The Fourteenth Army will attack the enemy beachhead on X day, 15 February 1944 at Y hour, with its main effort between 1.5 km west of Aprilia-Nettuno highway and the Fosso di Spaccasassi (F 9129 to 9034). The front will be pierced and the attacking forces will push through to Nettuno and destroy enemy forces of the beachhead.

Orders to the Corps: I Parachute Corps (4th Parachute Division and 65th Infantry Division) will concentrate all available forces on its east flank. It will attack from the sector west of Cle. Carroceto (F 869330) in a southerly direction and will cover the west flank of the entire attack. The LXXVI Panzer Corps (3d Panzer Grenadier Division, Infantry Demonstration Regiment, the 114th Jäger Division and the 715th motorized Infantry Division) will attack with the first wave. It will break through the enemy lines in the sector stretching from west of Aprilia-Nettuno highway to Fosso di Spaccasassi and will advance to Nettuno.

The 29th Panzer Grenadier Division and the 26th Panzer Division, including the 1st Battalion of the 4th Panzer Regiment and the 508th Tiger Battalion, will be held in readiness. They will be positioned so that they can be employed for a further thrust on Nettuno after a successful breakthrough or for mopping-up operations on the flanks. The sector east of Fosso di Spaccasassi will be held with a minimum of troops. Full use must be made of our strong artillery and armored forces. The date of the attack will be set later.

The I Parachute Corps will be organized as follows:

1. Large units

    a. 4th Parachute Division (only elements ready for action)
    b. 65th Infantry Division (less the 146th Grenadier Regiment, and the 4th Battalion of the 165th Artillery Regiment)
    c. Commander of Rome: 936th Security Battalion, Rome SS Police Battalion, 676th Regional Defense Battalion. Withdrawal of forces will be made only with Army approval.

2. Army troops

    a. 1027th Panzer Grenadier Regiment
    b. 590th Tank Destroyer Battalion
    c. One company of the 525th Tank Destroyer Battalion (Hornets")

3. Air Force troops

    a. Assault Gun Battalion, XI Air Force Corps
    b. 22d Air Corps Engineer Battalion

The Organization of the LXXVI Panzer Corps is listed below:

1. First Combat Wave

    a. Large Units

        (1) 3d Panzer Grenadier Division (less 103d Panzer Reconnaissance Battalion)
        (2) 114th Jäger Division
        (3) 715th motorized Infantry Division
        (4) Panzer Division "Hermann Göring" (temporarily, less the bulk of the Panzer Regiment and the staff of Panzer Grenadier Regiment "Herman Göring")
    b. Miscellaneous Units

        (1) 1st Parachute Division: 3d Battalion of the 1st Parachute Regiment.
        (2) 16th SS Panzer Grenadier Division: 2d Battalion of the 35th SS Grenadier Regiment and the reinforced 2d Battalion of the 36th SS Panzer Grenadier Regiment.
        (3) 362d Fusilier Battalion.

- 40 -

c. Army Troops

(1) Infantry Demonstration Regiment
    (horse-drawn)
(2) 1028th Panzer Grenadier Regiment
(3) 216th Assault Panzer Battalion
(4) 301st Radio Controlled Demolition
    Tank Battalion
(5) 525th Tank Destroyer Battalion
    (less 1st Company)
(6) 60th Engineer Battalion (motorized)
(7) 811th Armored Engineer Company
    (Goliath tanks)
(8) Staff, 543d Engineer Regiment
(9) 813th Armored Engineer Company
    (Goliath tanks)
(10) 840th Heavy Armored Bridge Column

d. Air Force Troops
(1) Parachute Demonstration Battalion
(2) 7th Air Corps Field Battalion
    (unattached)

2. Second Combat Wave

a. Large Units

(1) 26th Armored Division
(2) 29th Panzer Grenadier Division

b. Army Troops

(1) Staff of 69th Panzer Regiment
(2) 1st Battalion of the 4th Panzer
    Regiment (Panther tanks)
(3) 508th Panzer Battalion (Tiger tanks)

Full support by Air Force and Navy is requested for the
impending attack.

We must deceive the enemy as to the sector of our main
effort. To accomplish this it is ordered that: First, the
entire enemy front must be constantly raided, especially in
the the area of the Panzer Division "Hermann Goring" and
the 4th Parachute Division. Second, the 26th Panzer Division
will be assembled in the area Cisterna (G 0232) - Doganella
(G 106306) - Casale delle Castelle (G 007352) after they are
withdrawn from the front line. The 29th Panzer Grenadier
Division will be assembled in the area Velletri - Lanuvio -
Genzano (owns excluded). Raids by this division will be
made in the sector southwest of Cisterna. Third, the 26th
Panzer Division and the 29th Panzer Grenadier Division will
conduct reconnaissance, wearing black Tank Corps uniforms to
deceive the enemy that motorized forces are preparing attacks
in this area. Fourth, motorized troops from assembly areas,
in the rear, will be transferred only after the beginning of
the attack, to positions of readiness, behind the point of
main effort.

B. Intelligence Report

The 2d Battalion of the 157th Regiment, of the 45th Infantry
Division (US) has been located for the first time 1.5 km east of Cle.
S Lorenzo (F 780300). It has been confirmed, that the 2d Staffords

is employed in the area 1 km northwest of Cle. S Lorenzo. On their
right flank is the 5th Grenadier Guards, and next to them to the
northeast the remainder of the 1st Irish Guards. One American battalion under the command of the 24th Guard Brigade, is employed in
the area south of Lorenzo. The 2d Battalion of the 15th Infantry
Regiment of the 3d Infantry Division (US) is employed in the area,
Isola Bella (G 006294); this was confirmed by prisoner's of war.
All three battalions of the 168th Brigade, 56th Infantry Division (Br)
are employed in the Aprilia area and further east. The 3d Battalion
of the 157th Infantry Regiment, and the 3d Battalion of the 504th
Parachute Regiment are employed near Cle. S Lorenzo.

Prisoner's of war indicate that the 1st London Irish Rifles
and 10th Royal Berkshire are directly east of Cle. S Lorenzo. To
the east thereof is the 1st London Scots.

L Company 3d Battalion of the 179th Infantry Regiment, of
the 45th Infantry Division (US) is 1 km south of l'Osteriaccia (F 789283)
The regiment was employed on the southeastern flank one week ago.
Another regiment of the division is said to have been committed in
the western section of the beachhead.

C. Statistics

German losses: (less Combat Group "Gräser") 42 killed, 152
wounded, and 113 missing.

Allied losses:

Prisoners: 420 British, 1 American, 15 tanks
destroyed, 3 tanks put out of commission, and 4 heavy antitank guns
destroyed.

Captured: 10 antitank guns, 28 heavy mortars,
155 machine guns, 30 submachine guns, 22 motor vehicles, and 1 tank.

XVII. 10 FEBRUARY 1944

A. Operations Report

In the morning, the 65th Infantry Division succeeded in
taking the railroad station at Carroceto (F 865330), and the enemy
strongpoint on Hill 80 (F 865325). An enemy counterattack, supported by tanks, recaptured the hill, as well as the railroad station
at Carroceto and inflicted heavy losses. The station, however, was
retaken in the evening by Combat Group "Gräser".

Before dawn, the reinforced 26th Panzer Reconnaissance Battalion, occupied Cle Carroceto and destroyed the strongpoints north
of it, which had held out since the morning of 9 February. At night,
the 26th Panzer Division repelled an enemy attack in company strength.

The enemy attacked during the night, after heavy artillery
preparations, with the strength of two companies, in the sector of
the Panzer Division "Hermann Göring", and penetrated our main line
of resistance at a point 1 km south of Borgo Podgora(G 045240).
The enemy was repulsed by our counterattack. Another enemy attack
southeast of Aprilia (F 875333), was broken up by our artillery.

SOUTH ITALY GRID (BLUE)

TO GIVE A GRID REFERENCE ON THIS SHEET

Pay no attention to the smaller co-ordinate figures at the corners and in margins.
They are for finding full co-ordinates.

PAY ATTENTION TO LARGER MARGINAL FIGURES AND TO THOSE PRINTED ON THE FACE OF THE MAP.

POINT	Cava		F 844247	
	East		North	
	Take west edge of square in which point lies and read the figures printed opposite this line on north or south margin or on the line itself (on the face of the map)	84	Take south edge of square in which point lies and read the figures printed opposite this line on east or west margin or on the line itself (on the face of the map)	24
	Estimate tenths eastwards	4	Estimate tenths northwards	7
	East	844	North	247

Nearest similar reference on this grid 500 Km distant.

GRID DATA
Southern Italy Grid

Colour .... Blue
Projection .... Lambert Conical Orthomorphic
Spheroid .... Bessel
Origin .... 39°30′N 14°E of Greenwich
False Co-ordinates of origin .... 700,000 metres E
600,000 metres N

N O
3 55
Jan. 1943

Magnetic   True

Annual change 8′ East

CONVERGENCE

At the West Edge of this sheet Grid North is 0°59′West of True North
At the East Edge of this sheet Grid North is 0°40′West of True North

REFERENCE

Railways, two or more tracks with station
single track and electrified
narrow gauge or Tramway
Tram lines on a road
Cable railway
National Highways (Autostrade)
8 Metres wide, metalled
Main Roads (Strade Statali with route numbers)
6 Metres wide or over, metalled
Other Main Roads (Strade di grande comunicazione)
5 Metres wide or over, metalled
Secondary Roads
3–5 Metres wide, generally metalled
Other Roads and Cart Tracks, generally unmetalled
Mule Tracks
Paths
Boundaries, state
"   province
Canal
Aqueducts, over and underground
Wells, perennial, non-perennial
Marsh and Swamp
Church, Chapel, Cemetery
Names of physical features
Trigonometrical points
Heights in metres
Cliffs
Embankment or Dyke
Woods

Contours at 50 metres interval

No 7

ADJOINING SHEETS

149	150	151
F	G	
158	159	
L	170 M	

COMPARATIVE INDEX

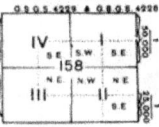

GSGS 4228 & GSGS 4226

IV		
S.E.	S.W.	S.E.
158		
N.E.	N.W.	N.E.
III		II
		S.E.

AREA REVISED
FROM AIR PHOTOS

AUTHORITIES
Copied from Carta Topografica
1/100,000 Sheet 158. 1933.
1/25,000 Sheets IV S.E., I S.W., I S.E.
III N.E., II N.W., N.E., S.E., 1936.
Instituto Geografico Militare
Partially revised for communications, 1943.

LITTORIA
N4120-E1227/20x30

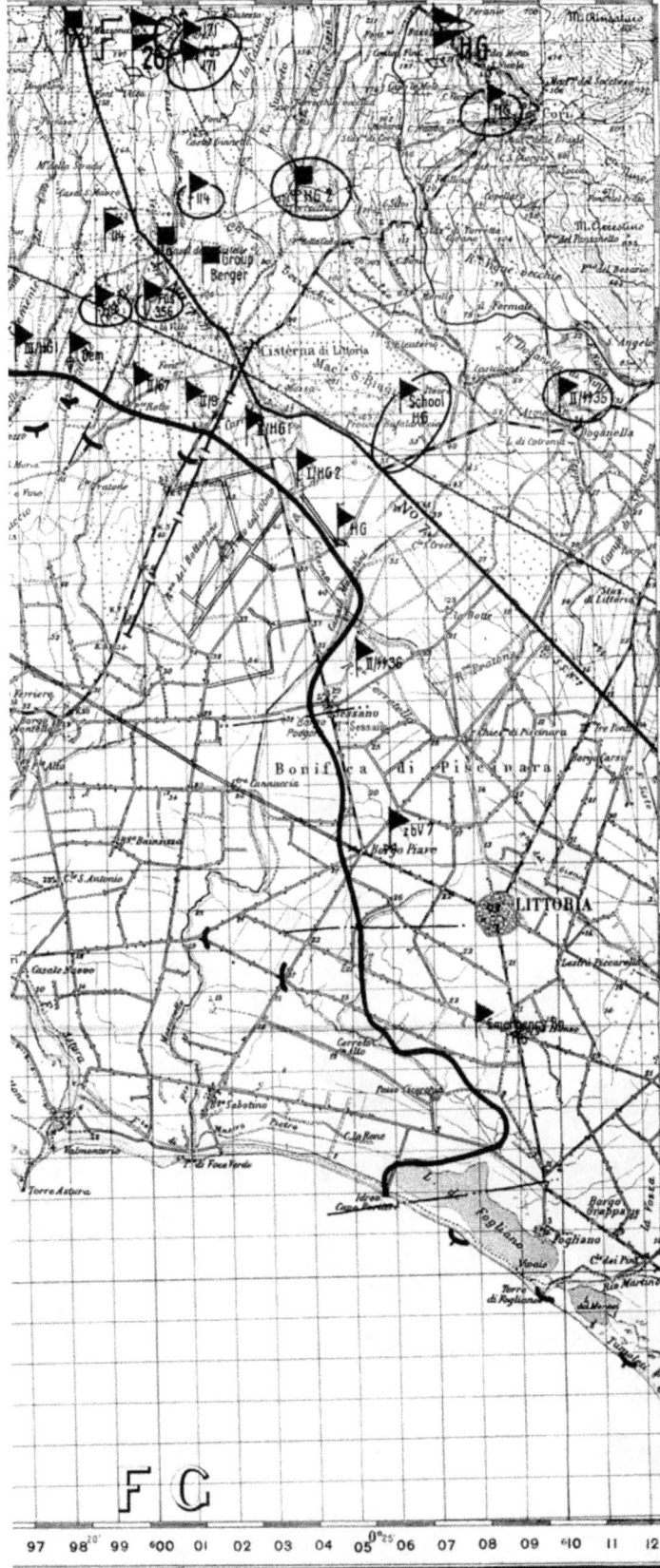

Reproduced under the direction of the Chief of Engineers by the Army Map Service,
U. S. Army, Washington, D. C., 1944 from GSGS
Second Edition 1943 Kodalines.

ARMY MAP SERVICE, U. S. ARMY, WASHINGTON, D. C. 113498

7   8 Miles
12   13 Kilometres

Longitudes are based on the meridian of Rome, which is 12°27′7·1″ East of Greenwich.

LITTORIA

F G

During the entire day, enemy artillery was very active, especially in the area of Aprilia.

B. Intelligence Report

The location of 1st London Guards, 1st Irish Guards, elements of the 894th Tank Destroyer Battalion (US), and 81st Tank Destroyer Battalion (Br), as well as 23d Engineer Company (Br) at Cle Carroceto, was confirmed.

According to information received from prisoners of war, the 1st Irish Rifles is between Cle Carroceto and Aprilia, and the 1st Battalion, 30th Infantry Regiment is in the Ponte Rotto (F 997314) area.

The 88th Infantry Division (US) arrived a short time ago at the beachhead, according to information from three deserters from the 2d Battalion, 7th Infantry Regiment.

It is believed that the 1st Special Service Force is emplaced along the Moscarello (G 0113 to G 0219).

Commander 1st Battalion of the 7th Infantry Regiment – Col. Sherman, is confirmed. Commander 2d Battalion of the 7th Infantry Regiment – Lt. Col. Devall.

Because of the considerable losses inflicted, especially upon the 1st Infantry Division (Br), during the last few days, the enemy has been forced to concentrate further forces in the Aprilia area, to prevent our breaking through. Since he would naturally attempt to prevent this, it must be assumed that, in addition to a determined defense, the enemy will counterattack in order to try to reconquer Aprilia.

C. Statistics

German losses: (less Combat Group "Gräser"): 18 dead, 61 wounded, and 16 missing.

Allied losses: 12 Americans captured (6 of them airmen) and 326 English captured.

Captured or destroyed: 20 tanks, 1 tank rendered immobile, 1 antitank gun, 3 prime movers, 1 machine gun, 12 submachine guns, 54 rifles, 2 heavy mortars with 500 rounds of ammunition, and 9 planes shot down.

Following are the total losses of the enemy, from 4 February 1944 to 10 February 1944, in the area of Aprilia: 2,563 prisoners, 53 tanks, 22 guns, 33 motor vehicles, 34 mortars, 168 machine guns, 42 submachine guns, 8 bazookas, and 20 planes.

XVIII. 11 FEBRUARY 1944

A. Operations Report

Since 0500, under cover of dense fog and artillery fire, the enemy attacked in strength, varying from one company to two battalions, supported by tanks. He attacked our positions at Aprilia (F 875333) and Carroceto (F 869330) from the southwest, south, and southeast and, in the afternoon, also from east of Aprilia. By the combined firing of our artillery, and particularly the self-propelled guns of the 103d Panzer Battalion, all attacks were repulsed; some only after close combat, in which the enemy suffered heavy losses. Flanking fire inflicted severe losses on the infantry. The main line of resistance remained unchanged. Due to repeated enemy attacks, the infantry was confronted with a serious ammunition shortage. If the attacks were to recur, the heavy weapons would have to bear the burden of defense. Heavy losses of the infantry, during the day, necessitated reinforcements. For this purpose, a combat engineer platoon was brought up, during the night, to be used as infantry.

Army Reserves consist of the 1st Battalion, 4th Panzer Regiment (Panther tanks); 301st Panzer Battalion (radio-controlled demolition vehicles, still in transit); 1st Battalion of the 93d Panzer Artillery Regiment (26th Panzer Division), 2d Battalion of the 29th Motorized Artillery Regiment (29th Panzer Grenadier Division). The last two are units received from the Tenth Army on exchange.

B. Eyewitness Report

As an enemy attack on Aprilia was expected, and therefore, the antitank defense in this sector had been especially reinforced. Our infantry was in position on the southern edge of the village. Only 12 assault guns and several heavy antitank guns remained in Aprilia. Although Aprilia was heavily shelled, our losses were comparatively small, because the assault guns took cover behind the houses, and waited for enemy tanks to come within close range before firing on them. The assault guns were very successful; 11 enemy tanks were destroyed, and 1 put out of commission. The fact that, despite repeated enemy attacks, the main line of resistance remained firm, gives credit to the excellent registration of our artillery. The "Hornets" due of their thin armor plating remained in the rear, but were also very successful in the antitank defense. They destroyed enemy tanks at a distance of 2.5 km.

C. Intelligence Report

Units of the 46th Tank Battalion (Br GHQ troops), were employed at Stazione Carroceto (F 865330). Their strength is approximately 48 tanks, mostly Shermans.

From prisoner of war reports, it ascertained that company A 1st Battalion of the 179th Infantry Regiment, of the 45th Infantry Division (US) is located at the Cle Carroceto (F 869330). The 2d Battalion 15th Regiment of the 3d Infantry Division (US) is located south of Ponte Rotto (F 997314). It is presumed that the disposition of the 3d Infantry Division (US) was approximately as follows: from Fosso delle Mole (F 9731) to the East, the 2d Battalion, 1st Battalion, 3d Battalion of the 30th Infantry Regiment; and from Ponte Rotto to the East, the 2d Battalion 15th Infantry Regiment, with the 2d Battalion 7th Infantry Regiment probably relieved. The enemy probably intends to renew his attacks in area Aprilia. 5 naval vessels, 4 freighters and several small vessels were observed off the coast of Nettuno.

D. Statistics

German losses (less Group "Gräser"): 40 killed, 115 wounded, and 15 missing.

Allied losses: 45 prisoners (22 British, 5 of them from the 46th Tank Battalion, and 23 Americans, one of them an aviator). 21 tanks destroyed, 2 tanks put out of commission, 1 antitank gun destroyed, and 2 ambulances captured.

XIX. 12 FEBRUARY 1944

A. Operations Report

Parts of the 65th Infantry Division and Combat Group "Gräser", which attacked at 0300, southwest of Cle Carroceto, (F 869330) were thrown back, after initial successes, by an enemy counterattack with armored forces. Numerous raids were executed by both sides during the night. In the forenoon, artillery and self propelled guns stopped an enemy attack from the southwest on Cle Carroceto and Aprilia (F 875330).

Fourteenth Army instructed the LXXVI Panzer Corps to prepare an attack on Isola Bella (G 006294), to deceive the enemy about the impending major attack along the Anzio and Aprilia road.

The German High Command commented on the planned attack as follows:

" The attack for 16 February is approved by Hitler. However, the final determination of D day depends upon favorable flying conditions. Mass employment of tanks cannot be afforded as it leads only to their loss. It is far better to keep tanks in reserve positions. Never commit tanks against concentrated antitank defenses, or pass through mine fields, antitank ditches, or swamps. If the infantry is properly concentrated, available forces will be sufficient for the mission."

The reinforced 956th Grenadier Regiment of the 362d Infantry Division, previously engaged in coastal defenses in the sector Cecina-mouth of Tiber, is allotted to the LXXVI Panzer Corps. Since the regiment is only suitable for defensive tasks, it will relieve elements of the Panzer Division "Hermann Göring" and the 1st Parachute Division in the sector southwest of Cisterna (G 0232), in order to free these units for the attack.

The following new units have arrived in the Army sector: 811th and 813th Armored Engineer Companies (remote controlled demolition vehicles "Goliath"); 1st and 2d Battalions, 741st Jäger Regiment; the greater part of 3d Battalion, 661st Artillery Regiment; and the 114th Engineer Battalion (114th Jäger Division); two companies of the 29th motorized Engineer Battalion; and one light and one heavy battery of the 313th Antiaircraft Battalion from the 29th Panzer Grenadier Division. The 4th Parachute Division received two companies of the Italian Parachute Battalion "Nembo", and one company of the Antitank Battalion from the 4th Parachute Division.

The 735th Grenadier Regiment, 715th Motorized Infantry Division, will relieve the 29th Panzer Grenadier Regiment the night of 12 to 13 February, in order that the latter unit can withdraw for rest and recuperation.

The 2d Battalion, 725th Motorized Grenadier Regiment has insufficient combat strength, and will be dissolved. The remaining troops of this battalion will be assigned to other parts of the regiment.

The 216th Assault Howitzer Battalion, in the sector east of Rome; the 811th and 813th Armored Engineer Companies (radio-controlled vehicles "Goliath"), in sector Frascati; and the Panzer Company "Meyer" (Tiger tank), in sector east of Frascati comprise the Army Reserve.

B. Personnel Strength of Fourteenth Army*

Army troops	Officers	Enlisted Men
Actual strength	2,556	59,918
Combat strength	986	33,355
Rear echelon troops of combat units	288	9,955
Supply troops	429	2,159
Air Force ground troops		
Actual strength	830	30,216
Combat strength	570	23,426
Rear echelon troops of combat units	159	4,926
Supply troops	136	2,801
SS troops		
Actual strength	22	1,703
Combat strength	21	1,408
Rear echelon troops of combat units	1	295
Total strength		
Actual strength	3,408	91,837
Combat strength	1,577	58,189
Rear echelon troops of combat units	448	15,189
Supply troops	565	4,960
Other units	Officers and Enlisted Men	
Italian Forces	181	
Italian Auxiliary Supply Units	265	
Russian Auxiliary Supply Units	887	
Other Auxiliary Supply Units	17	

* less 114th Jäger Division and 71st Infantry Division. Including the 362d Infantry Division (12,403 men) which is employed in coastal defense.

C. Intelligence Report

Company B 2d Foresters of the 3d Brigade 1st Infantry Division (Br) is again in the sector southwest of Cle Carroceto (F 879330). The other companies of the Battalion are in the same sector. The 24th Brigade is on the right of the 2d Foresters. The 191st Tank Battalion (US GHQ Troops) has been established at Cle Carroceto pursuant to prisoner of war reports. Prisoners of war further report that the 1st Irish Guards and 1st Scots Guards of the 24th

Brigade are located in the Cle Carroceto sector. They reconfirm the employment of the 80th Medium Artillery Regiment 1st Infantry Division (Br) west of Cle Carroceto.

The following American units are known to be on the beachhead: 45th Infantry Division, 3d Infantry Division, 1st Armored Division, 82d Airborne Division (elements only), 1st Special Service Force Regiment, 1st Ranger Battalion, 3d Ranger Battalion, 4th Ranger Battalion, 191st Tank Battalion (GHQ troops), 751st Tank Battalion (GHQ troops), 894th Tank Destroyer Battalion (GHQ troops), and the 601st Tank Destroyer Battalion (GHQ troops). In addition, these British units are also present: 1st Infantry Division, 168th Brigade 56th Infantry Division, and the 46th Tank Battalion (GHQ troops). These forces are reinforced, particularly by GHQ Artillery Units. At this time, there is no confirmation of the employment of the 88th Infantry Division (Br).

8 warships, 3 transports, 5 small vessels, and 10 LST's were observed in the harbor of Anzio - Nettuno.

The enemy situation:

As the major enemy attack, of 30 January, with main emphasis at Aprilia and Cisterna has failed, the tactical initiative is now in our hands. Our main line of resistance of 30 January has been restored by our counterattacks. The enemy has taken up defensive positions and is endeavoring to hold the beachhead by fortifying his positions. He has attempted to recapture Aprilia. Continued attacks in the area of Aprilia and Cisterna must be expected. Enemy positions around Aprilia and Cisterna are fortified in depth with mines and obstacles. The enemy keeps his local reserves near the front lines presumably to launch immediate counterattacks. With the exception of the 1st Armored Division (US), he does not appear to have any reserves for immediate employment. Generally, the counterattacks have been supported by tanks. However, tank attacks are not probable, since the present situation does not favor such operations.

Enemy forces which landed on the beachhead, have not succeeded in reaching their first objectives; namely, Via Appia, near Albano, and Cisterna. The enemy is now awaiting our major attack. He has detected our troop concentrations partly by air reconnaissance. This and terrain conditions lead him to expect our main blow from Aprilia and Cisterna. Aware of the tactical and political significances, the enemy will attempt to hold the beachhead positions by all possible means. Stubborn infantry defense, extensive antitank gun positions, and superior artillery fire is expected. The bulk of the artillery is in the woods 5 to 10 km south of Aprilia. Our repeated attacks will accentuate the enemy's shortage of personnel and materiel. His supply situation is worse than ours, because it depends largely on the weather, and is affected by our artillery fire. A withdrawal by the enemy is not probable. However, in such a case our air force and artillery will make the evacuation very costly.

Part of the enemy forces, especially the 1st Division (Br) and 3d Division (US), have suffered heavy losses, but they defend their positions stubbornly, particularly the British. According to a prisoner, the combat strength of the 3d Division (US) has been reduced considerably, and it has been necessary to send rear echelon troops to the front. Our attacks, particularly at Aprilia, resulted in the enemy's confusion and disorganization.

D. Statistics

German losses: 17 killed, 66 wounded, and 2 missing.

Allied losses: 30 killed, 29 British prisoners (including 3 aviators), 15 Americans, 8 tanks destroyed, and 5 airplanes downed by antiaircraft.

XX. 13 FEBRUARY 1944

A. Operations Report

During the night of 12 to 13 February 1944, Combat Group "Gräser" regained our former position at the railroad embankment and Hill 80 (F 863328), thus pushing forward the main line of resistance. This area, southwest of Carroceto (F 869330), was lost to the enemy the previous day.

Only active scouting and assault detachment activities on both sides occurred in the other sectors. An assault detachment of the 26th Panzer Division attacked Isola Bella (G 006294) and encountered strong enemy resistance. Two assault detachments of the Panzer Division "Hermann Göring" and of the 4th Parachute Division silenced 3 machine gun positions and took prisoners. During the night, the Luftwaffe raided the harbor of Anzio-Nettuno.

By order of Army Group C, the 1st and 2d Companies of 763d Artillery Battalion (caliber 170 mm) are allotted to the Fourteenth Army for employment on the beachhead.

By order of the Fourteenth Army, the LXXVI Panzer Corps attaches one company of the 129th Assault Gun Battalion to the I Parachute Corps for the planned major attack. The Fusilier Battalion of the 362d Infantry Division is being placed under the command of the LXXVI Panzer Corps. The reinforced 954th Infantry Regiment, previously employed in the coastal defense of northeastern Italy, is being transferred to the area of Pescara as Army Group Reserve.

Other strong units of the 114th Jäger Division arrived in the area south of Rome. The 2d Battalion of the Infantry Demonstration Regiment (Garrison: Döberitz near Berlin) arrived to replace the 1st Battalion of the 145th Grenadier Regiment, 3d Panzer Grenadier Division. However, the remaining parts of the regiment are still on their way.

For the month of February the Fourteenth Army will receive the following replacements:

For the 3d Panzer Grenadier Division	650 men
For the 3d Panzer Grenadier Division and 26th Panzer Division	850 men
For the 29th Panzer Grenadier Division	350 men
For the 65th Infantry Division	900 men
Total	2750 men

Order Number 2, issued by the Commanding General of the Fourteenth Army, directing an attack against the Nettuno beachhead.

No essential changes have been made in enemy dispositions, as far as known. To a great extent, bad weather conditions have prevented the reinforcement of the beachhead forces. However, under more favorable weather conditions, we expect a great amount of fresh troops to be brought up.

The Fourteenth Army will attack on 16 February, concentrating mainly along the highway, leading from Aprilia to Nettuno, and eastward of this highway. In this sector, the Army will force its way through the main enemy defense area, and then push onward to Nettuno. The main assault will be launched on 16 February at daybreak (0630). The exact hour will be given later. On 16 February at 0400, strong assault detachments will push forward along the entire frontline of both Corps to cut the enemy defenses. Simultaneously with the main attack, the LXXVI Panzer Corps will mount an attack in the sector of the Panzer Division "Hermann Göring". Strong forces of this division will push forward in the direction of Borgo Montello (F 976236), with Isola Bella as the first target. By an increased use of artillery, in support of this attack, we intend to give the enemy the impression that a decisive battle is to be expected at this point.

The following points are of decisive importance: First, the main attack of the I Parachute Corps' east flank, and particularly the LXXVI Panzer Corps' west flank, must be supported effectively by coordinated and accurate artillery fire. Due to ammunition difficulties, the artillery will be unable to fire rolling barrages. Therefore, in supporting the infantry attack, it will be necessary for all artillery, including antiaircraft, to shift to observed fire, after a short preparatory fire on recognized points of resistance. Second, the armored units, to be employed in the attack, will be echeloned in depth. The first wave will consist mainly of infantry and the second of motorized units. Detached tanks of the "Tiger" type will be required to support the assault howitzers.

The enemy's air superiority when weather conditions are favorable, will prevent our transporting motorized units over long distances. Therefore, the first wave of the two motorized divisions and the attached tank units must be deployed close to the assaulting infantry.

The entire operation, especially date and time of attack, is to be considered as top secret. Telephone calls revealing our intentions are prohibited. Officers of the Army High Command who are here in advisory capacity will be forbidden to communicate with their headquarters by telephone.

The forward Army Command Post will be located 4 km west of Lake Nemi, effective 16 February at 0600 hours.

B. Intelligence Report

The location of S Company, 2d Foresters Regiment at the hill 3 to 4 km northeast of Cle. Buonripso (F 859310) has been reconfirmed.

A prisoner identified the unit, at the crossing of the Fosso della Ficoccia (F 886333), to be the 2d Battalion, 180th Infantry Regiment of the 45th Infantry Division (US). According to another prisoner of war interrogation the whole regiment was in this area.

The 39th Infantry Regiment was located near Ponte Rotto (F 997???)
as confirmed by 2 wounded soldiers. Company C, 3d Regiment of the
1st Special Service Force was 1.5 km southwest of Borgo Piave
(G 053203). The 1st Special Service Force, consisting of 3 regiments (6 companies each) and a Headquarters Company with 3 platoons
(25 men each), had been employed on the beachhead for ranger tasks
since 2 February. The Command Post of the force was located
immediately east of crossroad (G 004182). This information was
from prisoners of war.

Although the enemy situation in general was unchanged, local
attacks at Aprilia (F 875333) and an attack near Cisterna (G 0232)
are possible. The enemy appeared reforming and regrouping his
forces near Aprilia.

C. Statistics

German losses: 42 killed, 121 wounded, and 26 missing.

Allied losses: 14 prisoners (5 British, 9 American), 1 aircraft downed by antiaircraft, 2 tanks, 2 ammunition carriers, 1
heavy machine gun and 3 light machine guns, 5 vehicles, and 3
ammunitions dump shot afire.

XXI. 14 FEBRUARY 1944

A. Operations Report

Except for reconnaissance and raids by both sides, no particular activities took place during the day. The enemy was observed reinforcing his main line of resistance, opposite the
sectors of the 4th Parachute Division, and Panzer Division "Hermann
Göring".

Our long-range artillery forced 2 destroyers to leave the
harbor of Anzio. The harbor and the airfield east of Nettuno were
placed under artillery fire.

The 26th Panzer Division was withdrawn to the rear of the
eastern flank of the LXXVI Panzer Corps. This division will constitute the corps reserve for the proposed attack. In addition to
its own area, the Panzer Division "Hermann Göring" took over the
sector of the 26th Panzer Division. The greater part of the 29th
Panzer Grenadier Division, previously employed with the Tenth Army
has arrived, and will be placed under the command of the LXXVI
Panzer Corps.

B. Intelligence Report

According to prisoner of war statements the organization of
the 894th Tank Destroyer Battalion (GHQ troops) includes one reconnaissance battalion, equipped with 12 antitank guns (7.62 cm).

1st Duke of Wellington Regiment, 3d Brigade, 1st British
Infantry Division, has been filled up to Table of Organization
strength. The 1st Scots Guard, 24th Brigade, received 360 men as
replacements. Previously, the strength of its individual companies
was only 40 men.

The fact that the enemy is entrenching, suggests that they plan further defenses. Increased traffic on the beachhead could be due to the movement of replacements and supply. Greater debarkation was observed. There were no indications of immediate large-scale attacks. However, local attacks, especially in the area south of Ardea (F 787350), at Aprilia (F 875333), and Cisterna (G 0232) were possible.

C. Statistics

German losses (less Combat Group "Gräser"): 18 killed, 82 wounded, and 24 missing.

Allied losses: 11 prisoners (British, Duke of Wellington), 1 aircraft downed by antiaircraft, and 2 light machine guns and 1 antitank gun (7.5 cm) captured.

XXII. 15 FEBRUARY 1944

A. Operations Report

With the exception of combat and reconnaissance patrols, there was no activity during the day. Around noon, our artillery fired on enemy tank concentrations and gun emplacements, south of Aprilia. The enemy fired a large quantity of smoke and phosphorous shells.

In the morning, Fourteenth Army Headquarters made the following additions and rescissions to the attack order dated 13 February 1944.

First it has to be assumed that the enemy expects our attack. His superior air force will enable him to ascertain our main points of effort. Special orders to assault detachments, as per order of 13 February, are hereby rescinded. Assault detachment activity during the night prior to the attack must be the same as usual. In order to achieve surprise, orders providing for the elimination of certain enemy combat outposts and advanced strongpoints are rescinded. Our attack must be sudden so as to be a surprise. H-hour will be given later.

Second, the commander of the air-ground support of the 2d Air Force will drown out the noise of the tanks, by the use of airplanes the night before the attack, between 2400 and 0400. As the sound made by the planes will be insufficient, it must be improved by artillery harassing fire. However, this fire must be the same as usual, in volume and type, in order not to alert the enemy.

H-hour for the main attack of 16 February is fixed at 0630 and will be announced to the subordinated units by Army.

The 71st Infantry Division withdrew from the beachhead front, and moved to the Tenth Army. The 114th Jäger Division (less 1st Artillery Battalion 114) arrived at the beachhead front. The 1st Battalion, 114th Artillery Regiment is south of Rome for refitting. The bulk of the 956th Grenadier Regiment of the 362d Infantry Division, previously assigned to coast defense, arrived at the LXXVI Panzer Corps and took over the sector of the 721st Infantry Regiment.

The reinforced 10th Parachute Regiment has, in addition to its own area, taken over the former sector of the 147th Grenadier Regiment of the 65th Infantry Division. The attachment of the 715th Motorized Infantry Division to Combat Group "Gräser" is rescinded. The 715th Infantry Division will assume command of the adjoining sector on the left of the 3d Panzer Grenadier Division.

B.   Intelligence Report

Pursuant to prisoner of war statements, C Company, 6th Gordons of the 2d Brigade of the 1st Infantry Division (Br) is deployed on the road 3 to 4 km south of Cle Carano (F 940309). Up to 2 days previously, which was dissolved to provide replacements for other heavily weakened companies of the battalion. The officers of C Company do not believe that a decisive operational success will result from the beachhead.

The continuous disembarkation and direct commitment of troops and materiel in the front emphasized the enemy's intention to reinforce his defense, as soon as possible. Until the present, there has been no confirmation that severely weakened units of the 1st Infantry Division (Br), in the Aprilia area, have been replaced by units of the 45th Infantry Division (US). Enemy entrenchments, naval activity, and his assignment of replacements indicate that he expects our attack with the main point of effort in the Aprilia area.

C.   Statistics

German losses   (less 3d Panzer Grenadier Division and 715th Infantry Division): 18 killed, 47 wounded, and 3 missing.

Allied losses: 3 prisoners (Br) of C Company 6th Gordons and 2 prisoners (US) of the 504th Parachute Regiment.

XXIII.   16 FEBRUARY 1944

A.   Operations Report

Our attack with the purpose of eliminating the enemy beachhead began.

The Commander in Chief of the Fourteenth Army, with his Chief of Staff moved at 0615, to the forward command post, located in a house 2.5 km southwest of Genzano. During the night of 15 to 16 February, our assault detachments engaged the enemy along the entire army sector.

The left flank of the I Parachute Corps and the right flank of the LXXVI Panzer Corps began the attack at 0630, after a short concentration of artillery and rocket projector fire. The Panzer Division "Hermann Göring", having been detached at midnight from the LXXVI Panzer Corps and placed under the immediate command of the Army, joined in the attack.

The 65th Infantry Division and the 1st Parachute Division seized the ridge south of Cle Buon Riposo (F 859310) and the Carroceto valley (F 8732) against strong enemy resistance, including flanking fire, which prevented a further development of the attack.

In order to pin down the enemy and diffuse his artillery fire, increased scouting and raiding was continued. The attacking 3d Panzer Grenadier Division and 715th Motorized Infantry Division progressed rather slowly, due to strong enemy resistance and artillery fire, supported by naval guns. The tanks, assault howitzers, and Goliaths employed to support the attack, could only advance along the roads and paths, as the terrain was not sufficiently hardened by the night frost. Furthermore, the advance in this terrain was obstructed by ditches extending perpendicularly to the direction of the attack. As a result, the brunt of the attack was borne by the infantry supported by artillery. Advanced units suffered considerable losses from enemy artillery fire and snipers.

The Panzer Division "Hermann Göring" attacking under support of heavy artillery fire, gained 1 km of ground, but it was then forced to dig in because of effective enemy defensive fire, which caused heavy losses. Combat Training Units of the Panzer Division "Hermann Göring" and the Parachute Demonstration Battalion were wiped out. The first unit had 80, the latter 110, casualties. Heavy, concentrated fire of enemy artillery and fighter bombers shelled and raided our points of attack, supply lines, artillery positions, and reserves. This action occurred mainly in the area of Aprilia (F 875333).

Toward evening, the Infantry Demonstration Regiment which had lost a large number of officers and noncommissioned officers, fell back about 500 m without permission. It was employed at the right flank of the 3d Panzer Grenadier Division.

Throughout the night, the enemy maintained observation of our rear area, by dropping parachute flares, and bombed observed traffic. Although Army Group C has suggested commitment of the 26th Panzer Division and 29th Panzer Grenadier Division, until now held in reserve, the Commanding General of the Fourteenth Army, at 1825, claimed the time had not yet come to employ these vitally important forces. It was originally intended to weaken the enemy with the divisions now in combat, and to push forward with the mobile reserve divisions, when the enemy began to fall back. Not all forces of our engaged divisions were as yet in combat. The 3d Panzer Grenadier Division and the 715th Infantry Division each kept one regiment in reserve.

In the evening, Fourteenth Army issued the following additional combat orders to its subordinate units.

Enemy strongholds still maintain a main line of resistance. From reliable sources, we learned that in some sectors our attack brought the enemy considerable confusion, and that he frequently called for reinforcements. It is assumed that the enemy suffered heavy losses. No counterattacks have as yet been made due to the shortage of forces on the beachhead. Reserves have not been brought up and tank reserves not yet been committed. It is possible that the enemy resistance will weaken on 17 February. Today, the Fourteenth Army has thrown back the enemy combat outposts, and captured the advanced strongholds along the entire front of attack. The Army will continue the attack on the night of 16 to 17 February.

It is of decisive importance, during the night of 16 to 17 February, that the attack be continued along the entire eastern flank of the I Parachute Corps and in the sector of the LXXVI Panzer Corps. Where conditions permit, armored vehicles must support the attacking infantry along all roads and paths. The objective of the attack is to establish a line running from Fosso Michele (F 828315 to F 345308) via Carrocetello creek (2 km south of Aprilia) to the southern edge of the small wood, 2.5 km southeast of Aprilia. Bridge-heads across the Carrocetello creek should be extended as far as possible. The Panzer Division "Hermann Göring" will continue the attack on its west flank. Strong assault detachments must attack the enemy along the entire beach-head front, except at the center of main effort. The enemy must be engaged throughout the night. He must not be allowed to gain time, which would permit him to strengthen his defense.

The objective of the I Parachute Corps is Ridge, west of Riserva Nuova (F 8530). The main effort of the LXXVI Panzer Corps is to be along the border of the 715th Infantry Regiment and the 114th Jäger Division. The initial objective for the assault elements of the I Parachute Corps and the LXXVI Panzer Corps is Highway Number 82 S Lorenzo (F 780300) – Cle Torre di Padiglione (F 922290). The LXXVI Panzer Corps must have the 26th Panzer Division in readiness to exploit a point of penetration. This division will not be committed without permission of the Army Commander. The 29th Panzer Grenadier Division is to advance east of the 26th Panzer Division towards the Campoleone (F 877386) – Cisterna (G 0232) railroad. An advance over the railroad will only be extended on army orders.

Guns listed below were available on 16 February for the attack:

Number each	Type of weapon	Caliber
114	howitzers	10.5 cm
46	howitzers	15 cm
39	guns	10 cm
6	guns	17 cm
3	howitzers	21 cm
2	railway guns	21 cm
2	railway guns	24 cm
54	rocket launchers	15 cm
14	rocket launchers	21 cm
172	antiaircraft guns	8.8 cm
Total 452		

Ammunition expenditure of long-range artillery on 16 February: 454 rounds caliber 17 cm and 50 rounds (railway guns) caliber 21 cm.

The Army Command believes that the unauthorized withdrawal of the Infantry Demonstration Regiment was due to unusually heavy artillery fire, which this regiment has encountered after having lost a great number of officers and noncommissioned officers. Although fifty per cent of the men in this regiment have already been in combat, they have not been in action for a long time. The regiment is expected to show an improved combat spirit, and to prove its courage in further actions. The Commanding General of the Fourteenth Army visited the regimental commander at his Command Post, during the afternoon of 16 February, and ordered an investigation of this incident.

Despite increased enemy air activities, such as the dropping of parachute flares throughout the night of 16 February, our troops succeeded in reaching their initial positions without heavy losses. The reconnaissance activity and raids carried out in the sector of the 4th Parachute Division divided the enemy defense, and considerably relieved our attacking forces. Our heavy losses were due to insufficient training of troops, heavy enemy artillery fire, frequent fighter attacks, and enemy sniper activity. Because of tank losses, Fourteenth Army ordered that tanks are to operate only within our lines, and under no circumstances in front of them. Our artillery could not completely neutralize the enemy artillery due to lack of ammunition.

B. Intelligence Report

A, B, and X Companies of the 9th Royal Fusiliers and the 8th Royal Fusiliers, both of the 167th Brigade of the 56th Infantry Division (Br) were established in the area north of Clo Carano (F 939313). Both Battalions relieved American units two days ago. A company of the 9th Royal Fusiliers was brought up to strength by inexperienced troops which arrived from England via Naples.

The 3d Battalion, 179th Infantry Regiment of the 45th Infantry Division (US), was placed southeast of Aprilia, according to prisoners of war of Companies K and M. Through prisoner of war interrogation and captured documents, it was ascertained that B Company, 1st Battalion of the 15th Infantry Regiment was 2 km eastwards of Isola Bella (G 006294), and that E Company, 2d Battalion of the 7th Infantry Regiment was west of Ponte Rotto (F 997314).

As expected, enemy resistance was strong and determined. The enemy prevented a breakthrough, despite several crises which arose during the morning at Aprilia and southwest of Cisterna (G 0232). The enemy made no attempt to recapture his positions except southeast of Aprilia. Local reserves, and especially tanks, were observed only southeast of Aprilia. It is assumed that he will not commit his small local infantry reserves, until his former combat positions are threatened with a breakthrough. Although we may assume that the enemy has suffered losses, strong enemy resistance and counterattacks along the entire front during 17 February must be anticipated.

C. Statistics

German losses (less the 715th Infantry Division): 324 killed, 1207 wounded, and 146 missing.

Allied losses: 224 prisoners (141 British, 60 American, and 23 nationality not yet determined), and 7 tanks destroyed.

XXIV. 17 FEBRUARY 1944

A. Operations Report

Against stubborn enemy resistance on the ground and in the air, it was possible during night and day attacks, to penetrate the enemy main line of resistance, and to win initial positions for further attacks on 18 February.

Today the enemy's artillery fire and air bombardment was the heaviest since his landing on the beachhead. He made continuous raids in waves of 30 to 40 planes throughout the day, attacking troops, artillery positions, and rear areas. The estimated Allied ammunition expenditure is 22,000 rounds.

The 4th Parachute Division advanced to the Appolonia area, 1.5 km west of Cle Buon Riposo (F 859310), and in the evening, it took the wooded area around Hill 67, 2 km northeast Cle. La Cogna (F 815292) and the northwest part of the Fossi di Buon Riposo sector, 1.5 km north Cle. La Cogna.

The 65th Infantry Division overcame stubborn enemy resistance and tank supported counterattacks, especially against the right flank. It captured a part of the defense system of Cle. Buon Riposo. After previous unsuccessful attacks, the stubbornly defended strong point of Cle. Carrocetello, 2 km southwest of Aprilia (F 875333), was taken by a frontal attack, during the night of 17 to 18 February.

In the afternoon, continued attacks enabled the 3d Panzer Grenadier Division to push further south and to cross the Carrocetello creek (2.5 km south Aprilia).

The 725th Grenadier Regiment, 715th Infantry Division overcame strong enemy resistance and advanced to Piscina Tombola and to 2 km northeast Fta Campo di Carne (F 862284).

The 114th Jäger Division took fortified Hill 61, 1.5 km southeast of Aprilia, by storm, and broke into the northern edge of the Macchia della Ficoccia Forest (2 km southeast of Aprilia); it held its gains against heavy, tank supported enemy counterattacks.

Our attack in the sector of Panzer Division "Hermann Göring" was stopped, after the road fork 250 m northeast of Colle del Pozzo (F 964312), was taken. The enemy put up a stubborn resistance from well fortified positions, supported by heavy weapons and tanks. There was increased sniper activity. Our antiaircraft defense was effective. Thirteen enemy planes were shot down. Enemy planes dropped bombs on Tiger tank dummies in the sector of the Panzer Division "Hermann Göring".

The morale of unseasoned troops was affected by the unusually heavy artillery fire. The initially poor fighting qualities of the Infantry Demonstration Regiment have improved.

The Commander in Chief Southwest issued the following order:

"On the first day of attack our artillery expended much ammunition. This large expenditure is not in proportion to our supply. The ammunition must be utilized to clear the way for our infantry by destroying enemy pockets of resistance. The infantry must make use of our artillery fire and the fire of its own heavy weapons in order to gain ground. It appears that fighting on the beachhead will last for several more days, and we cannot expend ammunition on secondary targets."

Orders of the Fourteenth Army for further attacks.

Although the 3d Panzer Grenadier Division and the 715th Infantry Division were able to penetrate deeply the enemy's battle positions, our attacks have not produced the anticipated results. Our task is to commit the second wave, whereby the initial penetration in the sector of the LXXVI Panzer Corps is to be expanded into a breakthrough, which will carry our forces to Nettuno. To accomplish this, the 26th Panzer Division and the 29th Panzer Grenadier Division will be attached to the LXXVI Panzer Corps. During the night of 17 to 18 February the forces previously committed will continue the attack. All commanders are advised that the battle of the Nettuno beachhead has reached its critical stage, that our troops must advance and pursue the enemy under all circumstances. Only a complete elimination of the beachhead ends our mission. During the night of 17 to 18 February, I Parachute Corps will insure the protection of the right flank of the LXXVI Panzer Corps, even if the Parachute Corps' right flank will have to be weakened for this purpose and will advance to Highway 82 (F 780300 to F 922290) during the night. The LXXVI Panzer Corps will continue the attack, with the divisions now committed, to gain as much ground as possible to the south, by the morning of 18 February. The Panzer Division "Hermann Göring" will pin down the enemy along its entire front.

The push to the south will be resumed by 0400; the east flank of the I Parachute Corps, the LXXVI Panzer Corps, and the west flank of the Panzer Division "Hermann Göring" participating. In the sector of the LXXVI Panzer Corps, the 26th Panzer Division and the 29th Panzer Grenadier Division will be brought up during the night. The units will be ready to launch the breakthrough towards Nettuno before dawn; they will move into the positions of the 3d Panzer Grenadier Division and the 715th Infantry Division during the night. It is most important that the east flank of the Corps be protected from enemy tank supported counterattacks. The 1st Battalion, 4th Panzer Regiment (Panther tank) will remain in reserve. This battalion will be prepared for defense against a tank attack from the general direction of Torre di Padiglione (F 921289).

B. Eyewitness Report

The success of the past two days would have been much greater if the terrain conditions had permitted the employment of tanks as planned. But as the tanks had to keep to the roads, the burden of the fight fell on the infantry. The infantry overcame enemy strongholds and pockets of resistance, but sustained heavy losses. Enemy resistance weakened rapidly, at points where tanks or assault guns could support the infantry. Enemy artillery fire was mainly responsible for the high casualties of our infantry. The strength of our infantry had already been weakened from continuous fighting. The combat strength of infantry battalions was approximately 120 to 150 men. Enemy aircraft did not excessively harass the infantry as his planes chose for their targets isolated houses or settlements, which were avoided by the infantry. However, enemy air action against our supply lines and artillery positions was very successful. For example, one well equipped antiaircraft unit, assigned to the 715th Infantry Division, was not able to participate fully in the attack, as enemy artillery and aircraft had inflicted heavy losses on troops and guns shortly after the start of the attack. The enemy fired a great number of white phosphorous shells, especially during the night. These shells did not produce actual damage, but they affected the morale of the troops. Once the men became accustomed to the phosphorous shells, they feared the high explosive shell more, as it caused higher casualties and inflicted more serious wounds.

C. Intelligence Report

The 9th Royal Fusiliers Regiment (Br) is in the sector north of Casale Vecchio, 1 km northwest of Cle La Cogna(F 815292). East of it is the 8th Royal Fusiliers. Adjacent to the south of Cle Buon Riposo (F 859310), is the 7th Oxfordshire and Buckinghamshire Light Infantry Regiment. They relieved the 2d Foresters Regiment a few days ago.

The 167th Infantry Brigade, previously in the Garigliano sector, landed in Nettuno on 14 and 15 February, and was immediately put into action. The brigade is to be supported by elements of the 81st Tank Destroyer Battalion of the 1st Infantry Division (Br). This was learned from prisoners of war. The 2d Battalion, 157th Infantry Regiment of the 45th Infantry Division (US) is in the area southwest of the railroad station at Carroceto (F 865330). 2d Battalion, 179th Infantry Regiment is near the road junction, 1.6 km east of Cle Carroceto (F 869330). E Company, 2d Battalion, 7th Infantry Regiment is in the area 800 meters west of Ponte Rotto (F 997314).

Flash ranging located six enemy batteries.

Active naval traffic and disembarkations in the harbor of Anzio have been observed. Two cruisers and three destroyers lie off the beachhead, and shelled Littoria (G 0818) around noon. 11 large and approximately 20 small naval units were outside Anzio harbor. A new landing point was observed 1 km northwest of Le Grottaccie (F 940 150).

The heavy losses of the day are expected to have weakened the enemy. However, continued resistance can be expected along the entire front.

D. Statistics

German losses (less 29th Panzer Grenadier Division and 725th Infantry Division): 222 killed, 635 wounded, and 35 missing.

Allied losses: 571 prisoners (245 Americans, 326 British), 19 airplanes shot down (13 by antiaircraft and 6 by fighters), 17 tanks destroyed, and 4 heavy antitank guns destroyed. Several vehicles were set afire.

XXV. 18 FEBRUARY 1944

A. Operations Report

Continuing our attack, the initial penetrations were enlarged in depth and width. However, no decisive breakthrough was achieved. Strong Allied counterattacks were halted by the I Parachute Corps, and the LXXVI Panzer Corps.

In the sector of the I Parachute Corps, the wooded area east of Hill 67, 2 km northwest of Cle Buon Riposo (F 853310), was cleared of the enemy. Along the 65th Infantry Division boundary, the enemy attacked supported by tanks, after an artillery and mortar barrage, and seized Hill 68, 1 km southwest of Cle Buon Riposo. A further attack was halted.

The 65th Infantry Division seized Hill 79, 1 km southwest of Cle Buon Riposo, and another Hill 79, 1.5 km southeast of Cle Cle Buon Riposo.

In the area of the LXXVI Panzer Corps, both the 26th Panzer Division and the 29th Panzer Grenadier Division were committed for the first time. After 0400, they fought along with the 3d Panzer Grenadier Division in the attack toward the south. A line, just north of Highway 82 (F 780300 – F 92229) was reached by the 29th Panzer Grenadier Division. Strong enemy resistance was overcome at Cle l'Ovile, 1 km east Cantoniera (F 864282), and at the foot of hills 73 and 69, 1200 meters northeast of Cle l'Ovile.

The 715th Infantry Division will be relieved from the area southeast of Aprilia (F 875333) and designated as Corps Reserve. By order of Fourteenth Army, this division is earmarked as reinforcement of the assault troops.

The 114th Jäger Division fought through the south edge of the Macchia della Ficoccia wood (2 km southeast Aprilia). After overcoming stubborn enemy resistance, they established a bridgehead over the canal. This position was held against heavy counterattacks.

The 1028th Panzer Grenadier Regiment seized the enemy strong point at Rosatelli (F 903320), but due to heavy artillery and mortar fire, the left assault group remained in the valley south of Spaccasassi (F 927330).

In the morning, Fourteenth Army reported to Army Group C that it required stronger fighter support to aid in the attack, and also increase the confidence of the troops. Our plans remain unchanged. New attacks towards the south, are to reach the wooded area south of Aprilia. The 1st Battalion of the 4th Panzer Regiment (Panther tanks) will remain in Army reserve. One Battalion of the 362d Infantry Division employed as coastal defense, will be attached to the Panzer Division "Hermann Göring". This will enable the latter division to form assault units, and to attach them to the western flank. It is the intention of the Army to detach similar forces from the 362d Infantry Division for the same purpose. The 1027th Panzer Grenadier Regiment will be withdrawn from coastal defense, south of the mouth of the Tiber, and employed on the left flank of I Parachute Corps.

B. Intelligence Report

On 17 February, the following units were identified, on either side of the Aprilia-Anzio Highway: the 1st Battalion, 157th Infantry Regiment, 2d Battalion 157th Infantry Regiment, and the 2d Battalion 179th Infantry Regiment. (adjoining the 157th Infantry Regiment on the east). On 15 February the 2d Battalion 157th Infantry Regiment relieved elements of the 1st Infantry Division (Br). The antitank company of the 179th Infantry Regiment was observed on the highway, 1 km northeast of Fta Campo di Carne (F 862284). During the last few days colored troops were engaged in bitter close combat at the Mussolini Canal.

We expect the enemy was to try to avoid a breakthrough on the highway to Nettuno by withdrawing all available forces from the less threatened sectors and by committing newly arrived troops. It is assumed that more tank supported counterattacks will be made. Positions still held north of the wooded area will be stubbornly defended in order to protect artillery emplacements. It may be assumed that enemy forces, echeloned in depth, are to be found particularly on highway 82 and between that highway and the northern edge

of the woods at Bosco di Padiglione (F 880260). Local counterattacks may be expected, especially against the flanks of our assault
groups. Heavy enemy losses are no indication that enemy resistance
will diminish.

C. Statistics

German losses: (less 29th Panzer Grenadier Division, 114th
Jäger Division and 715th Infantry Division): 63 killed, 350
wounded, and 21 missing.

Allied losses: 364 prisoners (293 Americans mostly from
179th Infantry Regiment and 2d Battalion 180th Infantry Regiment.)
14 tanks (4 Sherman) destroyed, 1 antitank gun destroyed, 4 airplanes
downed by antiaircraft guns, and 2 ammunition carriers and 4 personnel
carriers set afire. Captured: 4 Sherman tanks, 2 antiaircraft guns
(2 cm), 17 machine guns, 1 mortar, 1 bazooka with rockets, 30 rifles,
12 automatic pistols, and 1 antitank rifle.

XXVI. 19 FEBRUARY 1944

A. Operations Report

During the day, strong enemy counterattacks, supported by
tanks, forced partial withdrawals from newly gained positions.

Heavy enemy artillery fire resulted in great losses and halted
the attack of the 65th Infantry Division at Cle Buon Riposo (F 859310).
However, the 65th Infantry Division's left flank advanced towards
the south, and in a simultaneous attack from the east by parts of
the LXXVI Panzer Corps, the strongpoint Cle Buon Riposo was encircled.

During heavy night fighting, the bridgehead south of the forest
Macchia della Ficoccia, 2 km southeast Aprilia (F 875333), was enlarged. But in the afternoon, enemy counterattacks launched with
tank support, forced back the 114th Jäger Division into the northern
part of the forest. The division suffered considerable losses in
men and materiel. The village of Cle l'Ovile, 1 km east Cantoniera
(F 864282), was captured by combat patrols of the 26th Panzer and
29th Panzer Grenadier Divisions. It was lost again, during an
enemy tank attack, in the evening. Assault troops of the 29th
Panzer Grenadier Division crossed highway 82 (F 780300 - F 922290),
in a front 500 meters wide. The right flank of Panzer Division
"Hermann Göring", attacking Colle del Pozzo, 2 km west Cle Carano
(F 940309), was stopped in front of the enemy positions by concentrated
defensive fire. The left flank occupied two hills northeast of
Colle del Pozzo.

The 1028th Panzer Grenadier Regiment is attached to the 715th
Infantry Division. This Division was stationed in the region southeast of Aprilia as Corps Reserve. It now will take over the left
sector of the LXXVI Panzer Corps, adjacent to the 114th Jäger
Division as of 0800, 20 February 1944.

The enemy continued to place concentrated fire on the main line
of resistance and interrupted supply lines by heavy harrassing fire.
During our attack, Allied artillery fired barrages irrespective of
their own main line of resistance. The increased fire of enemy
artillery and the continuous air raids by bombers and fighter bombers

leads to the conclusion that the enemy intends to hold the positions on Highway 82. During the morning, Fourteenth Army informed Army Group by phone that a shift of the main effort to the east would require vast preparations, and would be advantageous to the enemy.

Therefore, we intend to destroy enemy forces isolated in the region of Cle Buon Riposo (F 859310), by a converging attack from all sides, and to consolidate the situation on the eastern flank of the IXXVI Panzer Corps (114th Jäger Division). All forces available will attack along highway Cle Carroceto (F 869330) - Torre di Padiglione (F 921289). Occupation of Highway 82 by surprise attacks will be attempted in the sectors of the LXXVI Panzer Corps, 3rd Panzer Grenadier Division, and 26th Panzer Division. After clearing the situation on both flanks of the attack group, Army intends to initiate, as soon as possible, a decisive southwesterly attack, in the sector of the 29th Panzer Grenadier Division.

The 26th Panzer Division will be made available for employment in the new offensive sector in the direction Torre di Padiglione, as soon as the situation on the western flank has been cleared up. The 362nd Division has been transferred from the coast defense sector Cecina - mouth of the Tiber to replace the Panzer Division "Hermann Göring" will be used for attacks in the sector of the LXXVI Panzer Corps. The former sector of the 362nd Infantry Division will be taken over by the newly activated 92nd Infantry Division, whose present strength is 4,242 men. The 954th Grenadier Regiment of the 362nd Infantry Division (Army Group C Reserve) will be transferred from the area of Pescara to an area south of Rome. The 2nd Battalion 1027th Panzer Grenadier Regiment and the Regimental Staff, until now employed in the coast defense sector Cecina - mouth of the Tiber, have been attached to the 65th Infantry Division.

The 146th Grenadier Regiment of the 65th Infantry Division, at present attached to the Tenth Army, will return to its division by 15 March. The combat strength of the 65th Infantry Division is 26 officers, and 871 enlisted men.

B. Intelligence Report

The following new units have been identified: 3rd Battalion 180th Infantry Regiment is located in the area east and north-east of Maccia della Fiocccia; the 514th Company Royal Army Service Corps of the 56th Infantry Division (Br) is near the highway in the region of Campo di Carne (F 870285).

The enemy artillery fired 30,000 rounds on 19 February 1944.

Our attacks have confused the enemy and also brought about emergency situations in some of his units. The enemy command has repeatedly called upon isolated and dangerously placed units to hold their positions, by promising reinforcements. Having determined the main direction of our attack, the enemy probably will concentrate all available forces in the region south of Aprilia to intercept the attack at the wood of Padiglione (F 890260). As the territory north of the forest has been lost, the enemy lacks observation posts. In addition, the loss of the northern edges of the forest has endangered his artillery positions. Stubborn opposition from key positions at the cross roads at Campo di Carne (F 863285), and Fta Padiglione (F 857242), and the traffic centers Torre di Padiglione (F 922289) and Le Ferriere (F 953342), is expected. Increased counterattacks, supported by tanks, against our flanks and especially southwest of Spaccasassi (F 917330) are imminent. It is estimated that large parts of the enemy's infantry and tank reserves were committed in today's counterattack, viz. the 1st Infantry Division (Br) and 1st Armored Division (US).

C. Statistics

German losses: (loss 4th Parachute Division, 3rd Panzer Grenadier Division, and 114th Jäger Division) 48 killed, 167 wounded, and 25 missing.

Allied losses: 83 prisoners, and 10 tanks destroyed.

XLVII. 20 FEBRUARY 1944

A. Operations Report

As a result of our attack from the west, the enemy was completely surrounded at Cle Buon Riposo (F 859310), and a defensive front toward the south was established. During the day, an enemy tank attack was repelled.

The 3rd Panzer Grenadier Division seized the eastern edge of the Gorge Campo di Carne (F 850890 to F 270290), the southwest edge of the Gorge Fosso di Carente, 700 meters northwest of Cantoniera (F 862282), and moved up to a line, 600 meters north of the crossroads of Cantoniera. The battalions of the 29th Panzer Grenadier Division (3rd and 1st Battalions 15th Grenadier Regiment), which had crossed Highway 82, east of Fta. Campo di Carne the day before, were either wiped out or were dispersed. The 114th Jäger Division in another attack from the northwest, seized the southern edge of the Macchia della Ficoccia forest, 3 km southeast of Aprilie (F 875333). An enemy tank attack towards Cle Rosatelli (F 908320) was repulsed.

We aim to destroy the enemy troops surrounded in the area of Buon Riposo (F 859310), and to prevent a breakthrough from the southwest, designed to assist these encircled troops. To avoid losses, Fourteenth Army ordered that the Panther tanks, brought up to clear the pocket of Buon Riposo, be used only as armored artillery.

In order to straighten the main line of resistance, on the eastern flank of the LXVI Panzer Corps, an attack will be launched, as early as possible on 21 February, to seize the enemy strongpoints Cle Biadaretto 2 km north of Cle Torre di Padiglione (F 921289) and Cle Carano (F 940309).

During our attempt to clear the pocket at Cle Buon Riposo (F 859310), the enemy bombarded his own positions with heavy artillery fire. His troops were protected against this, as they had taken shelter in the caves of the ravines to be found in that terrain. Our own fire could not reach them. Our units lost many radio sets, due to the heavy enemy artillery shells, the concussion of which destroyed the tubes.

It has become very difficult to evacuate the wounded. All ambulances, including the armored ones have been lost, making it necessary to use assault guns and Tiger tanks for the evacuation.

By early morning of 23 February, 2 Battalions of the 15th Panzer Grenadier Division, previously employed on the Cassino front, will be attached to the 29th Panzer Grenadier Division. The remaining elements of the 735th Grenadier Regiment 715th Infantry Division, i.e., 2 officers, 25 noncommissioned officers, and 158 men were assigned to the combat team of the 725th Grenadier Regiment.

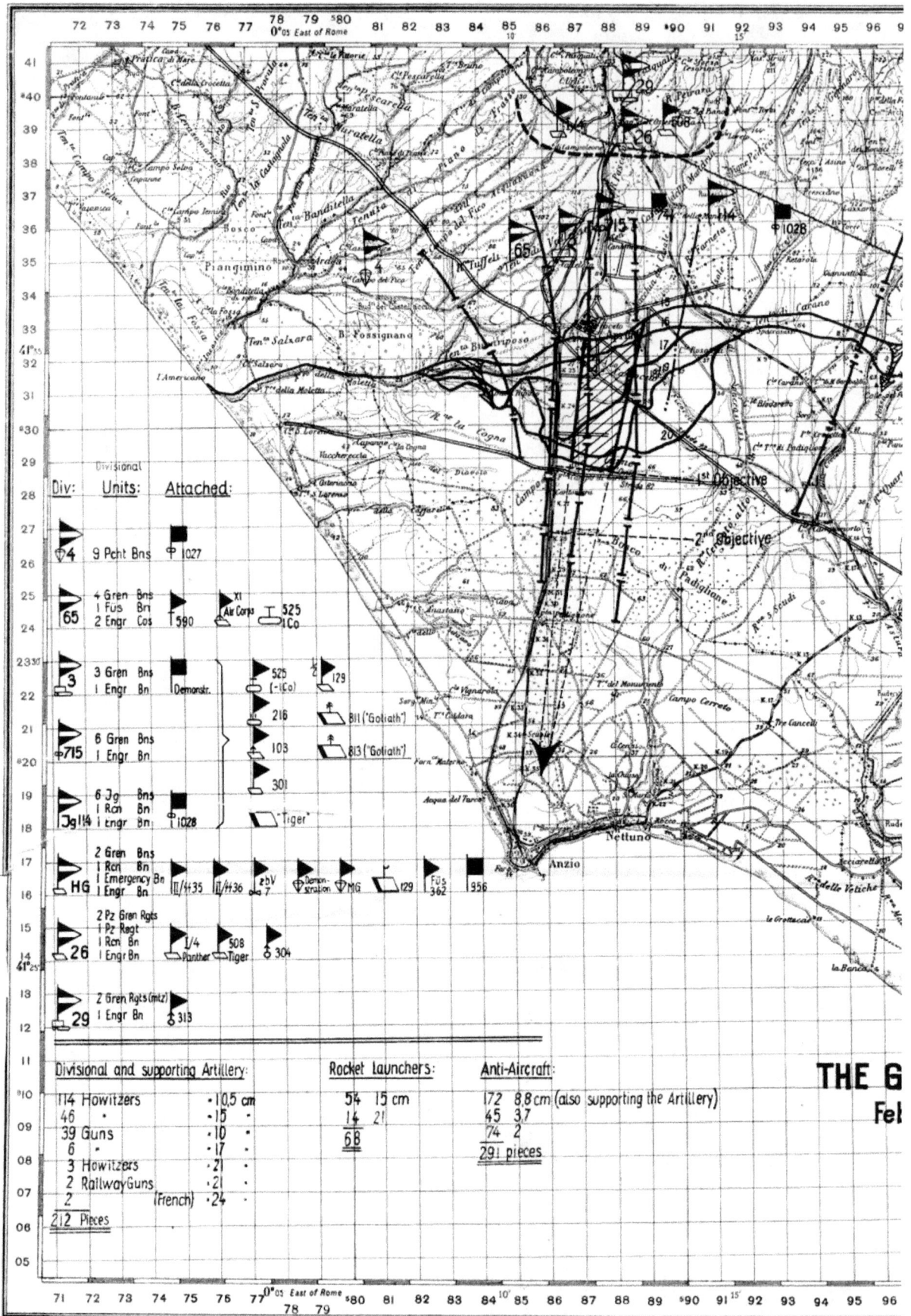

Div:	Units:	Attached:

4 — 9 Pcht Bns — 1027

65 — 4 Gren Bns / 1 Fus Bn / 2 Engr Cos — 590 — XI Air Corps — 525 1 Co

3 — 3 Gren Bns / 1 Engr Bn — Demonstr. — 525 (−1Co) — 129 — 216 — 811 ("Goliath")

715 — 6 Gren Bns / 1 Engr Bn — 103 — 813 ("Goliath") — 301

Jg 114 — 6 Jg Bns / 1 Rcn Bn / 1 Engr Bn — 1028 — "Tiger"

HG — 2 Gren Bns / 1 Rcn Bn / 1 Emergency Bn / 1 Engr Bn — III/++35 — II/++36 — zbV 7 — Demonstration — MG — 129 — Füs 362 — 956

26 — 2 Pz Gren Rgts / 1 Pz Regt / 1 Rcn Bn / 1 Engr Bn — I/4 Panther — 508 Tiger — 304

29 — 2 Gren Rgts (mtz) / 1 Engr Bn — 313

Divisional and supporting Artillery:

114	Howitzers	10,5 cm
46	"	15 "
39	Guns	10 "
6	"	17 "
3	Howitzers	21 "
2	Railway Guns	21 "
2	(French)	24 "
212	Pieces	

Rocket Launchers:

54	15 cm
14	21 "
68	

Anti-Aircraft:

172	8,8 cm (also supporting the Artillery)
45	3,7 "
74	2 "
291	pieces

1st Objective
2nd Objective

Anzio
Nettuno

THE G...
Feb...

GSGS 4164.
First GSGS Edition (AMS 1), 1941.
Second GSGS Edition (AMS 2), 1943.

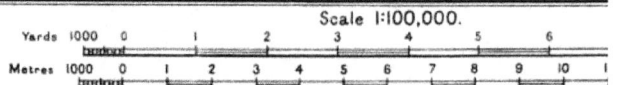

Scale 1:100,000.

Yards 1000 0 1 2 3 4 5 6
Metres 1000 0 1 2 3 4 5 6 7 8 9 10

SOUTH ITALY GRID (BLUE)

TO GIVE A GRID REFERENCE ON THIS SHEET
Pay no attention to the smaller co-ordinate figures at the corners and in margins.
They are for finding full co-ordinates.

PAY ATTENTION TO LARGER MARGINAL FIGURES AND TO
THOSE PRINTED ON THE FACE OF THE MAP.

POINT	Cava	F 844247

East		North	
Take west edge of square in which point lies and read the figures printed opposite this line on north or south margin or on the line itself (on the face of the map)	84	Take south edge of square in which point lies and read the figures printed opposite this line on east or west margin or on the line itself (on the face of the map)	24
Estimate tenths eastwards	4	Estimate tenths northwards	7
East	844	North	247

Nearest similar reference on this grid 500 Km. distant.

GRID DATA
Southern Italy Grid

Colour .... Blue
Projection .... Lambert Conical Orthomorphic
Spheroid .... Bessel
Origin .... 39°30'N., 14°E. of Greenwich
False Co-ordinates of origin .... 700,000 metres E.
                                        600,000 metres N.

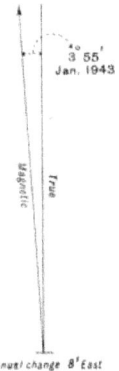

3°55'
Jan. 1943

Magnetic   True

Annual change 8' East

CONVERGENCE
At the West Edge of this sheet Grid North is 0°59'West of True North
At the East Edge of this sheet Grid North is 0°40'West of True North

REFERENCE

Railway, two or more tracks with station
single track and electrified
narrow gauge or Tramways
Tram lines on a road
Cable railway
National Highways (Autostrade)
   8 Metres wide, metalled   (2-way M.T.)
Main Roads (Strade Statali with route numbers)
   6 Metres wide or over, metalled
Other Main Roads (Strade di grande comunicazione)
   5 Metres wide or over, metalled   (Mostly 2-way M.T.)
Secondary Roads
   3-5 Metres wide, generally metalled   (1-way M.T.)
Other Roads and Cart Tracks, generally unmetalled
Mule Tracks
Paths
Boundaries, state
   province
Canal
Aqueducts, over and underground
Wells, perennial, non-perennial
Marsh and Swamp
Church, Chapel, Cemetery
Names of physical features .... M. Moncone
Trigonometrical points .... △ 170
Heights in metres .... · 160
Cliffs
Embankment or Dyke
Woods

Contours at 50 metres interval

No 7

ADJOINING SHEETS

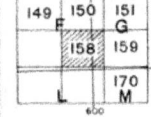

149 F	150 G	151
	158	159
L	170 M	

COMPARATIVE INDEX

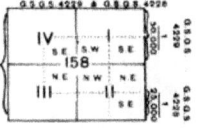

IV S.E.	S.W.	S.E.
	158	
III N.E.	N.W.	N.E.
		S.E.

AREA REVISED
FROM AIR PHOTOS

AUTHORITIES
Copied from Carta Topografica
1/100,000 Sheet 158. 1933.
1/25,000 Sheets IV S.E., I S.W., I S.E.
   III N.E., II N.W., N.E., S.E., 1936.
Instituto Geografico Militare
Partially revised for communications, 1943.

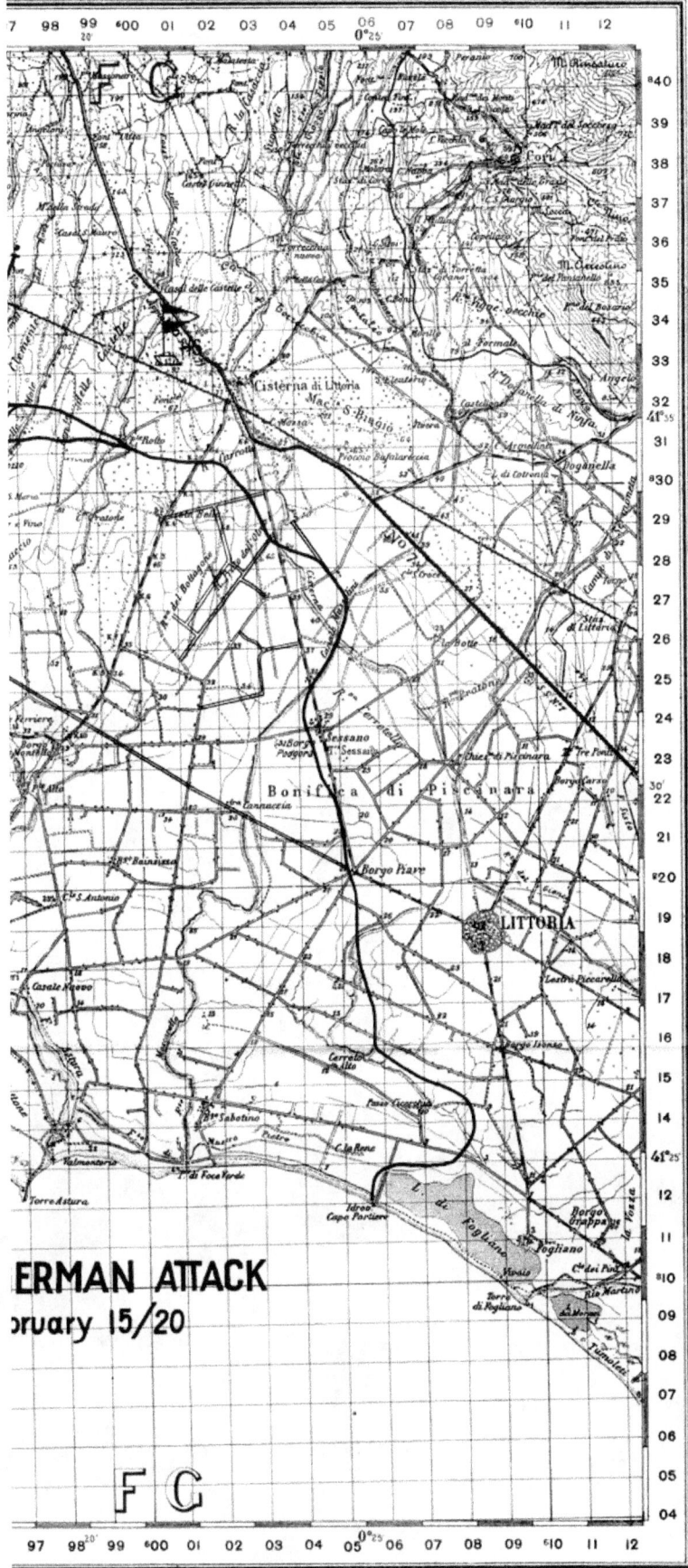

GERMAN ATTACK
February 15/20

F G

Reproduced under the direction of the Chief of Engineers by the Army Map Service,
U.S. Army, Washington, D.C., 1944 from GSGS
Second Edition 1943 Kodalines.

ARMY MAP SERVICE, U.S. ARMY, WASHINGTON, D.C. 113498
7-44   1944

LITTORIA
N4120-E1227/20x30

7   8 Miles
1   12   13 Kilometres

Longitudes are based on the meridian of Rome, which is 12°27'7·1" East of Greenwich.

B. Intelligence Report

According to reliable sources, the 6th Armored Infantry Regiment 1st Armored Division (US), with attached tanks, is in the sector of the 157th Infantry Regiment. One of the battalions of the 6th Regiment is employed west of the Aprilia-Nettuno Highway and two battalions east of it. The Commanding Officer of the 1st King's Shropshire Light Infantry is Lt. Col. Carelass, and the Commanding Officer of S Company 1st King's Shropshire Light Infantry is Major Mausabb. Major Brook commands Company C 1st London Irish Rifles.

On 19 February, the enemy supplied his surrounded troops, at Cle Buon Riposo, by air. Air reconnaissance reports show active disembarkation in the Anzio-Nettuno harbor.

C. Statistics

German losses (less 114th Jäger Division and 15th Motorized Grenadier Regiment): 61 dead, 211 wounded, and 8 missing.

Total losses from 16 to 20 February 1944 (dead, wounded, and missing): 5,389 men.

Allied losses: 62 prisoners (53 British, 9 Americans) and 1 tank put out of commission.

According to prisoner of war reports, the enemy lost many heavy infantry weapons.

XXVIII. 21 FEBRUARY 1944

A. Operations Report

In the evening of 20 February, preceded by heavy artillery fire, the enemy repeatedly attacked along the entire sector of the 29th Panzer Grenadier Division, and pushed back the left flank to a position some 2 km northwest of Torre di Padiglione (F 921289). There, a German counterattack, during the early morning hours, regained the formerly held positions at the Fosso delle Vallicelette, 3 km west of Torre di Padiglione.

At 0430, the 715th Infantry Division attacked to seize Cle Biadaretto, 2 km north of Torre di Padiglione, and Cle Carano (F940309). Heavy defense fire from the enemy stopped the attack. At 1730, after the enemy lines had been subjected to artillery fire and fighter bomber attack, another attack was attempted, but due to strong enemy defenses, the objective could not be reached. Enemy assaults in company strength, supported by tanks, were repulsed by the 114th Jäger Division.

Concentrated artillery fire destroyed enemy infantry and tank positions. Long-range artillery shelled the Anzio harbor, disembarkation points southeast of Nettuno, and supply depots. Antiaircraft artillery played an important role in the destruction of supply routes.

The enemy fighter bombers were less active than during the previous days. The Panzer Division "Hermann Göring", which is to be employed in the Spaccasassi sector (F 917330) for offensive operations, was relieved, at 1200, by the 362d Infantry Division. The Combat Team "von Corvin" consisting of: 1st Battalion 2d Panzer Grenadier Regiment "Hermann Göring", 2d Battalion 1st Panzer Grenadier Regiment "Hermann Göring", and Panzer Reconnaissance Battalion "Hermann Göring" was attached to the 715th Infantry Division.

Our aims are: First, the destruction of enemy positions at Cle Buon Riposo (F 859310) by the morning of 22 February. Second, the immediate relief of the forces of the 3d Panzer Grenadier Division west of the Aprilia-Nettuno highway, by the I Parachute Corps. Before the morning of 25 February, the 3d Panzer Grenadier Division will relieve the 26th Panzer Division and parts of the western flank of the 29th Panzer Grenadier Division. The 26th Panzer Division will be shifted to the area north of Cle Tre Spaccasassi (F 917330), before dawn of 26 February. Third, the seizure of the Colle del Pozzo, 2 km west of Cle Carano (F 940309), by the western flank of the 362d Infantry Division about 24 February.

B. Intelligence Report

The 1st Battalion 504th Parachute Regiment (US) is employed in the sector Fosso Formal del Bove, west of Colle del Pozzo. American infantry is on the right flank; on the left are additional paratroopers.

Increased naval activity was observed in the harbor of Anzio-Nettuno. Aerial reconnaissance reports indicate the presence of 6 merchant ships approximate tonnage: 10,000 to 15,000 tons each, 2 medium transports, one cruiser, and 7 destroyers.

C. Statistics

German losses: 85 killed, 236 wounded, and 8 missing.

Allied losses: 4 tanks destroyed, 1 tank rendered immobile, 1 radio station captured.

XXIX. 22 FEBRUARY 1944

A. Operations Report

The attack to destroy the enemy pocket at Cle Buon Riposo (F 859310), did not succeed. Under a heavy enemy barrage, the troops had to fight in difficult terrain with deep ravines. Up to the present, 150 prisoners have been brought in.

In the morning, and again in the afternoon, the 715th Infantry Division attacked Cle Biadaretto, 2 km north of Cle di Padiglione (F 921289), and the Cle Carano hills (F 940309). However, due to the enemy's defensive fire, these attacks were halted short of their objectives.

At 1900, the 3d Panzer Grenadier Division took over the sector formerly occupied by the 26th Panzer Division. The 67th Panzer Grenadier Regiment of the 26th Panzer Division, was attached to the 3d Panzer Grenadier Division.

To complete its mission successfully, the Fourteenth Army requested the Commander in Chief Southwest to strengthen it with one complete division ready for combat service, possibly a mountain division for greater mobility in wooded areas; one heavy mortar and one medium howitzer battalion; one engineer assault battalion; and additional portable radio sets, of which the Army has a shortage of 468.

We intend to shorten the main line of resistance on the east flank of the LXXVI Panzer Corps by seizing the Biadaretto and Carano hills, as well as to destroy, as quickly as possible, all enemy units still in the area Cle Buon Riposo (F 859310), in order to relieve units of the 3d Panzer Grenadier Division in the area west of the highway.

After the 3d Panzer Grenadier Division has taken over the present sector of the 26th Panzer Division and parts of the western flank of the 29th Panzer Grenadier Division, it will be attached to the I Parachute Corps. When fighting has ceased, in the area of Ble Biadaretto, the remaining units of the 715th Infantry Division will be withdrawn in order to take over the sector of two battalions on the eastern flank of the 362d Infantry Division. All forces committed south of that area will be attached to the 715th Division.

On or about 26 February the Army plans a breakthrough to the Mussolini Canal, from the north, crossing a general line from Pte della Crocetta (F 950296) to Isola Bella (G 006294). Units to participate in this attack will be: 362d Infantry Division, Panzer Division "Hermann Göring", and the 26th Panzer Division. The attack will be made from the west flank of the 362d Infantry Division. If this action meets with success, the Army intends to push on to the lower Spaccasassi creek (F 9229 to F 992253). The two battalions of the 15th Panzer Grenadier Division (earmarked for the 29th Panzer Grenadier Division) which are at present in transit will be held initially as Army reserve in the area west of Velletri. After the 29th Panzer Grenadier Division has been withdrawn from its present front sector, it will be used either for the attack against Fosso di Spaccasassi and to roll up the enemy lines southwest of Cisterna (G 0232) from the west; or to make a surprise attack from north of the area of Borgo Podgora (G 045240) against the enemy units fighting in the area of Isola Bella.

Experience has shown that the enemy reacts very quickly to a regrouping of our forces. It is, therefore, imperative that the regrouping be concealed, and it is of particular importance that the enemy be engaged along the entire line by continuous raids. These raids will have the secondary purpose of improving the local front. By means of all types of deceptive measures, the enemy must be misled as to the actual assembly area of the assault divisions. To aid this deception further, the I Parachute Corps will erect dummy tanks in the area around Ardea (F 787350).

By order of Hitler, tank assaults in small groups will be made prior to the attack from and south of the area of Borgo Podgora in the direction of the Mussolini Canal. The tanks of the Panzer Division "Hermann Göring", used for this purpose, will return to their division shortly before the attack begins.

The objective of this attack is to push back the beachhead in the sector of the LXXVI Panzer Corps toward the general line from Fosso di Leschione (F 885300 to F 917289) to Fosso di Spaccasassi up to the point where it joins the Mussolini Canal, 1.5 km west of Borgo Podgora.

B. Intelligence Report

2d Company, 7th Queens (169th Brigade, 56th Infantry Division) (Br) located in Fosso della Bottaccia, 1 km northwest of Fta Campo di Carne (F 862284) has been identified by 16 prisoners of war. Presence of the entire Brigade is confirmed by captured documents. 1st Battalion Irish Guards 24th Brigade, is located 150 meters southeast of Puntoni, 1 km northwest of Cantoniera (F 863282). During the night of 21 to 22 February, the 1st Irish Guards came from south of Campo di Carne to this new area, and relieved an unidentified American unit. Three days before, the 3d Company received 30 replacements from supply troops of the Battalion; the 1st Company, reduced to 38 men, was absor ed by the 3d Company. The 1st Scots Guards and the 5th Grenadier Guards 24th Brigade were committed in the night of 21 to 22 February according to prisoners of war.

Reliable sources report the enemy expects an impending attack near Campo di Carne and to the east.

C. Statistics

German losses: 86 killed, 232 wounded, and 84 missing.

Allied losses: 265 prisoners (75 from Cle Buon Riposo), 5 tanks destroyed, 1 self propelled antitank gun destroyed (75 mm), and 2 tanks put out of commission. Captured material: 1 antitank gun (50 mm), 11 machine guns, 1 mortar, 1 antitank rifle, and 1 bazooka.

XXX. 23 FEBRUARY 1944

A. Operations Report

After brief artillery preparatory fire, the 65th Infantry Division renewed its attack at 0530, against the encircled enemy at Cle Buon Riposo (F 853310). Supported by self-propelled guns, we succeeded in penetrating the enemy's defensive system, and occupied the houses at Cle Buon Riposo. With the exception of enemy remnants we cleared out the valley. Two enemy relief attacks, in battalion strength from the south, were repulsed after heavy fighting. Our artillery shelled infantry and artillery targets, and supported the attack on Cle Buon Riposo with blocking fire towards the south.

During the night of 22 to 23 February, the 725th Grenadier Regiment 715th Infantry Division, was relieved by the 2d Battalion 1028th Panzer Grenadier Regiment, and transferred to Fosso Presciano, 4 km northeast of Campoleone (F 860406) as reserve. Combat Team "von Corvin", which had been attached to the 715th Infantry Division on 21 February, was now placed under the command of the 114th Jäger Division. At 1200, the 362d Infantry Division was attached to the LXXVI Panzer Corps.

B. Intelligence Report

According to prisoners, the 509th Parachute Battalion (US) is now located 1.5 km north of the Colle del Pozzo (2 km west of

Cle Carano F 940309). The Battalion is attached to the 3d Infantry Division (US). On its right is the 7th Infantry Regiment 3d Infantry Division; on its left, the 180th Infantry Regiment of the 45th Infantry Division (US).

According to interrogation of prisoners of war and captured documents, the 167th Infantry Brigade and the 169th Infantry Brigade landed on 11 and 19 February respectively.

For the past week, the boundary between the English and American sectors ran along the Aprilia-Anzio Highway. Reliable sources report that the Royal Scot Greys Armored Battalion is in the area east of the highway.

Counterattacks from the area southwest of Aprilia (F 875333), strongly supported by armor, are to be expected. Reliable sources report that part of the enemy armored forces are assembled in this area.

C. Statistics

German losses (less 3d Panzer Grenadier Division, 9th and 1027th Panzer Grenadier Regiments): 33 killed, 184 wounded, and 8 missing.

Allied losses: 402 prisoners (majority from 2d Battalion 157th Infantry Regiment, and 2d Company 7th Queen's Own), and 1 tank put out of commission.

XXXI. 24 FEBRUARY 1944

A. Operations Report

Reconnaissance and combat patrols were conducted by both sides during the period. In the sector of the I Parachute Corps, an enemy attack in company strength and a tank assault were repelled. The pocket of Cle Buon Riposo (F 859310) was cleared, with the exception of a few dispersed Allied troops. At 2030, the 10th and 11th Parachute Jäger Regiments began an attack to straighten the main line of resistance at the boundary of the 4th Parachute Division and the 65th Infantry Division.

The 3d Panzer Grenadier Division will be attached to the I Parachute Corps at noon on 25 February 1944; the Infantry Demonstration Regiment, 998th Heavy Artillery Battalion, 10th Company Artillery Demonstration Regiment, and one Company of the 525th Heavy Antitank Battalion (Hornets) are attached to this division. The new boundary line of the I Parachute Corps and the LXXVI Panzer Corps is: Stazione di Campoleone (F 877385) - Aprilia (F 875333) - Cle l'Ovile, 1 km east of Cantoniera (F 862282). Tenth Army will supply the 3d Panzer Grenadier Division with ten armored personnel carriers for the evacuation of the wounded.

One company of the 653d Antitank Battalion (Ferdinand tanks) will be attached to the LXXVI Panzer Corps. The 3d Battalion of the 1st Parachute Regiment previously committed in the sector of the Panzer Division "Hermann Göring", will return to the 1st Parachute Division (Tenth Army). The Parachute Demonstration

Battalion, up to now with the Panzer Division "Hermann Göring" will be attached to the 4th Parachute Division.

B. Intelligence Report

According to prisoner of war statements the 6th Cheshire of the 56th Infantry Division (Br) landed on 16 February. It consists of four companies and one Headquarters Company. Each company is equipped with 12 heavy machine guns. Lt Col Birch is the Commanding Officer of the battalion.

Heavy traffic on Highway 82 (F 780300 to F 922289) indicates further regroupings. It is probable, that elements of the 1st Infantry Division (Br), which are being kept in reserve, will be committed to relieve the weaker sectors of the 45th Infantry Division (US).

C. Statistics

German losses (less 3d Panzer Grenadier Division and 715th Infantry Division): 91 killed, 343 wounded, and 55 missing.

Losses of Fourteenth Army from 16 to 22 February 1944 (including materiel turned in for repair): 450 submachine guns, 430 light machine guns, 93 heavy machine guns, 6 light mortars, 56 medium mortars, 1 heavy mortar, 2 light infantry guns, 12 light antitank guns (1 salvagable), 1 medium antitank gun, 8 heavy antitank guns, 13 light field howitzers (12 salvagable), 7 heavy field howitzers (7 salvagable), 3 guns 10 cm (3 salvagable), 1 light gun, 6 guns 7.5 cm, 1 howitzer 22 cm, 5 antiaircraft guns 2 cm (2 salvagable), 5 rocket launchers 15 cm, and 10 rocket launchers 21 cm.

Allied losses: 59 prisoners (this makes a total of 650 prisoners, taken in the pocket of Cle Buon Riposo) and 2 tanks put out of commission.

A. Operations Report

During the night, the 4th Parachute Division and 65th Infantry Division succeeded in pushing the main line of resistance forward, despite heavy enemy artillery and mortar fire. This attack was part of the operation to straighten the line.

Late in the evening, the enemy attacked the sector of the 65th Infantry Division at the Michele Gorge (F 828315 to F 845308), and 1 km northwest of Cantoniera (F 863282). At both points the attack was made under support of heavy artillery fire, but was stopped by the coordinated fire of our artillery. No major operations, except raids, took place in the sector of the LXXVI Panzer Corps.

The following is an order for a new attack against the beach-head:

On 28 February, the Army will resume its attack against the beachhead. The LXXVI Panzer Corps will attack at 0400; in the sector of the 362d Infantry Division the attack will begin at 0545. The objective is to drive the enemy into the sea. To achieve surprise, deception and secrecy are paramount.

The I Parachute Corps is to feign preparations for an impending large-scale attack in its sector, as well as to increase activity by assault detachments, during the night of 27 to 28 February. Roving guns are to be employed in the area of Ardea (F 787350) to simulate the concentration of a new artillery group. The arrival of strong, motorized forces in the area of Ardea is to be simulated during the 26th, 27th, and in the night of 27 to 28 February. For this purpose combat vehicles of the 3d Panzer Grenadier Division will be used. Individual vehicles will be ordered to blink their lights while moving up, during the night, but this must not be done in a clumsy way. In the evening of 27 February, an attack to seize Hills 78 and 79, 1 km north of Fta. Campo di Carne (F 862284), is to be executed.

At 0530 on 28 February, our artillery will shell known enemy assembly areas, in which there will probably be heavy troop concentrations.

The LXXVI Panzer Corps is to simulate an impending strong attack in the direction of the Mussolini Canal, by tank supported raids and the use of roving guns. These operations will not be extended farther than Borgo Piave (G 053203).

In the sector where the actual attack is planned, raiding and scouting will be carried out in usual strength only. No units, other than those at present employed in these sectors, will be used in these operations. Scouting or raiding by mobile units is prohibited. During the attack, it will be important that bridge-heads are established on the south bank of the Astura creek. These bridgeheads will serve as bases for further attacks.

The enemy forces remaining on both flanks of our Assault Group must be wiped out in a frontal attack by the reserves of the Army Group.

The Air Force is requested to provide air-ground support for our attacking forces, and to chase off enemy artillery observation planes, especially on 28 February.

The 65th Infantry Division reported that as a result of recent actions the conditions of its infantry is such that only an immediate relief can prevent complete exhaustion. The combat strength on 23 February was: 33 officers, 81 noncommissioned officers, and 559 enlisted men. This number includes two regimental staffs, and some regimental units. Nearly all competent noncommissioned officers and specialists were lost during recent actions. The Division will receive 400 to 800 men as replacements (surplus personnel of the 362d Infantry Division). Fourteenth Army suggests that according to development of the situation, single battalions be withdrawn for ten to fourteen days, as the current situation does not warrant the withdrawal of entire divisions.

At 1200 hours, the 715th Infantry Division took over the sector of the 362d Infantry Division which was withdrawn for the coming offensive. The divisions designated for the attack on 28 February are already in their respective assembly areas. The 1st and 2d Battalion of the 115th Panzer Grenadier Regiment arrived in the area of Cori (G 095380). These two battalions were part of the 15th Panzer Grenadier Division (Tenth Army), and are now attached to the Fourteenth Army as reserve.

B. Intelligence Report

During the last days, the enemy attempted to regroup his disorganized units. It was established that American units were relieved by the 56th and 1st Infantry Division (Br), which now hold the line extending from the coast to the eastern side of the Aprilia-Anzio Highway. Adjoining is the 45th Infantry Division (US), with a front line extending to the area of Cle Carno (F 940309). On the latter's right flank is the 3d Infantry Division (US). Regrouping and moving up of replacements continued. The main defensive centers are still on both sides of Fta. Campo di Carne (F 862284).

C. Statistics

German losses: (less 65th Infantry Division) 18 killed, 51 wounded, and 9 missing.

Allied losses: 46 prisoners.

XXXIII. 26 FEBRUARY 1944

A. Operations Report

Last night, an enemy attack in company strength supported by artillery and mortar fire, succeeded temporarily in penetrating the main line of resistance, in the sector of the 4th Parachute Division. Our immediate counterattack reestablished the main line of resistance and relieved one platoon of the 10th Parachute Regiment, which had been encircled. Except for reciprocal combat patrols, the other sectors were quiet.

At 1200, the 735th Grenadier Regiment of the 715th Motorized Infantry Division took over the sector of Group "Heidebreck", of the Panzer Regiment of the Panzer Division "Hermann Göring".

The Fourteenth Army High Command ordered that in the coming

attack, in addition to previous plans, a tank group is to push forward on the highway Spaccasassi (F 917330) - Ponte della Crocetta (F 950297). In this operation it is imperative that Carano (F 940309) be seized, during the first night, by a surprise raid. The main line of resistance at the southern flank of the LXXVI Panzer Corps is to be pushed forward, during the night 26 to 27 February, at least as far as the present line of our combat outposts. From this line, assault-detachments, supported by assault guns or tanks, will thrust forward toward the Mussolini Canal. These assaults are to be made on as broad a front as possible. The line of combat outposts will be advanced to the Mussolini Canal, or at least as close as p possible to the canal.

B. <u>Intelligence Report</u>

The 1st Battalion 157th Infantry Regiment of the 45th Infantry Division (U S) was confirmed to be in the area of the Lwschione bridge, 1 km west of Cle Tre di Padiglione (F 921289).

C. <u>Statistics</u>

German losses: 53 killed, 156 wounded, and 32 missing.

Allied losses: 19 prisoners.

XXXIV. 27 FEBRUARY 1944

A. <u>Operations Report</u>

No activity took place on either side, except reconnaissance and assault detachment operations. The enemy carried out reconnaissance and combat patrols against the sector held by the 715th Infantry Division. Fourteen enemy artillery batteries were located by reconnaissance. Most of them are in the western sector.

The date for the intended attack is changed from 28 to 29 February. The plans remain unchanged. Beginning the night of 27 to 28 February, the 29th Panzer Grenadier Division will be withdrawn from the front, and concentrated in the area Lanuvio-Genzano-Palomba. These movements are to be completed before dawn 1 March. The 146th Grenadier Regiment, which is arriving from the Cassino area, will take over the sector of the 29th Panzer Grenadier Division. Elements of the 129th Reconnaissance Battalion (motorized), one light artillery battalion, and elements of the 525th Antitank Battalion ("Hornets") will remain in this sector.

B. <u>Intelligence Report</u>

Company A 2d Battalion 5th Queens (169th Brigade/56th Britishh Infantry Division) is in the area of Michele Gorge (F 828315 to F 845308), according to prisoner of war interrogations.

C. <u>Statistics</u>

German losses: 44 killed, 177 wounded, 15 missing.

Allied losses: 39 prisoners, 1 tank destroyed by a mine, and several machine guns and small arms were captured.

A. Operations Report

Following up the attack by the 65th Infantry Division on 25 February, the left flank of the 4th Parachute Division pushed forward at the eastern end of the Michele Gorge (F 828315 to F 845308). In a sudden raid in the morning, the 65th Infantry Division took the group of ruined houses 1 km southwest Cle Buon Riposo (F 859310). Simultaneously, a second attacking group advanced in the Campo di Carne gorge, south of Cle Buon Riposo, to a line even with the first attack force. Enemy counterattacks on the group of houses were stopped by artillery fire. In addition, our artillery silenced five enemy batteries. Explosions were observed at four targets.

At 2000, the I Parachute Corps took over the sector of the 146th Grenadier Regiment; two artillery battalions of the 29th Panzer Grenadier Division were withdrawn.

Fourteenth Army ordered the 29th Panzer Grenadier Division to make a road reconnaissance on 29 February, for a possible attack at daybreak 1 March, the objective of which would be to occupy the Astura sector, between the road Borgo Podgora (G 045240) – Borgo Montello (F 976236) and the coast. This does not interfere with the original plan to employ the Division at the center of the LXXVI Panzer Corps' attack.

The Commanding General Fourteenth Army made the following report to the Commander in Chief Southwest:

"The divisions and regiments with little combat experience or insufficient training are not suited for difficult offensive operations. The 65th Infantry Division, 114th Jäger Division, and the 715th Motorized Infantry Division suffered heavy losses. Most casualties are inflicted by enemy artillery fire. Shell fragments are responsible for 75 percent of all wounds, while 10 to 15 percent of the casualties have been caused by enemy air attacks. The fact that due to insufficient training, the men do not know how to handle themselves properly in battle, has increased our casualties. The planning for attacks, the redeployment of troops, and the offensive operations now take longer, due to heavy losses among officers and noncommissioned officers."

B. Intelligence Report

According to prisoners of war, the 1st Battalion 180th Infantry Regiment of the 45th Infantry Division (US) is located at the northeastern edge of the Vallicelle Grandi woods. On its left is the 179th Infantry Regiment. The 1st Duke of Wellington Regiment and 2d Foresters Regiment are employed in the front line, while the 1st King's Shropshire Light Infantry Regiment is in a reserve position. Replacements from Naples increased the strength of the companies to 150 men.

The enemy seems to have transferred his attention from the Aprilia sector to the Cisterna-Littoria sector.

C. Statistics

German losses: (less 114th Jäger Division and the 362d Infantry Division) 37 killed, 116 wounded, and 18 missing.

Allied losses: 135 prisoners (130 British, 5 Americans), and 2 tanks put out of commission.

A. Operations Report

At 0400, the LXXVI Panzer Corps started the new attack against the beachhead with the 114th Jäger Division, 362d Infantry Division, 26th Panzer Division, and the Panzer Division "Hermann Göring".

The enemy had been pinned down and confused as to our intentions by I Parachute Corps' raids and local attacks along the entire front. Over one hundred prisoners were taken during these operations.

It was difficult to bring up the units of the LXXVI Panzer Corps to their initial positions, due to mud from the continuous rains. The attacks of the divisions, especially the 362d Infantry Division and 26th Panzer Division, were hampered as their troops were exhausted from marching in the mud. The attack was limited to local penetrations of the enemy's main line of resistance, because the defense area was stubbornly defended and strengthened by mines and barbed wire entanglements. The employment of tanks by the 362d Infantry Division was not possible, as the ground conditions were unfavorable. The 26th Panzer Division was unable to employ its tanks fully, because the Ponte Rotto bridge (F 997314) had been destroyed.

Several attacks of the 362d Infantry Division against the Cle del Pozzo, 2 km east of Cle Carano (F 940309), were unsuccessful in spite of a concentration of all forces. Raids by the 741st Jäger Regiment of the 114th Jäger Division wiped out two strongpoints in the area west of Torre di Padiglione (F 921289), and brought back 10 prisoners. Several attacks on Cle Carano (F 940309) were repulsed by strong defensive fire. Six tanks were lost during these attacks.

The right flank of the 26th Panzer Division, after crossing its own main line of resistance, was stopped by strong enemy resistance with very high losses. The 9th Panzer Grenadier Regiment on the left flank, attacked along the road running southwest from Ponte Rotto. After clearing mine fields on both sides of the road, it advanced and captured the crossroads, 1 km southwest of Ponte Rotto at 1230. Supported by tanks, it made several attempts to capture Hill 77 , 1.5 km west of Ponte Rotto, suffering heavy losses in officers and tanks; it was unsuccessful. The attack to seize the adjacent Rubbia Heights was halted by heavy fire.

Units of the Panzer Division "Hermann Göring" reached the line, 300 meters southeast of Isola Bella (G 006294), to S. Alberto (1 km southeast of Isola Bella), to benchmark 43 1.5 km southeast of Isola Bella. The right flank of the Division made little progress due to strong enemy resistance. At 1200, several tanks reached the north edge of Isola Bella.

The 715th Infantry Division sent assault troops to take the crossings over the Fosso di Cisterna, 3.5 km north of Borgo Podgora (G 045240), and the Mussolini Canal, 1 km north of Borgo Podgora. These assaults met strong enemy resistance, and did not reach their desired objectives. During the evening, the enemy pushed back our advanced positions to the old line of resistance at the left flank of the Division.

been heavily attacked by enemy artillery fire, which had increased before our attack began. Apparently, the enemy believed our main effort was going to be in this area. Our deception appeared to have been successful. However, enemy artillery was regrouped during the day, after which concentrated fire was laid in front of our attacking forces.

Fire from all of our artillery positions, supported by anti-aircraft and rocket fire at the points of main effort, was directed at enemy strongholds, pockets of resistance, and flank positions. Our artillery subjected the enemy's supply lines, assembly and unloading areas, mainly in the sector of Casale Campomorto (F 941270) and Le Ferriere (F 963242) to harassing fire throughout the entire day. Our counterbattery fire was successful in neutralizing the enemy's artillery. The enemy's rear area was subjected to constant shelling with all available long-range guns. Several direct hits on ships were observed. One ship was sunk in the harbor entrance to Anzio.

We aim to prevent the enemy from transferring troops from the front of the I Parachute Corps. Strong raids will be made on this front. It is also necessary that the LXXVI Panzer Corps establish one or more bridgeheads across the Astura as soon as possible. Combat teams supported by tanks will make the attack. The 29th Panzer Grenadier Division is transferred to the LXXVI Panzer Corps for employment on the east flank of the attacking force.

German Artillery Employed on the Beachhead

Number of Pieces	Type of Weapon	Caliber
151	howitzer	10.5 cm
61	howitzer	15 cm
46	guns	10 cm
8	light guns	7.5 cm
12	guns (Russian)	7.62 cm
18	guns	17 cm
12	heavy howitzers (Italian)	
20	captured enemy guns	
3	howitzers	21 cm
9	howitzers (French)	22 cm
2	railway guns	21 cm
51	rocket projectors	15 cm
7	rocket projectors	21 cm
	39 AA batteries	8.8 cm
Total: 400		

Allied artillery ammunition expenditure was 66,500 rounds, while the German artillery ammunition consumption was 1,183 tons, of which the following number of rounds were expended by the weapons indicated: Rocket projectors (15 cm) 817 rounds, rocket projectors (21 cm) 144 rounds, guns (17 cm) 600 rounds, and railway guns (21 cm) 12 rounds.

B. Intelligence Report

Enemy Information: According to prisoner of war reports, Company L, 3d Battalion 7th Infantry Regiment of the 3d Infantry Division (US) was in the area southwest of Colle del Pozzo 2 km west of Cle Carano (F 940309).

C. Statistics

German losses (minus 362d Infantry Division): 143 killed, 429 wounded, and 269 missing. Allied losses: 180 prisoners and 3 airplanes downed.

ITALY 1:100,000.

For use by
War and Navy Department Agencies only
Not for sale or distribution

LITTORIA

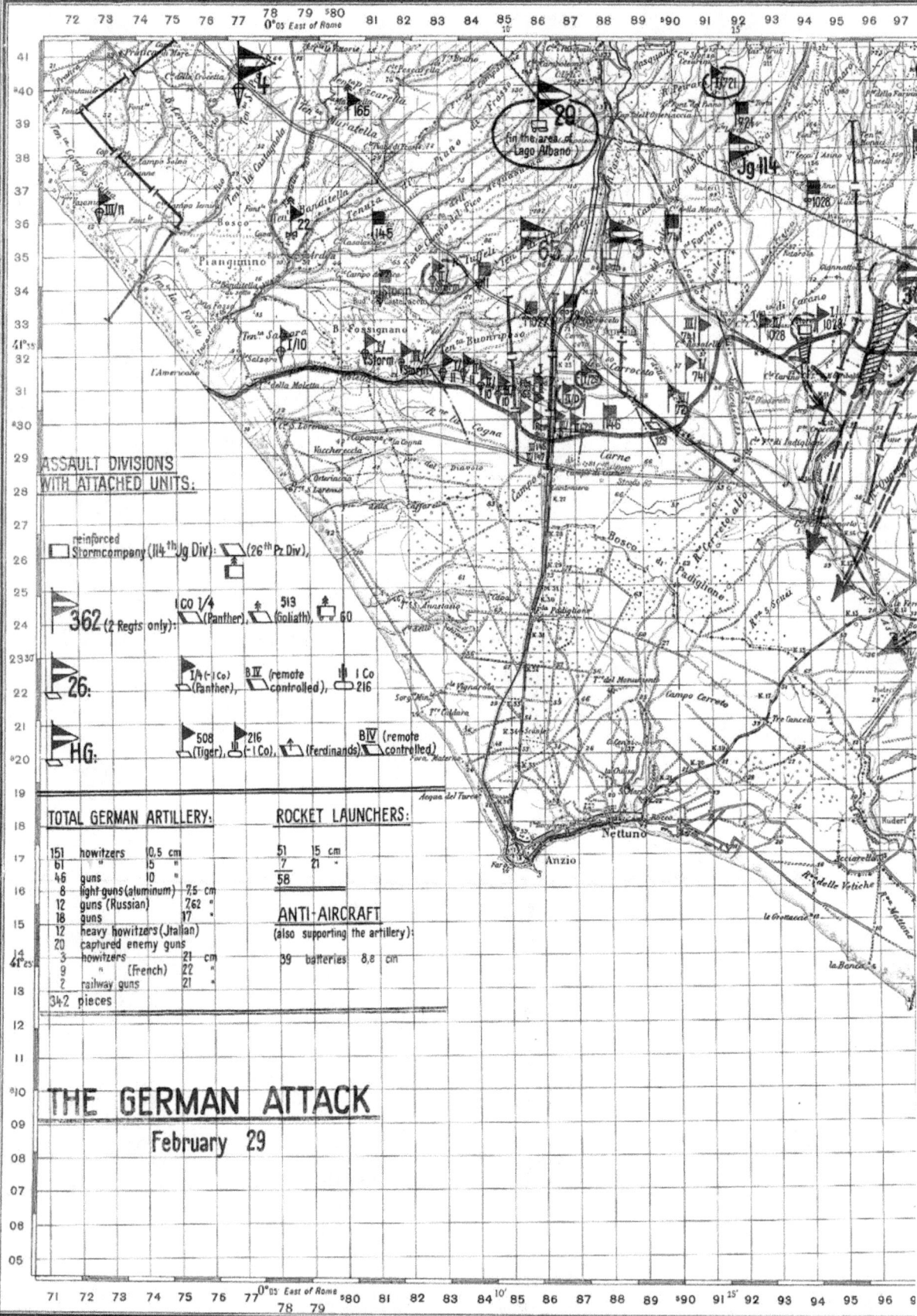

ASSAULT DIVISIONS
WITH ATTACHED UNITS:

reinforced Stormcompany (114th Jg Div):   (26th Pz Div),

362 (2 Regts only):   1 CO 1/4 (Panther),   513 (Goliath),   60

26:   1/4 (-) Co) (Panther),   B IV (remote controlled),   1 Co 216

HG: 508 (Tiger),   216 (- 1 Co),   (Ferdinands),   B IV (remote controlled)

TOTAL GERMAN ARTILLERY:

151	howitzers	10,5 cm	
61	"	15 "	
46	guns	10 "	
8	light guns (aluminum)	7,5 cm	
12	guns (Russian)	7,62 "	
18	guns	17 "	
12	heavy howitzers (Italian)		
20	captured enemy guns		
3	howitzers	21 cm	
9	" (french)	22 "	
2	railway guns	21 "	

342 pieces

ROCKET LAUNCHERS:

51	15 cm
7	21 "
58	

ANTI-AIRCRAFT

(also supporting the artillery):

39 batteries   8,8 cm

THE GERMAN ATTACK

February 29

GSGS 4164.
First GSGS Edition (AMS 1), 1941.
Second GSGS Edition (AMS 2), 1943.

Scale 1:100,000.

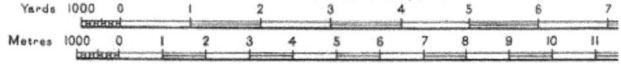

Yards 1000 0 1 2 3 4 5 6 7

Metres 1000 0 1 2 3 4 5 6 7 8 9 10 11

SOUTH ITALY GRID (BLUE)

TO GIVE A GRID REFERENCE ON THIS SHEET

Pay no attention to the smaller co-ordinate figures at the corners and in margins.
They are for finding full co-ordinates.

PAY ATTENTION TO LARGER MARGINAL FIGURES AND TO
THOSE PRINTED ON THE FACE OF THE MAP

POINT	Cava	F 844247	

East		North	
Take west edge of square in which point lies and read the figures printed opposite this line on north or south margin or on the line itself (on the face of the map)	84	Take south edge of square in which point lies and read the figures printed opposite this line on east or west margin or on the line itself (on the face of the map)	24
Estimate tenths eastwards	4	Estimate tenths northwards	7
East	844	North	247

Nearest similar reference on this grid 500 Km. distant.

GRID DATA
Southern Italy Grid

Colour .... Blue
Projection .... Lambert Conical Orthomorphic
Spheroid .... Bessel
Origin .... 39°30' N., 14° E. of Greenwich
False Co-ordinates of origin .... 700,000 metres E
600,000 metres N.

3 55
Jan. 1943

Annual change 8' East

CONVERGENCE
At the West Edge of this sheet Grid North is 0°59' West of True North
At the East Edge of this sheet Grid North is 0°40' West of True North

REFERENCE

Railway, two or more tracks with station
single track and electrified
narrow gauge or Tramway
Tram lines on a road
Cable railway
National Highways (Autostrade)
8 Metres wide, metalled
Main Roads (Strade Statali with route numbers).
6 Metres wide or over, metalled
Other Main Roads (Strade di grande comunicazione).
5 Metres wide or over, metalled)
Secondary Roads.
3-5 Metres wide, generally metalled

Other Roads and Cart Tracks, generally unmetalled

Mule Tracks
Paths
Boundaries, state
province
Canal
Aqueducts, over and underground
Wells, perennial, non-perennial
Marsh and Swamp
Church, Chapel, Cemetery
Names of physical features
Trigonometrical points
Heights in metres
Cliffs
Embankment or Dyke
Woods

Contours at 50 metres interval

ADJOINING SHEETS

149	150	151
	158	159
		170

COMPARATIVE INDEX
GSGS 4229 & GSGS 4228

AREA REVISED
FROM AIR PHOTOS

AUTHORITIES
Copied from Carta Topografica
1/100,000 Sheet 158. 1933.
1/25,000 Sheets IV S.E., I S.W., I S.E.
III N.E., II N.W., N.E., S.E., 1936.
Instituto Geografico Militare
Partially revised for communications, 1943.

LITTORIA
N4120-E1227/20x30

8 Miles
12   13 Kilometres

Reproduced under the direction of the Chief of Engineers by the Army Map Service,
U. S. Army, Washington, D. C., 1944 from GSGS
Second Edition 1943 Kodalines.

ARMY MAP SERVICE, U. S. ARMY, WASHINGTON, D. C. 113496
7-44   1944

Longitudes are based on the meridian of Rome, which is 12°27'7·1" East of Greenwich.

A. Operations Report

Operations, to harass the enemy by raids along the entire front of the I Parachute Corps, were continued. After the enemy received reinforcements, he attacked all important sectors of the LXXVI Panzer Corps. The Corps was forced to give up part of the ground gained the previous day.

At daybreak, the enemy made an attack on the 362nd Infantry Division, in the course of which he reached the Fosso di Carano (F 940309) and seized Hill 63, 800 meters northwest of Colle del Pozzo (F964312). We regained the height in a counterattack. An enemy assault at the Colle del Pozzo was halted by our artillery fire. The enemy forced the 26th Panzer Division to withdraw from the Rubbia Woods (F 984313), which we had taken in the morning. Due to enemy attacks and heavy casualties, the Panzer Division "Hermann Göring" lost the ground gained the day before.

The following order from Marshal Kesselring was received:

"Today's (20 February) successes did not meet our expectations, despite the fact that we had achieved surprise, that enemy artillery fire was light, and his air raids delayed.

Again and again, I have noticed an overestimate of the enemy. This has resulted in lack of aggressiveness by both officers and men. We are all aware that the importance of this attack is not only confined to this theater of war. However, we will succeed, only if officers and men regain their former self confidence as in olden days, inspired by an impetuous urge to attack.

It is necessary to keep on pushing forward even if adjacent troops have been stopped, and enemy strongpoints have to be bypassed. We must continue attempting to establish bridgeheads across the Mussolini Canal and the Astura Creek."

The Commanding General of the Fourteenth Army reported to the Commander in Chief Southwest that the failure, of the previous day, was mainly due to the deficiencies enumerated on 27 February, which are: insufficient training of troops, and young replacements, who are not qualified to meet the Allied troops in battle. Due to this, the Army will be unable to wipe out the beachhead with the troops on hand. The tactics which have been employed, viz. to reduce the beachhead gradually by concentrated attacks by several divisions, cannot effectively be continued much longer. New tactics must be employed, in order to enable us to meet the eventual enemy large-scale attack from the beachhead with an adequate number of troops and materiel. This attack will probably be made in connection with an offensive against the Tenth Army and, possibly, simultaneously with the main invasion in Western Europe if the weather conditions turn for the better. It will be the mission of the Army to harass the enemy and to keep him in the dark concerning our intentions, and to improve our positions in order to reduce the beachhead so as to place us in a favorable position to counter the eventual major enemy attack.

A message was sent from the Commander in Chief Southwest to the Commanding General Fourteenth Army at 1840. This message stated that contrary to the weather predictions, it has been raining continuously for 18 hours. The ground is so muddy that neither tanks nor horse-drawn vehicles can be moved. Therefore, all concentrated attacks must be halted. The divisions will continue to mount carefully-prepared local raids. Units which are not needed for these actions will be withdrawn for rest and replacements.

Order from Fourteenth Army to subordinate units

Since the attack on the 29 February did not lead to the desired result, our next operation will be to launch minor well-prepared attacks to push our lines forward and to reduce the enemy beachhead. The 26th Panzer Division and the 29th Panzer Grenadier Division will be withdrawn from the front as tactical reserve.

In general, the orders to the Corps were to engage the enemy along the entire front. At least two raids a night will be launched in every division-sector. Attacks, in company to battalion strength, will be carried out with the twofold purpose of improving our positions and inflicting heavy losses on the enemy; the objectives for attacks will be chosen with those points in mind. These actions will start immediately. Especially selected and equipped assault companies or battalions will be formed in all divisions. Recent days have shown that the different arms are not cooperating sufficiently in battle. It is imperative that during the coming attacks mistakes be pointed out to the troops, so that they will learn from experience. After the attacks, the newly occupied lines will be fortified and mined immediately to prevent effective enemy counteraction. These preparations must not lower the spirit of aggressiveness. On the contrary, they should only be considered as an aid for the continuance of our offensive operations.

In the sector of the I Parachute Corps it is most important to gain ground on the western flank of the 4th Parachute Division, in order to further reduce the beachhead in this sector. It will be necessary to push forward the main line of resistance to the Buon Riposo and Botaccia gorges. To achieve this, the Corps will make attacks, in company to battalion strength, on 2, 4, and 6 March. On each of these days one attack will be made.

In the sector of the LXXVI Panzer Corps, the front must be pushed forward, particularly in our current offensive sector. Possible objectives for these operations are Cle Biadaretto (F 918307), Cle Carano, Colle del Pozzo, the Rubbia Woods and the Rubbia hill, Isola Bella, and the little woods 1 km northeast of Isola Bella. The 29th Panzer Grenadier Division will be withdrawn as soon as possible. The 26th Panzer Division will withdraw in the near future. The 29th Panzer Grenadier Division will move to the area Cisterna-Velletri, and the 26th Panzer Division will move to the area Cecchina-Genzano-Albano. Both of these divisions will become Fourteenth Army Reserve.

The mission of the artillery, including antiaircraft is to support the offensive operations of the Corps, shell the enemy artillery systematically, annihilate all observed enemy points of resistance, fire on all profitable moving targets, and shell enemy ships, harbor installations, and disembarkation points.

Beginning 2 March, the following tank forces of the 69th Panzer Regiment, which have been attached to the LXXVI Panzer Corps, will be brought to their original assembly areas southward and eastward of Rome: 301st Panzer Battalion (radio controlled demolition vehicles), 508th Tiger Battalion (including a company of Ferdinand tanks), 1st Battalion 4th Panzer Regiment (Panther tanks), and the 216th Panzer Battalion.

The I Parachute Corps and the LXXVI Panzer Corps will form the following alert-units to be ready to move within 2 or 4 hours, in order to reinforce the units employed in coastal defense, in case of a possible enemy landing in the area of Civitavecchia: one company of the 50th Motorized Engineer Battalion, one company of the 22nd Airforce Engineer Battalion, one Panther tank company, one company of the 1st Antiaircraft Battalion, 12th Regiment, one company of the 590th GHQ Tank Destroyer Battalion, and infantry reserves as the condition demands (at present 145th Grenadier Regiment and 1 battalion 71st Motorized Grenadier Regiment).

B. Intelligence Report

The GHQ Tank Battalion 4th Queens Own Hussars (Br) is reemployed in the Campo di Carne sector, according to a captured map.

Further attacks against our advanced points must be expected.

C. Statistics

German losses: 202 killed, 707 wounded, and 465 missing.

Allied losses: 132 prisoners (66 British and 66 Americans), several machine guns, 1 truck and 1 radio set captured.

Tanks and self propelled guns fit for combat:

	Available evening 28 February	Available evening 1 March
Hornets	25	29
Tanks	165	147
Tigers	(32)	(14)
Panthers	(53)	(53)
Assault Howitzers	29	21
Assault Guns	46	58
Ferdinands	11	3

XXXVIII. 2 - 4 March 1944

A. Operations Report

Due to strong enemy counterattacks, one company of the 4th Parachute Division, which had occupied the eastern part of the Ciocca gorge (F 820305), was wiped out by the enemy. The group of houses, 1 km southwest of Ponte Rotto (F 997314), which had previously been taken by the 26th Panzer Division, had to be abandoned after a struggle of several days. In the course of this struggle, the houses changed hands several times.

In other sectors, scouting and raiding were the only activities. Enemy artillery fire has been generally light. However, during the morning of 2 March the enemy brought the sectors of the 114th Jäger Division and the 362nd Infantry Division under an artillery barrage.

During numerous heavy air raids on our rear areas and artillery positions, the enemy systematically neutralized our antiaircraft.

The following subjects were considered in a meeting of the Commander in Chief Southwest and the Commanding Generals of the armies: First, Marshal Kesselring believes that minor operations in the Mediterranean Theater, probably in Southern France, will precede the main invasion in Northern France. Nevertheless, heavy diversionary attacks at Livorno and Genoa are possible. Landing operations on the Adriatic coast are not likely at the present; the possibility of tactical landings at Pescara and Civitavecchia remains. Second, the mission of the Commander in Chief Southwest still is to defend central Italy and to reduce gradually the Nettuno beachhead. Third, the Fourteenth Army will transfer the following forces to the Tenth Army: 114th Jäger Division, one regiment before 20 March and the majority of the division by 25 March; 1st and 2nd Battalions of the 115th Motorized Grenadier Regiment, beginning on 8 March; 1st Battalion of the 71st Projector Regiment, formerly the Projector Demonstration Battalion, by 12 March; 450th Heavy Artillery Battalion, by 12 March; and the Panzer Division "Hermann Göring" to Group "von Zangen" for employment in the area of Livorno. The 3d Panzer Grenadier Division will get back from the Tenth Army the reinforced 8th Motorized Grenadier Regiment, by 8 March.

The German High Command intends to reinforce the Fourteenth Army with one railway battery (280 mm), and one Czechoslovakian railway battery (320 mm).

The Commander in Chief Southwest has ordered the immediate construction of a second line of defense ("C" line) from Macchia Idrovora (F 740343) in a northeasterly direction to the east coast. The line will be ready for occupancy, particularly in the threatened sector, by 30 April. The Fourteenth Army is responsible for the fortification from the west coast to the neighborhood of Artena.

On 3 March the Italian Marine Battalion "Barbarigo", consisting of Battalion Staff and four companies with strengths of 650 men, arrived at the 715th Infantry Division. It will be stationed in the area northeast of Littoria.

Army reserve: 29th Panzer Grenadier Division (less the elements currently employed in the front line) to be assembled in the area north of Volletri.

B. Intelligence Reports

The 2nd Company, 6th Queens Own, 169th Brigade 56th Infantry Division (Br), is located in the Michele gorge (F828315 to F845308) as confirmed by prisoners of war from Company C. The Battalion relieved the 10th Royal Berkshire Regiment on the 29 February. The 1st King's Shropshire Light Infantry (3rd Brigade 1st British Infantry Division) is now employed in the sector 1.5 km northwest of the road crossing Campo di Carne (F850890 to F270290). Prisoners of war state that Company C has been in this area for ten days.

The chart on page 79 shows estimated Allied ammunition expenditures for the period 16 February 1944 to 3 March 1944.

ALLIED ARTILLERY AMMUNITION EXPENDITURE

By Rounds for the Period 16 February to 3 March 1944

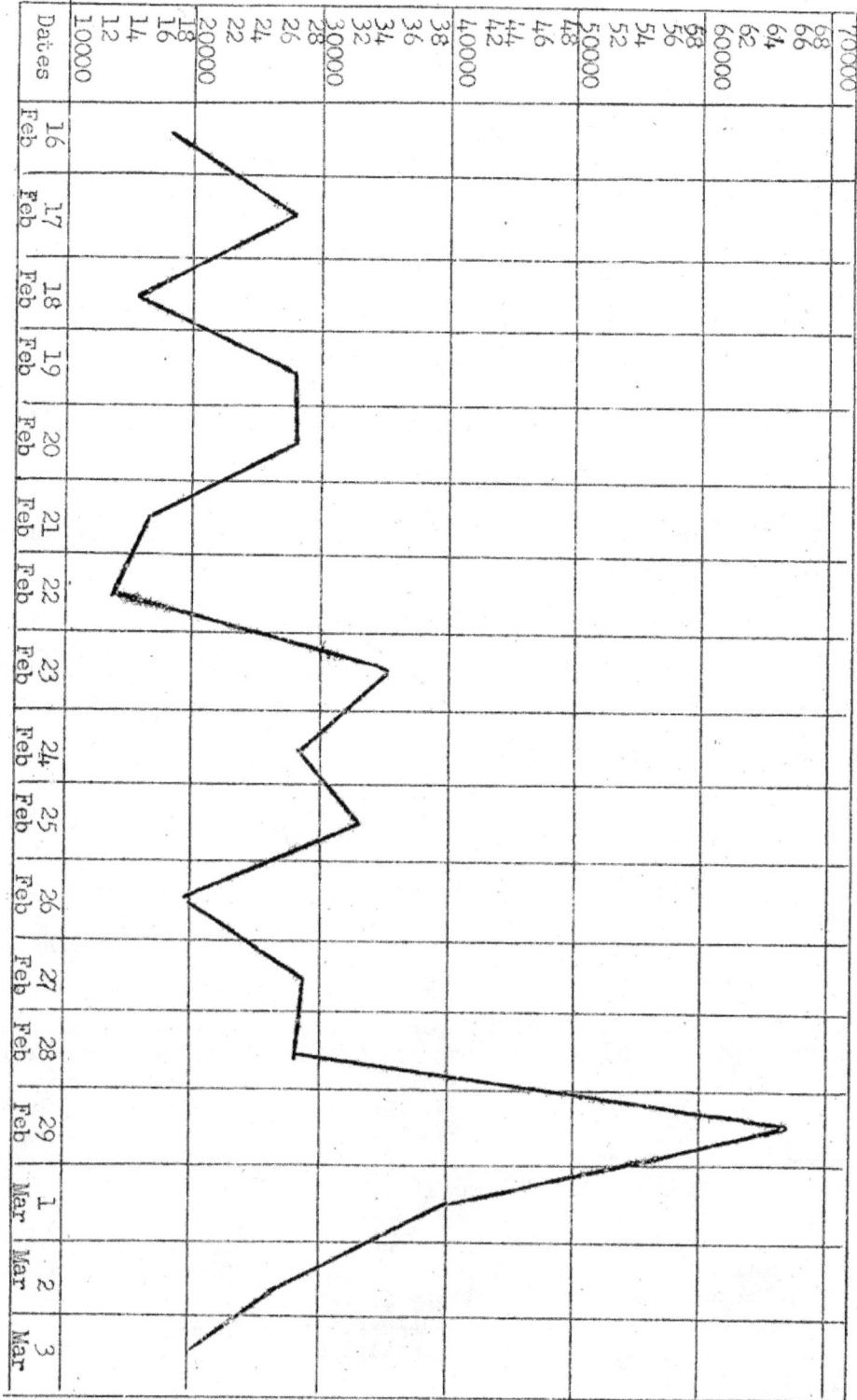

C. Statistics:

German losses: 156 killed, 667 wounded, and 209 missing.

Allied losses: 38 prisoners, 7 airplanes downed by anti-aircraft, several machine guns and small arms captured.

XXIX 5 to 9 MARCH 1944

A. Operations Report

During the entire period, combat and reconnaissance patrols were active on both sides.

Enemy bombing and strafing raids on 6 March against artillery emplacements in 362nd Infantry Division's sector met with no success. At 1200 on 6 March, the 26th Panzer Division took over the former sector of Panzer Division "Hermann Göring", which, in turn, was moved to Livorno, less its antiaircraft and armored units.

On 5 March, one company of Italian Marines, Battalion "Barbarigo", was committed in the sector of the 2nd Battalion of the 36th SS Panzer Grenadier Regiment, attached to 715th Infantry Division. This unit could not be employed for special missions because it lacked sufficient infantry training. The 114th Jäger Division, earmarked for mountain warfare on the southern front, will be equipped with mountain artillery.

On 7 March, the 114th Jäger Division's attack on the enemy stronghold at Cle Biadaretto, 2 km north of Cle Tre di Padiglione (F 921289), failed, due to the heavy barrage and the strongly defended and mined positions of the enemy.

During the night of 7 to 8 March 1944, enemy attacks against the 10th Parachute Regiment's right flank by about two companies, launched after two hours of artillery preparation, were repelled in hard fighting.

On 9 March, several enemy assaults, partly supported by tanks, launched at the boundary between the 65th Infantry Division and the 3rd Panzer Grenadier Division, were repulsed by determined counterattacks.

Enemy artillery fire was very heavy, at times increasing to barrage pitch, especially along the Aprilia-Anzio highway and in the Cle Buon Riposo area (F854310). The enemy fired an extraordinary number of smoke shells. He also employed a new type of shell for the first time, which explodes about 150 meters from the ground, ejecting four smoke pots in different directions, that produce heavy smoke after hitting the ground some 50 meters apart.

Our artillery bombarded the enemy's strongpoints, positions, supply traffic and gun emplacements. Good results were observed in several cases. Long-range artillery, supported by antiaircraft artillery, bombed the harbor at Anzio. Two merchant vessels were hit, one of them pouring out great quantities of smoke. Violent explosions were also observed.

During the night of 8 to 9 March our air forces launched a heavy aerial attack on the Nettuno area.

The Commander in Chief Southwest foresees the possibility of major airborne and seaborne enemy landings in the very near future, coordinated with an offensive against the Tenth Army's front. The following reserves are available for the defense: 29th Panzer Grenadier Division (Fourteenth Army Reserve); Elements of 3rd Panzer Grenadier Division (I Parachute Corps); and the 26th Panzer Division (LXXVI Panzer Corps Reserve). These units will be on a two hour alert status from 2100 to 0300 daily. Reconnaissance for possible commitment in the Civitavecchia area was to be executed at once. The following units are subject to the same alert status: 3rd Battalion 2nd Artillery Demonstration Regiment; 1st Company 590th Anti-tank Battalion, 1st Battalion 4th Panzer Regiment (Panther tanks), and the 60th Engineer Battalion.

Repeated observations confirmed that the frequently erroneous release of our artillery barrages was due to the use of flare signals by the enemy. For this reason, flare signals changing daily, at noon, will be introduced immediately.

Dispersion and echelonment in depth of enemy artillery positions render our artillery's counter fire more difficult. To remove this obstacle, the Chief Artillery Officer, Fourteenth Army, requested the attachment of a howitzer battalion and a heavy flat-trajectory gun battalion (Schwere Flachfeuer-Abteilung).

The Commanding General, Fourteenth Army, reported to the Commander in Chief Southwest, that no suitable tunnels as air protection were available for the employment of the two railway artillery batteries promised by the German High Command. The tunnel, farthest to the south, gives an effective range of only 3 kilometers in front of our own main line of resistance. In case the batteries must operate from the tunnels, the Army will have to forego their employment.

Enemy fighter-bomber activity is continually causing considerable losses in motor vehicles. Considering the difficulty of replacing motor transport, Fourteenth Army again points out that all convoy traffic by day must be reduced to the minimum.

B.   Intelligence Report

Prisoners of war report that the 40th Royal Marine Commando is established 1.5 km northwest of Fta Campo di Carne (F 862284). The Commandos, 300 men strong, had disembarked at Anzio on 3 March. During the night of 5 to 6 March, they relieved the 2nd Foresters. Same source stated that the 43rd Marine Commando (Br), who came ashore with the first wave on the bridgehead, were withdrawn to Naples several weeks ago. It was also established from prisoners of war that the 3rd Battalion 30th Infantry Regiment of the 3rd Infantry Division (US), is at Fossa della Pedata, 1 km west of Cle Carano (F 940309), and has occupied this position for the last ten days. The 7th Infantry Regiment 3rd Infantry Division (US), is newly established 1.5 km southwest of Ponte Rotto (F 997314). Prisoners taken belonged to the antitank platoon, the Headquarters Company, and the Engineer Company. The Regiment has occupied this position for the last two days. Lt. Gen. Truscott, previously commanding the 3rd Infantry Division (US), was transferred to the VI Corps, as Commanding General. General McDaniel is mentioned as the new commanding officer of the 3rd Infantry Division (US), with Col. Sherman as Chief of Staff.

There were no indications of the arrival of new units. Commitment of the 1st Armored Division (US) in the Cisterna sector (G 0232), is to be expected.

C. Statistics

German losses: 162 killes, 646 wounded, and 66 missing.

Allied losses: 27 prisoners, 2 tanks destroyed, 2 anti-tank guns destroyed, and 1 airplane downed.

XL 10 to 14 MARCH 1944

A. Operations Report

Shortly after midnight on the 14th March, the enemy attacked in battalion strength supported by tanks. The attack, which was directed against our positions west of the Aprilia-Anzio highway was turned back with heavy enemy losses. During the same night, two more attacks from the gorges Caronte (F 854297) and Campo di Carne, south of Clo Buon Riposo (F 859310), succeeded in making several penetrations. However, by immediate counterattacks, the original line was reestablished by early morning. Enemy raids were turned back on the entire beachhead front. Our reconnaissance and raid operations were successful in taking prisoners. One scouting party of 5 men succeeded in taking 36 prisoners.

Enemy artillery fire was comparatively light. Since the beginning of March, the enemy has extensively been employing artillery observation planes, especially in the area of Cisterna (G 0232), and south of Aprilia (F 875333). Our artillery firing white phosphorous shells, caused a fire in an enemy motor pool at Le Ferriere (F 963242), and our long range artillery shelled enemy supply traffic. It was observed that three transports were hit, and that several ships were forced to withdraw from their berths in the harbor.

Throughout the entire period there was considerable enemy air reconnaissance, and fighter-bombers were active. Our main defensive area and artillery positions were bombed and strafed. Fires were observed at Anzio and Nettuno after air raids.

On 13 March, in the Fourteenth Army sector, the remaining elements of the Panzer Division "Hermann Göring", consisting of antiaircraft regiments and Panzer regiments, were sent to the new operational area at Livorno. The staff of the 26th Panzer Regiment took over the command of the coastal sector of the IXXVI Panzer Corps, in the area of the 715th Infantry Division, and the 26th Panzer Reconnaissance Battalion was attached to the 715th Infantry Division in the area southeast of Littoria.

On 14 March, the 362nd Infantry Division relieved the 67th Panzer Grenadier Regiment and elements of the 2nd Battalion 9th Panzer Grenadier Regiment. The bulk of the 25th Panzer Division has now been taken from the front and made Army Reserves. One regimental group is in the area of Cori (G 093380) and another is in the area of Genzano - Velletri.

By order of the Commander in Chief, Southwest, the 29th Panzer Grenadier Division will move to the area south of Rome, between the Tiber and the Via Appia, as Army Group reserve.

Army Reserve is comprised of the staff of the 69th Panzer Regiment, with the following units: the 1st Battalion 4th Panzer Regiment, the 508th Heavy Panzer Battalion (Tiger tanks), the 653rd Heavy Tank Destroyer Battalion (Ferdinands), and the 216th Assault Howitzer Battalion.

During the present lull in the fighting, an opportunity has been given to improve deficiencies in close antitank combat techniques. Such training has been given; 13 officers, 73 non-commissioned officers, and 177 men have finished the course. The training is mainly concerned with the employment of rocket launchers (bazookas) and antitank grenades.

At the present, the divisions are equipped with the following:

Unit	Rocket Launchers (Bazookas)	Antitank Grenades
4th Parachute Jäger Division	25	200
65th Infantry Division	40	327
3rd Panzer Grenadier Division	12	336
362nd Infantry Division	59	180
26th Panzer Division	76	425
29th Panzer Grenadier Division	20	635
Total	232	2,103

After Fourteenth Army was regrouped, it was possible to relieve the battalions in the line according to schedule. Of three battalions in a regiment, two stayed in position, and the third was sent to the rear area to rest and receive newly arrived replacements in its units. These battalions were also used to erect switchpositions in the rear. With this system, it was possible for each battalion to have approximately 10 days rest after having been at the front for three weeks. During this period, outstanding soldiers were given the opportunity to spend two days in Rome with hotel accommodations.

Personnel strength of the Fourteenth Army is depicted in the chart below:

Units	Officers	Enlisted men
Army troops		
Actual strength	3,711	101,466
Combat strength	1,632	50,113
Rear echelon troops of combat units	348	16,464
Supply troops	1,063	16,769

Units	Officers	Enlisted men
Air Force Ground troops		
Actual strength	779	25,018
Combat strength	400	12,896
Rear echelon troops of combat units	187	5,088
Supply troops	111	3,053

Units	Officers	Enlisted men
SS troops		
Actual strength	24	1,527
Combat strength	17	769
Rear echelon troops of combat units	1	232

Total strength		
Actual strength	4,514	128,011
Combat strength	2,049	63,778
Rear echelon troops		
of combat units	536	21,784
Supply troops	1,174	19,822

Other units	Officers and Enlisted Men
Italian units	2,129
Italian auxiliary supply units	248
Russian auxiliary supply units	655
Other auxiliary supply units	341
Total	3,373

B. Eyewitness Report

The enemy artillery observation planes which were in the air every day, were harassing our troops, because each moving object was at once fired upon. Night, was the only time that commanders could make an inspection of the main line of resistance and get in touch with their men. The defense against artillery observation planes was very difficult, because the planes stayed about 500 meters from our main line of resistance. Due to their manoeuverability, they could not be followed by our antiaircraft guns.

C. Intelligence Report

It has been learned from prisoners of war that the 6th Seaforth 17th Brigade of the 5th Infantry Division (Br) is in the Michele gorge (F 823315 to F 841310). The Battalion came from Naples and landed at Anzio on 9 March. It relieved parts of the 1st London Scots on 10 March. The strength of each company is 110 men. One week ago, this Battalion was employed at Garigliano and later relieved by the Americans. After 5 days of rest south of Naples, it assembled, probably with the entire 17th Brigade.

The 14th Foresters is in the Bottacia gorge. (vicinity of F 854297) This battalion was employed in the Middle East and came via Algiers and Naples to Anzio, where it landed on 20 February. It belonged to the 18th Independent Infantry Brigade and consists of four infantry companies, a Heavy Company, and a Headquarters Company. Its strength is approximately 600 men. Companies A, B, and C are committed. The 9th King's Own Yorkshire Light Infantry Buffs, strength unknown, and the 14th Foresters, belong to the 18th Infantry Brigade. The 9th King's Own Yorkshire Light Infantry landed at Anzio at the beginning of March, after having been employed in Africa for 2 years. On 7 March they relieved the 1st King's Shropshire Light Infantry 310th Brigade of the 1st Infantry Division (Br). The 5th and 51st Infantry Divisions (Br) are probably in England.

The 1st Ranger Battalion of the 1st Special Service Force is 1 km east of Isola Bella (G 006294), according to captured documents.

The heavy traffic in the area south of Aprilia is probably due to the arrival of the 5th Infantry Division (Br).

D. Statistics

   German losses: 121 killed, 372 wounded, 65 missing.

   Allied losses: 173 prisoners (163 British), 20 machine
guns, and 140 small arms captured.

XLI The German Command's Mid-March Estimate of the Situation And German Intentions

A. Enemy Situation, according to report of 13 March 1944 from Fourteenth Army to Commander in Chief Southwest.

   After our major attacks were discontinued in the beginning of March, the enemy has shown increased activity. His frequent reconnaissance and combat patrols have the twofold task of procuring intelligence and concealing regroupments; lately these patrols have also taken place in the Littoria area.

   In addition to replacements for depleted units the following new units have been brought up to the beachhead: 40th Royal Marine Commando, elements of 17th Brigade of the 5th Infantry Division (Br), and the 14th Foresters.

   From the western flank to Borgo Podgora the defensive positions are well fortified and manned at all times. The bulk of reserves, estimated at ten to eleven British infantry battalions and six to eight American battalions, is believed to be in the area south of Aprilia. There, the enemy places his main emphasis both for the offensive as well as the defensive; his secondary emphasis lies in the region southwest of Cisterna. A local attack in the Littoria sector aiming to force the German artillery positions further away from disembarkation points appears to be possible.

   As yet we have no knowledge of a specific date for an Allied offensive. Such offensive action is to be expected in combination with major strategic operations and an attack on the southern front. The enemy continued to reorganize his forces as evidenced by the relief of front units. The enemy's knowledge of weakened German forces must have strengthened his intentions for an offensive on the beachhead.

B. Enemy order of battle, as given by the intelligence officer Fourteenth Army.

       VI Corps (US) under Fifth Army Command
       1st Special Service Forces Brigade (US)
       504th Parachute Regiment of the 82nd Airborne Division (US)
       3rd Infantry Division (US)
       509th Parachute Battalion (US)
       751st Tank Battalion (US)
       1st and 3rd Ranger Battalions (US)
       23rd Tank Brigade (Br)
       Tank Battalion "Greys" (Br)
       1st Armored Division (US)
       45th Infantry Division (US)
       Tank Battalion (4th Hussars) (Br)
       1st Infantry Brigade (Br)
       18th Infantry Brigade (Br)
       5th Infantry Division (Br)
       56th Infantry Division (Br)
       191st Tank Battalion (US)
       36th Engineer Regiment (US)
       4th Ranger Battalion (US)

C. German Intentions

As the 114th Jäger Division has been transferred to the Tenth Army and the Panzer Division "Hermann Göring" has been withdrawn to the area of Livorno, the German Command cannot plan a major attack for the elimination of the beachhead within the near future. German divisions are battle weary and have suffered considerable losses. The following effective combat strength was reported by General Hartmann of the German Army High Command, after his visit to the front on 4 to 6 March: 65th Infantry Division, consisting of 145th and 147th Infantry Regiments, 2,680 men; 114th Jäger Division, 4,582 men; 1028th Panzer Grenadier Regiment, 1,218 men; and the 715th Infantry Division, 3,099 men. This gave a total of 11,579 men.

Our artillery is weakened considerably. Statistics of 15 March show the following ready for action:

Type of Weapon	Caliber	Number of Pieces
Artillery:		
Light Artillery:		
Guns	up to 99 mm	
Howitzers	up to 129 mm	158
Medium artillery:		
Guns	100-209 mm	
Howitzers	130-209 mm	
Howitzers (Mörser)	210-249 mm	99
Heavy-Superheavy:		
Guns	210 mm and up	
Howitzers	210 mm and up	
Howitzers (Mörser)	250 mm and up	2
Rocket Projectors:		
Medium	110-159 mm	24
Heavy	160-219 mm	18
Antiaircraft artillery:		
Light	up to 36 mm	419
Medium	37-59 mm	35
Heavy	60-159 mm	140

Transportation difficulties often delay the arrival of ammunition allotments.

The enemy regrouped his artillery pulling back emplacement positions. Therefore, the range of our howitzers and antiaircraft guns is too short to reach enemy artillery positions, and only the few 100 mm guns at our disposal can do so.

Number of tanks and assault guns as of 24 March.						
	Pz III (50mm)	Pz IV (75mm)	Pz V (Panther)	Pz VI (Tiger)	Flame thrower	Assault guns
216th Assault Pz Bn						35
26th Panzer Division	5	51			7	
29th Panzer Gren Div	8	18				
3rd Panzer Gren Div						25
1st Bn 4th Pz Regt			40			
508th Pz Bn				32		
Assault Gun Bn XI Air-force Corps						17 (Italian)
Total	13	69	40	32	7	77

Due to their weakened condition the forces employed in the front line cannot be considered fit for any major attack at this time. Only the 26th Panzer Division and the 29th Panzer Grenadier Division are capable of any large scale operations. Both units presently constitute the Army Group Reserve, located south of Rome. Tank units, attached to the staff of the 69th Panzer Regiment with the exception of the Panther Battalion are brought into forward positions as a countermeasure against tank supported attacks of the enemy. Two groups are formed: First, "Group West" in the area of Cle Campoleone (F 860406), composed of two companies of Tiger tanks and one company of assault guns. Second, "Group East", between Genzano and Velletri, consisting of one company of Tiger tanks, two companies of assault guns, and one company of heavy self-propelled antitank guns.

Since the German units are considerably weakened and the enemy is constantly fortifying his positions, the German command can only plan a gradual reduction of the beachhead. An order dated 16 March from the German Army High Command emphasized this fact, as follows: "....we must continue to attack in the Nettuno sector, in order to keep the initiative. Attacks must be made continuously in small sectors so that the beachhead is steadily reduced....We have experienced in the past that our failures were due mainly to enemy artillery. Further attacks must be executed according to the tactics of the Ludendorff offensive in 1918."

Fourteenth Army will receive 12 howitzers (210 mm), seven batteries of 122 mm - 152 mm guns, from Germany, two batteries of 210 mm guns from artillery reserve France, and one railway artillery battery of 320 mm guns. The ammunition supply will be increased even though it means reducing rations. Part of the required food is to be procured locally.

On 13 March, the Commanding General Fourteenth Army recommended to Army Group the following two plans for attack, either of which can be put into effect after 29 March, provided the ground has dried. First, attack against the northern flank of the beachhead with the objective of gaining the line, Buon Riposo gorge 2 km south Cle Buon Riposo (F 859310) - crossroads Cantoniera (F 863282) - south edge of wood Vallicelle Grandi, 2 km west of Tre di Padigliano (F921289) .5 km north of Tre di Padiglione - Cle Savrini (F 920296) - Cle Carano (F 940309). The attack is to be carried out in three limited assaults. Secondly, an attack with the objective of gaining the line; bench mark 67, group of houses 1 km southwest of Ponte Rotto (F 997314) - bench mark 60, on hill with windmill 1 km west - northwest of Isola Bella (G 006294) - Isola Bella Borgo Podgora (G 045240). A successful outcome of this attack will assist further action to establish bridgeheads across the Mussolini Canal and an eventual breakthrough to the Astura.

Both attacks would involve the commitment of the 26th and 29th Divisions now in Army Group Reserve. If the latter plan is executed, it is feared that one of the assault divisions will have to be committed to hold the newly captured ground. In addition, the Fourteenth Army is confronted with the following problems: First, enemy landings may occur at Terracina (codeword "Thea"); between the front line of the I Parachute Corps and the mouth of the Tiber (codeword "Rückendeckung"); and the coastal defense sector Cecina - Mouth of the Tiber (codeword "Caecilie"). Detailed orders were issued concerning the fortification of the coastal defense sectors, the plan for tactical countermeasures, and the organization of alert units in case of enemy airborne operations. The 92nd Infantry Division which is in activation is to defend the coast line from the mouth of the Tiber to the boundary of the Fourteenth Army at Cecina. Secondly, due to the lack of safety in Rome, strict orders concerning entrance into the city limits are issued. Rome has been declared an "Open City"

and all service units will be moved outside the city. Only
medical and quartermaster units which operate bakeries, butcher
shops, tailor shops, etc., will remain. Thirdly, the partisans,
consisting of communists, Badoglio followers, and prisoners of
war at large, endanger the areas south of Perugia and east of
Orvisto. The 103rd Reconnaissance Battalion has been dispatched
to these areas.

XLII 15 - 19 MARCH 1944

A. Operations Report

Particularly at night, during this period, routine reconnaissance and raiding activities took place.

Early on 15 March, the Allies captured the strongpoint at
K 9, 1.5 km southeast of Tre Spaccasassi (F 917330), with overwhelming forces. Despite a counterattack, during which we suffered
heavy losses, the group of houses could not be retaken.

Withdrawal of the 26th Panzer Division was completed on 15
March. The 362nd Infantry Division took over this sector. The 26th
Panzer Division will be assembled as Army Reserve, in the area di-
rectly west of Velletri.

The relief of the 114th Jäger Division by the 1028th Panzer
Grenadier Regiment began on 13 March, and will be completed by 20
March. On 19 March, the present sector of the 114th Jäger Division
will be taken over by the 3rd Panzer Grenadier Division (I Parachute
Corps).

On 18 March, our assault troops succeeded in penetrating enemy
positions in the wooded area at the Moletta gorge (F 813313). Infantry weapons were captured. The enemy had considerable losses and
his position was destroyed.

At 0730, 19 March, after very heavy artillery preparatory fire
which extended to the Cisterna sector (G 0232), the enemy attacked
at several points southwest of Aprilia (F 875333). These attacks
were continued throughout the day, at times in battalion strength.
They were repulsed partly by close combat and partly by immediate
counterattacks. Forty-five prisoners were taken.

B. Intelligence Report

It has been learned from prisoners of war that the 36th Combat
Engineer Regiment is located south of Torre della Moletta (F 774312).
The 1st Battalion of this regiment is committed north of Highway 82;
2nd Battalion is in reserve; 3rd Battalion is located on the coast.

It also was learned from prisoners of war of B Company that the
2nd Cameronians (13th Brigade 5th Infantry Division (Br)) is located
in the area west of Michele gorge (F 828315 to F 845308). It landed
at Anzio on 12 March, and is replacing the 56th Infantry Division (Br).
On 14 March, part of the Queen's Royal Regiment was relieved. A and C
Companies of this unit have not as yet been committed. In the morning
of 19 March, the 43th Tank Battalion (Br), attached to 1st Infantry
Division (Br), took part in an attack west of the Aprilia-Anzio Highway. E and G Companies 30th Infantry Regiment of the 3rd Infantry Division (US) are committed on both sides of Cle Carano (F 940309). The
1st Battalion is held in reserve.

Continuous convoy activity was observed in the harbor area
of Anzio-Nettuno with a daily average of 30 to 40 units, including
LST's, transports, several large freighters, tankers, destroyers,
and escort vessels.

By smoke screens, the enemy tried to conceal the reorganization
and replacement of his troops. The enemy seems to be preparing further
attacks.

C. Statistics

German losses: 150 killed, 646 wounded, 76 missing.

Allied losses: 78 prisoners, 2 tanks put out of commission,
2 planes downed by antiaircraft, and heavy and light infantry
weapons captured.

XLIII. 20 - 24 MARCH 1944

A. Operations Report

On the front, the only activity was scouting and raiding. Reconnaissance patrols reported the construction of new barbed-wire
entanglements by the enemy. For this reason, raids by both sides
were rather unsuccessful. During the mopping up of the Michele
gorge near Appolonia (F 828314) on 20 March, 35 British dead were
found. Their small arms, machine guns, and mortars were brought
in.

The artillery continued the usual harassing fire on recognized
objectives. The enemy ammunition expenditure was much larger than
ours. After our artillery shelled the enemy rear areas, explosions
and fires were observed. It was assumed that large ammunition dumps
were hit. Our long-range artillery fired on ships lying in the harbor of Anzio-Nettuno, and occasional direct hits were observed.

B. Intelligence Report

It has been learned from prisoners of war that the 2nd Camer-
onians 13th Brigade of the 5th Infantry Division (Br) was in the
Michele gorge (F 823315 to F 845308), and was replaced by the 2nd
Battalion Inniskillings 13th Brigade of the 5th Infantry Division
(Br) on 21 February. The 14th Foresters 18th Independent Infantry
Brigade (Br), is located 1 km north of the Campo di Carne cross-
road (F 862284).

Captured documents yielded the following information:

On the front is the 6th Seaforth 17th Brigade, in second line
the 2nd Wiltshire 13th Brigade; both of the 5th Infantry Division
(Br).

Documents taken from dead enemy soldiers revealed that the
1st Reconnaissance Battalion of the 1st Infantry Division (Br) is
stationed in the sector northeast of Campo di Carne. (F 850270 to
F 890270).

Daily disembarkations of reinforcements for the beachhead have
been observed. On 21 March, for the first time, enemy propaganda leaflets were shot into our lines at Cisterna (G 0232); on the following

days this also happened in other sectors. In several sectors white phosphorous shells were used by the enemy.

C. Statistics

German losses: 110 killed, 394 wounded, and 16 missing.

Allied losses: 8 prisoners, 1 tank put out of commission, 1 airplane downed, and small arms captured.

XLIV. 25 - 29 MARCH 1944

A. Operations Report

Raid, reconnaissance, and artillery activities continued on both sides. Combat patrols often clashed in no-man's land. Results were negligible and losses relatively high.

On the morning of 26 March, the enemy captured a German strongpoint north of the Rubbia forest, 1.5 km west of Ponte Rotto (F 997-314), with an attack in company strength. He was repulsed after hand-to-hand fighting.

The coastal defense sector north of Castiglione and west of Grosseto up to Cecina was separated from the Fourteenth Army.

In the sector of the 65th Infantry Division, the 165th Infantry Battalion was relieved by the 2nd Battalion 1027th Infantry Regiment on 28 March. In the sector of the 362nd Infantry Division, the 362nd Fusilier Battalion was relieved by elements of the 1028th Panzer Grenadier Division on 27 March. The 556th Ost Battalion was transferred to the 362nd Infantry Division and assigned to 955th Infantry Regiment as 3rd (Ost) Battalion. The 1st Battalion of the Italian Assault Brigade "Barbarigo" was assigned to 715th Infantry Division.

At noon on 29 March, Army Group issued codeword "Caecilia I", i.e., enemy landings are imminent in the Tarquinia-Civitavecchia area. Consequently, during the night, the 29th Panzer Grenadier Division was transferred from the assembly area, 12 km south of Rome, to the vicinity of Bracciano lake; only the 71st Panzer Grenadier Regiment remained.

B. Intelligence Report

Newly established: The 1st Green Howards 15th Brigade of the 5th Infantry Division (Br) is with Company D at Torre di Moletta (F 774312). On 24 March, this Battalion relieved the 3rd Battalion of the 36th Engineer Regiment (US). The 2nd Royal Inniskilling Fusiliers 13th Brigade of the 5th Infantry Division (Br), committed on 21 March, was relieved by the 2nd Royal Scots Fusiliers 17th Brigade of the 5th Infantry Division (Br) on the 27 March. This Battalion landed at Anzio with 2 other battalions of the 17th Brigade, viz. the 2nd Northamptonshire and the 6th Seaforth Highlanders) on 12 March.

On the 14 March, the 2nd Battalion of the Royal Scots Fusiliers and the 2nd Battalion of Northamptonshire Regiment were attached as reserve to the 40th Royal Marine Commando. The 6th Seaforth, on the left of the 40th Royal Marine Commando, was withdrawn from the frontline. Company strength was 60 men. In the southern sector of the

Riserva Nuova gorge, 1 km southwest Cle Buen Riposo (F 859310), one prisoner belonging to the 1st King's Shropshire Light Infantry 3rd Brigade of the 1st Infantry Division (Br) was taken. On 23 March, Company C of this battalion relieved parts of the 1st King's Own Yorkshire Light Infantry 15th Brigade of the 5th Infantry Division (Br).

On 26 March, for the first time, elements of the newly arrived 34th Infantry Division (US) were identified. According to statements by prisoners of war, the 2nd Battalion 168th Infantry Regiment of the 34th Infantry Division (US) was transferred 5 days ago from Naples to Anzio. Two days ago the Battalion with a company strength of 200 men each was committed in the Isola Bella area (G 006294) which was the original sector of the 15th Infantry Regiment of the 3rd Infantry Division (US).

Documents from dead enemy soldiers revealed that the 2nd and 3rd Battalion 7th Infantry Regiment of the 3rd Infantry Division (US) were stationed in the sector 1.5 km west of Ponte Rotto (F 997-314).

According to statements of two prisoners from Company L the position of the 3rd Battalion 168th Infantry Regiment of the 34th Infantry Division (US) was established north of the Mussolini Canal in the former sector of the 2nd Battalion 504th Parachute Regiment. The 504th Parachute Regiment was supposed to have been withdrawn and replaced by elements of the 34th Infantry Division (US). Prisoners stated that the Fosso Carano (F 955328 to F 940310) is the boundary between the 45th and 34th Infantry Division.

In the harbor area of Anzio-Nettuno, heavy shipping traffic (a daily average of 50 to 60 units) has been observed.

Because of the drying up of the terrain and the appearance of the 34th Infantry Division (US) on the beachhead, it can be assumed that the enemy intends an attack presumably in a northerly direction.

D. Statistics

German losses: 93 killed, 397 wounded, and 32 missing.

Allied losses: 17 prisoners, infantry arms captured, 3 barrage balloons shot down over Anzio, and 2 ammunition dumps destroyed by direct hits.

XLV. 30 MARCH – 3 APRIL 1944

A. Operations Report

Patrol activity continued on both sides. Enemy outpost positions on the north side of the Michele gorge (F 824315 to F 841310), were captured by our scouting parties on 31 March, and held against strong enemy counterattacks.

The main line of resistance in the sector of the 3rd Panzer Grenadier Division southwest of Aprilia was considered a disadvantageous position in case of large scale enemy attacks. For that reason, it was strengthened in depth, while the main line of resistance was held with reduced forces. On 30 March, we succeeded in destroying the bridge 1.5 km southwest of Borgo Piave (G 053203) with remote-controlled demolition vehicles (Goliath). Thirteen prisoners were taken.

There was the usual artillery activity with occasional surprise barrages. Long-range artillery employed in shelling disembarkation points, ran short of ammunition at the end of the month. In the beginning of April, the ammunition supply was replenished. Shelling was resumed and hits were observed.

The 1st Battalion 4th Panzer Regiment (Panther Tanks), less the 1st Company which remained in the Cassino sector, was shifted to Pratica di Mare (F 735410), to replace the 29th Panzer Grenadier Division.

Terrain conditions were so poor that they were comparable only with the mud on the Russian front, during the worst period of the year. The level of surface water continued to rise. On 23 March, it was decided that the attack planned for 29 March would have to be postponed for several days, because of terrain conditions and the difficulty of ammunition supply. The Army now ordered the preparation for an offensive from the east, to reduce the beachhead. An attack of this kind was thought to be more promising, particularly in the Borgo Podgora sector (Sossano) (G 045240) – Borgo Piave (G 053204). The aim was to thrust across the Mussolini Canal toward the Astura. On the second day, to execute a flanking thrust from the south against the enemy positions in front of Cisterna (G 0232). However, for the latter action, a third assault division is required.

A Fourteenth Army summary concerning the fighting qualities of its units gave the following estimates: Units falling into Combat Quality Classification I are the 3d Panzer Grenadier Division, 26th Panzer Division, 29th Panzer Grenadier Division, Infantry Demonstration Regiment, and General Headquarters Panzer and Antitank Battalions. Those falling into Classification II are the 4th Paratroop Division, 362d Infantry Division, 1027 Panzer Grenadier Regiment, and the 1028 Panzer Grenadier Regiment. Combat Classification III consists of the 715th Infantry Division, 92d Infantry Division (in activation).

Attached Italian units were evaluated as follows: (1) Paratroop Battalion "Nembo", (2) Battalion "Barbarigo", and (3) 1st Battalion Italian Assault Brigade.

Comparison of Artillery Strength: With his units up to full strength, the enemy has on the beachhead more than 442 artillery pieces, not including antiaircraft artillery, compared to our 323 pieces, only 226 of which were ready for action on 31 March. Even if we include the 109 antiaircraft guns and the 61 rocket launchers, whose ammunition supply is limited, the Allies would still have a numerical superiority of 46 pieces, excluding the artillery of the 34th Infantry Division (US), which is in transit.

B. Intelligence Report

Prisoners of war reveal that the 1st York and Lancaster Battalion of the 5th Infantry Division (Br) is in the area west of the Ciocca gorge (F 853310). A prisoner of war confirmed that the 9th Kings Own Yorkshire Light Infantry of the 18th Infantry Brigade (Br) is south of Cle Buon Riposo (F 853310).

The 24th Guard Infantry Brigade is said to have been sent to Naples for a rest period. They are expected to return on 4 April to relieve the 18th Independent Brigade (Br).

The Allied relief schedule is : 10 days front-line, 2 days 2d line, 6 days rest.

Along the canal, cigarette packages were found, which exploded when opened.

C. Statistics

German losses: 147 killed, 420 wounded, and 12 missing.

Allied losses: 29 prisoners and small arms captured.

XLVI.   4 - 8 APRIL 1944

A. Operations Report

No activity except the usual patrols. A derelict enemy vessel (LCA) with two machine guns was brought in, north of the mouth of the Tiber.

The enemy artillery was somewhat more active. His surprise fire often increased to heavy barrage fire, especially in the area of Ardea (F 787350) and Cisterna (G 0232). 18 cm guns with a high burst effect were observed in the northern sector. Explosions and fires were seen after our artillery fired on enemy rear areas and landing places. It is assumed that large enemy dumps were located there.

Air activity was heavy. Fighter units of 15 to 24 planes repeatedly attacked artillery, antiaircraft artillery positions, and traffic centers.

Due to strongly fortified positions and the alertness of enemy troops, surprise raids in force were nearly impossible. The raids that were made resulted in heavy casualties and had little success. on 7 April 1944, the Army ordered such raids to be prepared very thoroughly and to be supported by heavy artillery fire, even at the expense of the element of surprise. Reconnaissance patroling was to be continued, in order to have a clear picture of the enemy situation at all times.

The 216th Assault Tank Battalion, with 15 cm assault howitzers, was transferred to the area Pisa - Lucca as Army Group Reserve.

On 7 April, after operations against partisans south of Perugia were completed, the 103d Reconnaissance Battalion relieved the 129th Reconnaissance Battalion in the area west of Terracina.

B. Intelligence Report

Prisoners of war state that the 2d Battalion Stafford 2d Brigade of the 1st Infantry Division (Br) is now in the new operational area north of Highway 82 at (F 876285).

The 133d 135th, and 168th Infantry Regiments of the 34th Infantry Division (US) are now on the beachhead and in action.

Artillery ammunition expenditure is estimated at 51,000 rounds.

The enemy fired propaganda leaflets into our lines. A new type of shell was observed in the east sector. The shell exploded 50 meters above the ground and broke into 3 smaller shells which left green smoke trails.

Due to less naval and ground activity on the beachhead, and increased artillery fire on our command posts and observation posts, it is assumed that enemy preparations for the attack have been completed.

C. Statistics

German losses: 140 killed, 421 wounded, and 18 missing.

Allied losses: 20 prisoners, machine guns and small arms captured, 1 tank put out of commission.

XLVII. 9 - 13 April 1944

A. Operations Report

Continued reconnoitering took place during this period. During the night 13 April, six sudden artillery concentrations, using all artillery and antiaircraft artillery at the disposal of the Fourteenth Army, were directed at enemy rear areas and particularly at identified ammunition and fuel dumps approximately 8 km north of Nettuno. At the same time enemy antiaircraft artillery positions were shelled in order to protect our participating aircraft.

All convoy traffic south of the line Piombino - Ancona has been suspended during daylight hours because of the losses inflicted by enemy fighter-bombers.

Army Group ordered on 9 April, that the 26th Panzer Division be moved to the area between Nemi Lake and Segni, to act as Army Group Reserve, available for the central Italian front also. Elements of this division were utilized during the day to consolidate the C-Line. However, the 93d Artillery Regiment of the 26th Panzer Division and the 304th Antiaircraft Battalion are to remain in the front line.

Since the Staff of the 69th Panzer Regiment was transferred to Commander in Chief, West (France), the local tank reserves for immediate counterattacks were reorganized as follows: "Group Cori" : One platoon of the 653d Antitank Battalion (Ferdinands), and one company of the 1st Battalion 4th Panzer Regiment (Panther tanks); "Group East": Located between Genzano and Velletri, with one company of the 508th Panzer Battalion (Tiger tanks), and one company of the 653d Antitank Battalion (less one Platoon); "Group West" : Situated at Campoleone (F 875405), with the 508th Panzer Battalion, less one company (Tiger tanks), and 1st Battalion 4th Panzer Regiment (less one company) at Pratica di Mare (F 734410).

On 10 April, the Commanding General Fourteenth Army decided that, at the present time, the complete Army Reserves should not be committed in an attack against the eastern position of the beachhead. Therefore, the planned attack was to be carried out merely as a counterattack after the expected Allied offensive. A strength report by Fourteenth Army dated 10 April, showed a total combat strength of 70,400 men in comparison to 65,800 for the previous month. This included all attached units of the Air Force, SS, SS-Police in Rome, Antiaircraft, Paratroopers, but no rear echelon troops, supply units, or foreign auxiliary (Hilfswillige).

B. Intelligence Report

Documents found on dead enemy soldiers established the location of the 238th Engineer Company of the 1st Engineer Battalion of the 1st Infantry Division (Br), 1.5 km north of Milestone 11 on Highway 82 (F 782300 to F 922289). An artillery observation plane was observed landing 4 km southwest of Borgo Montello (F 976236). Thus the existence of the advanced airfield which was recognized on aerial photographs was confirmed.

The use of 4 cm rapid-fire guns, probably self-propelled, west of Fta Campo di Carne (F 863284) was observed. At several points, the enemy employed phosphorous shells with combination fuse.

C. Statistics

German losses: 82 killed, 403 wounded, and 14 missing.

Allied losses: 11 prisoners.

<h1 style="text-align:center">XLVIII. 14 - 18 APRIL 1944</h1>

A. Operations Report

On 15 April, the enemy captured two advanced strong points 6 km southwest of Littoria (G 0818). After a preparatory artillery fire he attacked with two companies, each supported by 6 tanks. German losses were 3 killed and 46 missing in the 735th Infantry Regiment, 16 Italians of Battalion "Barbarigo" were also missing. 3 Allied tanks were destroyed by mines. It is not planned to recapture these strongpoints due to lack of forces in this sector. On 18 April, the enemy repulsed a raid on a strongpoint, 1.75 km northwest of Borgo Piave (G 053203), and pushed forward into our main line of resistance. He was thrown back by a counterattack. Our artillery activity remained unchanged.

During the night of 17 April, both battalions of the 16th SS Panzer Grenadier Division employed on the beachhead front, (2d Battalion 35th SS Regiment, and 2d Battalion 36th SS Regiment were relieved by the 1028th Panzer Grenadier Regiment, and transferred to the area of Florence.

In the sector of the 1028th Regiment, on the right flank of the 362d Infantry Division, the I Parachute Corps took over the area vacated by the battalion furthest on the right. The Corps boundary now runs in a northsouth line through the western edge of Cle Carano (F 940309). To protect the area of Terracina against a landing a strong point is being established at the road junction 8 km northwest of Terracina, and switch positions in the mountains north of Terracina are being prepared.

B. Intelligence Report

According to prisoners of war, the 1st and 2d Battalion 30th Infantry Regiment of the 3d Infantry Division (US) have been withdrawn from the front, and are now in the area north of Anzio. The enemy organized an assault detachment from volunteers of several companies of these units. This assault detachment was ordered to take over a sector temporarily, and to launch raids from it.

On 18 April, during an attack on the Aqua Bianca road, between the Mussolini Canal and Littoria (G 085190), phosphorescent smoke, which adheres to clothing and weapons, was encountered for the first time. The estimated enemy ammunition expenditures, 84,000 rounds. Two ammunition dumps were hit and set on fire.

During the last few days, the enemy tactics changed in the northeastern and eastern part of the beachhead. In the Carano sector (F 940309) artillery shelling increased to heavy barrages. Enemy

reconnaissance patrols were more active. A prisoner of war
stated that the 3rd Infantry Division (US) is in action again.
Whether this is in preparation for an attack or to relieve the 45th
Infantry Division (US), has not been ascertained.

C. Statistics

German losses: 97 killed, 342 wounded, and 82 missing.

Allied losses: 12 prisoners and 4 tanks destroyed.

XLIX. 19 - 23 April 1944

A. Operations Report

In addition to the usual raids along the entire beachhead front,
hard fighting developed for the German strongpoint in the northern
section of the Vallicelli Grandi woods at (F 898294), 4.5 km southeast of Aprilia. After preparatory mortar fire, the enemy temporarily penetrated the strongpoint during the night 21 to 22 April.
During the following night, an enemy attack in battalion strength
was repulsed. On 23 April, the enemy advanced behind a smoke screen
and succeeded in penetrating the southern part of the position.

On the eastern front enemy thrusts were repelled and supporting
tanks turned away by our own artillery fire.

During the night 22 to 23 April, all available artillery of the
Fourteenth Army fired surprise concentrations on enemy positions,
according to plan "Blumenkohl", with good results. Subsequently, it
was ordered to discontinue all scouting for 48 hours to confuse the
enemy as to our intentions. The enemy replied by heavy artillery
fire.

The 3rd Panzer Grenadier Division has requested relief from
front line duty. The division has been employed at the front since
the landing in January and has sustained more than 4,000 casualties.
The Commanding General of the Fourteenth Army suggested replacement
by the 29th Panzer Grenadier Division, as at present no major engagements are expected on the beachhead front.

B. Intelligence Report

According to prisoner of war interrogations, the 13th Brigade
is located in the western coast sector. The 15th Brigade joins the
right flank of the 13th Brigade. The 56th Infantry Division (Br) has
been withdrawn from the front. The bulk of the division is at Naples
for shipment to England. The 5th Infantry Division (Br) has received
the heavy weapons and vehicles of the 56th Infantry Division and has
marked the vehicles with its own insignia.

Prisoners of war of the 2nd Cameronians state that Company B 2d
Cameronians of the 13th Brigade of the 5th Infantry Division was wiped
out and has not been reactivated. Several officers of the battalion
were said to be on leave in England.

6th Gordons 2d Brigade of the 1st Infantry Division (Br) is
located 2 km west of Tre di Padiglione (F 920282) according to
prisoners of war of Company C. The battalion is said to have been
in the front line for one week.

According to a captured officer of the 7th Infantry Regiment
3d Infantry Division, the 45th Infantry Division (US) was relieved

by the 3·d Infantry Division 8 days ago and is in rest north of Anzio.

The 3.d. Battalion 30th Infantry Regiment of the 3·d Infantry Division is located at Cle Carano (F 940309), according to captured documents.

Barking dogs north of the Rubbia wood, 1.5/west of Ponte Rotto (F 997314), seemed to indicate employment of watch-dogs.

Estimated enemy ammunition expenditure: 78,000 rounds.

The German High Command, Propaganda Section, rebroadcast the following British report:

"Beachhead at Anzio was 3 months old on the 22 April. During this time, 3,889 enemy soldiers were taken prisoner. The Germans fired an average of 2,000 artillery rounds a day, while the Allies fired many times that amount."

C. Statistics

German losses: 107 killed, 340 wounded, and 48 missing.

Allied losses: 9 prisoners, 3 aircraft downed by small arms, 1 tank destroyed, and 3 trucks destroyed.

During the three months since his landing at Nettuno, the enemy suffered the following losses:

prisoners counted: 6,700 (of which 2,350 are American)
estimated killed : 7,000
estimated wounded: 23,000
tanks and armored scout cars (destroyed) : 249
heavy infantry weapons (captured) : more than 500
airplanes downed: 235
8 warships and 60,000 Register tons of shipping sunk.
39 warships and 376,000 Register tons of shipping damaged.

L.   24 - 28 APRIL 1944

A. Operations Report

The enemy penetrations into the northern part of the Vallicelle Grandi Forest (F 898294) could not be pushed back, during 23 and 24 April, nor could a smaller enemy penetration south of Spaccasassi (F 917330) be prevented. Only on 25 and 26 April, were these two penetrations wiped out. At the Vallicelle Grandi Forest, the 30th Regiment 3·d Infantry Division (US) was granted a one hour truce on 25 April to recover their dead and wounded. In the morning of 25 April, after heavy artillery preparations, tank supported enemy attacks were repelled 2 km east of Cle Carano (F 940310). Covered by a smoke screen, the enemy withdrew.

On the 25th, 26th, and 27th, concentrated artillery fire was directed at enemy batteries and supply depots. Extensive fires and effective hits were observed.

Air activity was livelier than ever. In the evening of 28 April, about 20 enemy vessels and 3 motor torpedo boats were observed off the mouth of the Tiber. The 3d Panzer Grenadier Division claimed that the heavy losses, during the last few days, were caused by heavy infantry weapons and not by artillery fire which previously had inflicted 80 percent of all losses.

Commencing on 21 April, Fourteenth Army Command issued various orders: Only defensive measures are considered. The centers of main effort are expected at Aprilia (F 975333) and Cisterna (G 0232). The enemy will lay down a tremendous barrage on our main defense area prior to his major attack. Thereby, he will attempt to break through our front line with a minimum loss of his own troops. For this reason, the defense area is ordered to be enlarged to a depth of 3 to 4 km . It will contain strong points and switch positions, on which artillery fire will be less effective; after a day long heavy barrage fire, some strong points will still be operative. Each artillery battalion will place in reserve one battery which will not fire at present.

Orders were given for the construction of several switch positions between the eastern front of the beachhead and the mountains; e.g. Borgo Isonzo (G 090158) - Sezze, Cisterna (G 0232) - Norma, etc., in order to block the coastal plain against attacks from the south. In case that the beachhead breaks open, the two divisions committed in that area will delay the enemy approach to line C, as long as feasible.

The reinforced 71st Panzer Grenadier Regiment, located about 10 km south of Rome, returned to its division. Thus, the complete 29th Panzer Grenadier Division was assembled northwest of Bracciano Lake, as Army Group Reserve. The 90th Panzer Grenadier Division, less the reinforced 200th Regiment, formerly with the Tenth Army, will be transferred on 26 April, into the area between the mouth of the Tiber and the beachhead, as Army Group Reserve.

Elements of the 26th Panzer Grenadier Division, mainly, the 9th Panzer Grenadier Regiment, will be transferred to the area east of Sezze on 26 April as Army Group Reserve.

B. Intelligence Report

The presence of the Duke of Wellington Regiment 3d Brigade of the 1st Infantry Division (Br), was confirmed 1.5 km northwest of Cantoniera (F 863282) from prisoners of war. This battalion relieved units of the 18th Brigade on 21 April, after it had been brought up to full strength.

The presence of the 1st Battalion 30th Infantry Regiment, of the 3d Infantry Division (US) was confirmed north of Cle Biadaretto, 1 km north of Cle Padiglione (F 921289). The 2d Battalion is on the right, and the 3d Battalion is in reserve according to prisoners of Company C. The Biadaretto Highway (F 919308), towards the northwest, is probably the boundary between the 7th Infantry Regiment and the 30th Infantry Regiment of the 3d Division. The 15th Infantry Regiment is probably employed on the right flank of the 30th Infantry Regiment in the area of Carano. In the last few days, the enemy increased his propaganda with loudspeakers and leaflets inviting our troops to desert.

The enemy fired smoke shells, ejecting smoke pots which screen the entire area over which the shells explode. Shells were observed bursting in the air, leaving 2 smoke trails, and releasing red and green smoke after impact.

Local reliefs took place mostly in battalion strength. It is assumed that two-thirds of the 5th and 1st Infantry Divisions (Br) are committed on the front, and one-third is held as local reserve. Total strength of the American reserves is unchanged. The 3d Infantry Division (US) relieved the 45th Infantry Division (US). It is imperative in order to give a correct estimate of the enemy situation to know the location of the 56th Infantry Division (Br).

Even if this division has not been withdrawn from the beachhead, but is located in the area of Anzio for rest, no major enemy attack can be expected within the next few days.

In a detailed statistical report, the Intelligence Officer made the following calculations: From 29 February to 25 April, the strength of the Fourteenth Army, including the coastal defense units of Tarquinia, and the rear areas were reduced by 42,800 men, by about 170 guns and 125 tanks through transfers and losses. The Allies, however, increased their forces on the beachhead by about 13,000 men, 48 guns, and 104 tanks. The statistics gave the actual strength of German units, the Allied figures were based on the T/O strength of the organization identified.

C. Statistics

German losses: 116 killed, 447 wounded, and 56 missing.

Allied losses: 43 prisoners, 5 tanks destroyed, and 1 airplane downed by small arms fire.

LI. 29 APRIL – 3 MAY 1944

A. Operations Report

Patrol activity continued. At the northern edge of the Michele Gorge (F 835318) and at the Vallicelle Grandi Forest (F 898294), there was stubborn fighting for advanced outposts, which resulted in local successes for our forces. The enemy suffered heavy losses during counterattacks. On 29 April, our advanced strongpoint at (G 035284) 4 km southeast of Cisterna was recaptured with the help of Goliaths. On 1 May, an enemy assault supported by tanks 4 km southwest of Littoria (G 085189) was repelled.

Enemy artillery and naval guns were very active especially during the night. Dummy batteries and other deceptive measures were employed to mislead artillery fire. In the morning of 30 April, enemy ships 20 to 30 km off the mouth of the Tiber were observed. The enemy Air Force was very active.

On 3 May, in the presence of Marshal Kesselring, Fourteenth Army Staff and the Divisional Commanders conducted a war game, which was based on the following estimate of the enemy situation in Italy as of 30 April:

Regrouping of enemy units on the main front is continuing. The sector of the British Eighth Army has been broadened to the south. Three to four infantry divisions and one to two armored divisions have been assembled behind the US Fifth Army. An offensive against the southern flank of the Tenth Army may be launched, simultaneously with an envelopment of the southern flank by a landing at Gaeta. In connection with these operations, there is the possibility of a landing at Terracina and Cap Circeo to connect the two fronts. It is also possible that available Allied Reserves will be used for a landing between the beachhead and the mouth of the Tiber, or farther to the north at Tarquinia, Civitavecchia, or Palo. In each of these cases, attacks from the beachhead, probably with the main effort at Aprilia (F 875333) are anticipated.

B. Intelligence Report

According to prisoners of war, the 13th and 17th Brigades are employed in the area of the 5th Infantry Division (Br). Prisoners of the 2d Inniskillings stated that the 2d Cameronians were on the left of the 2d Wiltshire on the right flank of their unit. These units all belonged to the 13th Brigade. Prisoners from the 2d Northamptons were taken 1 km north of Highway 82 at (F 825295); they stated that the 6th Seaforth and the 2d Royal Scots Fusiliers had joined their unit. All are elements of the 17th Brigade.

It was assumed that in the beginning of April, 1,000 men arrived from England. Of these, 400 landed at Anzio on 15 April. A troop transport convoy from England with 50,000 men is supposed to be on its way to the Mediterranean Theater. Captured documents of the 9th King's Own Yorkshire Light Infantry indicated that elements of the Independent 18th Infantry Brigade were still available for commitment.

Estimated enemy ammunition expenditure: 93,000 rounds.

C. Statistics

German losses: 132 killed, 531 wounded, and 11 missing.

Allied losses: 140 killed, 23 prisoners, 2 tanks destroyed, and 1 airplane downed.

LII. 4 - 8 MAY 1944

A. Operations Report

All infantry battalions of the 92d Infantry Division were committed in strongpoints of the coastal sector Castiglione - Mouth of Tiber. Units of the 29th Panzer Grenadier Division were drawn up closer to the coast to strengthen the defense. Frequent enemy light bomber attacks were reported. Chiefly scouting and raiding occurred in the main sectors of the beachhead. During the night of 6 to 7 May, several enemy attacks, in company strength, were repulsed on the northwestern front of the beachhead.

During the morning of the 8th, an attack, by a company and 10 tanks, near the Rubbia wood (F 984313) was forced to withdraw.

Enemy artillery activity remained static, with occasional surprise barrages. There was considerable increase of artillery fire during raiding operations. Naval artillery fired intermittently on the right flank.

Enemy aerial activity was strong when weather conditions permitted.

B. Intelligence Report

Prisoners of war of the 1st Loyal and 2d Brigade of the 1st Infantry Division (Br) stated that their battalion relieved the 6th Gordons of the same Brigade. This unit is in the area 1 km north of Highway 82 (F 893285).

C. Statistics

German losses: 106 killed, 410 wounded, and 5 missing. Allied losses: 5 prisoners, 2 tanks destroyed, and 2 planes downed.

A. Operations Report

In comparison with the past few weeks, scouting and raiding has decreased. Minor enemy attacks were repulsed. Our raid to blast the bridge .75 km east of Isola Bella (G 006294), failed. Generally, the terrain is considered to be passable for tanks. The enemy airforce has been very active. Complaints have been made about the weakness of our aerial defenses. Heavy air raids were reported from northern and central Italy.

Artillery activity on both sides was the same except for occasional enemy surprise bombardments of shift points. Estimated enemy ammunition expenditure: 89,000 rounds. At 2300 on 11 May, the enemy artillery began concentrated firing preparatory to the offensive on the main front in Italy, which began on 12 May. Simultaneously, the shelling lasted for an hour on the whole beachhead front and increased to heavy barrage fire in the northern sector. The enemy repeated the shelling on the morning of 13 May. At noon, on 12 May, Terracina was shelled by 1 cruiser and 2 destroyers. In the evening of the same day, all troops not committed in the front line were ordered to be ready to move. The impending major attack from the beachhead and landings north and south of the beachhead were expected at any hour. It was ordered that land mines be laid behind the lagoons between the beachhead and Cap Circeo.

The 90th Panzer Grenadier Division, except for one assault gun battalion which is attached to the I Parachute Corps, was marched in the direction of Frosinone in the Tenth Army Sector in the evening of 13 May. The GHQ 525th Heavy Antitank Battalion (Hornets) parts of which had been committed at the front of the I Parachute Corps also was marched to the Tenth Army sector. One company of the 1st Battalion 4th Panzer Regiment (Panther tanks) was transferred to the Tank "Group West", to replace these units.

B. Intelligence Report

From captured documents it was established that Company E, 2d Battalion 157th Infantry Regiment of the 45th Infantry Division (US) was at Biadaretto, 1 km north of Torre di Padiglione (F 921289), and that Company C, 133d Infantry Regiment of the 34th Infantry Division (US), was .5 km north of Borgo Podgora (G 045240).

Since 11 May, naval activity in the Anzio-Nettuno harbor has increased. Movements of large freighters and landing craft indicates the arrival of large reinforcements.

C. Statistics

German losses: 77 killed, 357 wounded, and 27 missing. Some who had been reported as missing have deserted. Most deserters are from Italian units.

Allied losses: 4 prisoners, 1 tank destroyed, and 1 spitfire captured in emergency landing.

A. Operations Report

Usual patrol activity, with small forces, took place on both sides. On 17 May, the enemy attacked in battalion strength 4 km south of the east edge of Cisterna (G 0232). The attack was repelled.

Artillery activity consisted of heavy surprise concentrations. Coordinated fire, from 20 to 25 enemy batteries, occurred several times daily, mostly in the early hours of the morning. Our artillery shelled enemy lines and targets in the rear area. Total enemy ammunition expenditure: 125,000 rounds.

Air activity increased over the front with frequent attacks by fighter-bombers in the sector of Sabaudia - Terracina, and heavy air raids on coastal towns north of the Tiber.

During the morning of 15 May, Terracina was shelled from the sea. On 14 May, in connection with the Allied offensive on the main front in Italy, Field Marshal Kesselring issued a proclamation to the soldiers of the Army Group C. This was accompanied by the following order of the day by the Commanding General of the Fourteenth Army:

"Soldiers of the Fourteenth Army!

You who fence in the enemy on his beachhead and you who guard the coast:

On 12 May, the enemy launched his offensive against our comrades of the southern front. This tremendous attack between the coast and Cassino will not be a separate action. At any time, the enemy may also begin an attack against us. We are prepared.

In months of hard work you have dug in well. Enemy barrages will not break our defense line. But do not relax during these barrages.

Our defense is well planned and organized. Our artillery will do its utmost to help the infantry soldiers and the paratroops at the front. Lately, we have used less ammunition, and, therefore, have been able to save enough for the expected major attack.

No tank must penetrate our main line of resistance. Keep your antitank weapons ready and use them when they will be most effective.

There will be no withdrawals either on the beachhead or on the coast. Penetrations might occur, but enemy breakthroughs cannot be tolerated.

Once again, check all preparations, weapons, and supplies. In case reinforcements or materials are needed, request them immediately.

The decisive battle is imminent. We must and we will succeed. I have full confidence in you, my gallant soldiers, because the past five years of war have shown in an amazing way to what extent the German soldier is capable of almost miraculous performances.

Long live the Führer!

von Mackensen."

The piecemeal withdrawal of Fourteenth Army reserves, for the Tenth Army continued even though the Fourteenth Army Chief of Staff repeatedly complained about it to the Army Group.

On 15 May, one company of the 26th Panzer Regiment was transferred to the Tenth Army. On 16 May, the 1st Battalion of the 9th Panzer Grenadier Regiment was transported to Fondi in the Tenth Army sector, via the railroad tunnel north of Terracina. On 17 May, the remainder of the Regiment and the 26th Panzer Reconnaissance Battalion were moved to Pico, 25 km north of Terracina.

On the morning of 18 May, the Commanding General Fourteenth Army called Field Marshal Kesselring by telephone and reported as follows:

"All indications, including enemy orders intercepted on 17 May, lead to the conclusion that the enemy offensive is imminent. While the Tenth Army can withstand enemy attacks by withdrawing step by step without operational danger, the Fourteenth Army must unconditionally hold its present main line of resistance, and must prevent further landings. These landings are to be expected between the main front and the beachhead. A strategic landing north of the Tiber seems improbable at the present moment, unless troops are moved up from North Africa.

A large part of the tactical reserves has been removed from the Fourteenth Army. The Commanding General of the Fourteenth Army requested that at least one reinforced regiment of the 29th Panzer Grenadier Division still stationed as Army Group Reserve north of the Tiber, be attached to him. (Field Marshal Kesselring declined, but he agreed that the 67th Panzer Grenadier Regiment of the 26th Panzer Division should be transferred to the area of Pontinia. There it can be used as local reserve for the east front of the beachhead and will also be available for both the area of Terracina and the right flank of the Tenth Army)."

During the evening of 18 May, the remainder of the 26th Panzer Division, less two battalions of the 93d Artillery Regiment was moved to the Tenth Army. To replace the 67th Panzer Grenadier Regiment, the reinforced 1027th Panzer Grenadier Regiment was transferred from the northwestern front of the beachhead to Pontinia. Staff and two companies of the 1st Battalion 4th Panzer Regiment (Panther tanks) were transferred into the area of Littoria. One company of "Panther" tanks was moved up to Cori and only one remained at Pratica di Mare.

B. Intelligence Report

Prisoners of war state that the 5th Reconnaissance Battalion, 5th Infantry Division (Br) is located north of Highway 82 (at F 809297).

Prisoners of the Royal Electric and Mechanic Engineers 17th Brigade of the 5th Infantry Division (Br) state that their Battalion is employed at the north edge of Anzio. Company F 2d Battalion 179th Infantry Regiment of the 45th Infantry Division (US) is located at the Campo dei Pesci.

The 3d Battalion 180th Infantry Regiment of the 45th Infantry Division (US) is now employed northwest of Carano. It is assumed that this Battalion has taken over the sector of the 2d Battalion 30th Infantry Regiment.

A small vehicle which ejected a jet 60 meters wide, probably phosphorous, was observed near Cle Carano (F 940309) approaching the main line of resistance. Two minutes later, the vehicle exploded.

C. Statistics

German losses: 92 killed, 334 wounded, and 5 missing.

Allied losses: 31 prisoners and 2 planes downed by small arms.

LV. 19 - 22 MAY 1944

A. Operations Report

On the beachhead, action continued in the same manner as it had since March.

During the evening of 19 May an enemy attack against the strong-point at the northern edge of the Vallicelle Grandi forest (F 898294) was repelled. On the 20th the enemy succeeded in penetrating the main line of resistance for a short time 2 km north-northeast of Borgo Podgora (G 045240). The penetration was made under cover of smoke screens in the sector of an Italian unit. Fifteen Italians were shot for cowardice in the face of the enemy. Subsequent attacks at that point on 20 and 21 May were repulsed or wiped out by counter-thrusts. On 21 May attacks, partly in battalion strength, between Borgo Podgora and the coast were halted. Every day the enemy artillery repeatedly fired surprise concentrations of 20 minutes in duration.

The enemy Air Force was very active during clear weather, encountering little opposition. Road traffic east of the beachhead had to cease during daylight hours.

While the situation remained unchanged at the beachhead proper, conditions on the left flank of the Fourteenth Army became more and more serious. On 19 May, the German units on the southern flank of the main Italian front were already badly mauled and had been pushed northwest into the mountains. This left the left flank of the Fourteenth Army unprotected, except by the 103d Reconnaissance Battalion stationed around Fondi.

On 20 May, General von Mackensen asked Field Marshal Kesselring during several telephone conversations to assign him the 29th Panzer Grenadier Division in order that the rapidly developing gap north of the Terracina-Fondi sector might be closed. The Field Marshal only complied in the evening after air reconnaissance reports had shown that there was no enemy activity in the vicinity of Corsica or Sardinia, which would point to intended enemy landings north of the Tiber. However, at the same time, the boundary between Tenth and Fourteenth Army was moved to the line Sperlonga-Fondi-Vallecorsa-Castro dei Volsci i.e. it now ran in a northerly direction from the coast. This added to the Fourteenth Army zone the southern flank of the main front, which was continuously widening as the enemy advanced in a northwesterly direction. For this reason, the transfer of the 29th Panzer Grenadier Division could not improve the situation at the beachhead front, nor was it made in time to save the situation north of Terracina.

As replacement of the 1027th Panzer Grenadier Regiment (which

had been a reserve unit for the east flank of the beachhead)
the 71st Panzer Grenadier Regiment, with one Artillery Battalion
from the 29th Panzer Division, was moved up during the night of
20 May. Upon its arrival on 21 May it had to be committed north
of Terracina.

B. Intelligence Report

The enemy situation remains unchanged.

Estimated Allied ammunition expenditure: 107,000 rounds.

C. Statistics

German losses: 62 killed, 234 wounded, and 20 missing.

Allied losses: 10 prisoners, and 1 airplane downed by small
arms.

German artillery losses:

The following guns were lost at the beachhead between
21 April and 21 May. Most of the pieces were destroyed by direct
hits of enemy artillery or bombs, and a few were destroyed by
muzzle bursts: 10 Light guns or light infantry howitzers (7.5 cm),
8 Anti-tank guns 40 (7.5 cm), 6 Anti-tank guns 37 (8.8 cm), 42 Light
field howitzers (10.5 cm), 21 Medium field howitzers (15 cm), 9 Heavy
infantry howitzers (15 cm), 5 Gun 18 (10 cm), 2 Gun 390 (Russian)
(12.2 cm), and 2 Howitzers 18 (21 cm). A total of 107 pieces.

LVI. 23 MAY 1944

A. Operations Report

After very extensive artillery preparations, the enemy launched
the offensive, supported by numerous tanks and aircraft, against the
front of the 362nd Infantry Division and on the right flank of the
715th Motorized Infantry Division. Simultaneously he carried out
feints and holding attacks along all other front sectors.

By night, the enemy had succeeded in crossing a section 4 km
wide of the railway line in the center of the 362nd Infantry Division's
sector. His tank units thrust forward to the Cle Fiammingo area, 1 km
east of Cle Lazzaria (F 953365). The attack against the left flank
and the rear of the 3rd Panzer Grenadier Division was sealed off 1.4
km east and 2 km northeast of Spaccasassi (F 917330). In the 715th
Infantry Division's sector, the enemy advanced to the railway bridge
over the Mussolini Canal, 5 km southeast of Cisterna (G 0232). Three
attacks on the 715th Infantry Division's central sector were repulsed,
the enemy suffering heavy casualties.

On the I Parachute Corps sector, the enemy attacked the right
flank of the 4th Parachute Division simultaneously disembarking infantry units in the rear of this division, by local landings. He
thereby succeeded in taking the wooded dunes lying between the former
main line of resistance and l'Americano (F 758315).

At noon, the Commanding General, Fourteenth Army, reported to
the Commander in Chief Southwest, the enemy's breakthrough to the Via

Appia, 5 km southeast of Cisterna (G 0232) and outlined the proposal of the Commander, LXXVI Panzer Corps, which aimed at withdrawing the left flank of the beachhead to the Sezze line. The Commanding General, Fourteenth Army pointed out, that he had no reserves, strong enough to rectify the situation on the LXXVI Panzer Corps' right flank. The proposal was rejected by Field Marshal Kesselring. The situation is to be stabilized by local reserves.

Panzer Division "Hermann Göring" stationed in the Livorno area, left for commitment at the beachhead. Its arrival was expected within two days.

At 1230, Fourteenth Army gave orders that one reinforced Regiment Group of the 92nd Infantry Division, viz. two battalions and one light artillery battalion, commanded by the staff of the 1060th Grenadier Regiment was to relieve the 4th Parachute Division's elements, from their present coastal defense assignment, for commitment with the LXXVI Panzer Corps. In addition, the I Parachute Corps was to withdraw one Regiment Group of the 65th Infantry Division, two battalions with heavy weapons, by the morning of 25 May. This Regiment Group is to be committed as the situation requires.

I Parachute Corps was to move the 29th Panzer Grenadier Division's 129th Motorized Reconnaissance Battalion to the right flank of the LXXVI Panzer Corps.

In the evening, the Commanding General of the Fourteenth Army, ordered that the strongpoint in the Cle Vallicelle Grandi forest (F 898294), be evacuated during the night. In order to shorten the front line, the left flank of the I Parachute Corps was to be withdrawn to a secondary line; Cle Buon Riposo (F 853310) is to be held.

At 2200, I Parachute Corps reported to Fourteenth Army that it believed the enemy was to extend his attack on l'Americano (F 719369). Fourteenth Army assented that the 1st Battalion of the Parachute Assault Regiment should remain in its present sector.

During the night, the Commanding General of the Fourteenth Army, gave the following written order:

"On 24 May, it is of prime importance, to concentrate all forces to prevent an enemy breakthrough.

All heavy antitank guns, assault guns and tanks will be committed at the points where the enemy concentrates his tanks, by ruthlessly depleting all sectors not affected by the attack.

The danger of breakthrough to Velletri necessitates the reinforcement of the severely crippled fighting power of the 362d Infantry Division.

I Parachute Corps will release the following 65th Infantry Division units to the LXXVI Panzer Corps: 65th Fusilier Battalion, 1165th Assault Gun Battalion, and 165th Engineer Battalion (less 1 company). One antitank company of the 92d Infantry Division will also be released to this Corps.

By order of Army Group C, the 94th Infantry Division formerly with the Tenth Army, is subordinated to the 29th Panzer Grenadier Division of the Fourteenth Army effective at 1600 hours. The Division is left with 200 combat men.

B. Intelligence Report

No new enemy units were identified.

The major attack supported by additional Infantry and Armored Units will continue.

C. Statistics

German losses: 15 killed, 35 wounded, and 1 missing.

362d Infantry Division lost 50 per cent of its fighting power. 1028th Panzer Grenadier Regiment of the 715th Motorized Infantry Division lost 40 per cent of its fighting power. 725th Grenadier Regiment of the 715th Motorized Infantry Division lost 40 per cent of its fighting power. 735th Grenadier Regiment of the 715th Motorized Division lost 10 per cent of its fighting power.

Equipment lost: 15 antitank guns 7.5 cm, 12 infantry howitzers 7.5 cm, 30 medium and heavy mortars, and 2 howitzers.

Allied losses: 66 captured, 20 tanks destroyed, and 1 airplane downed.

LVII. 24 MAY 1944

A. Operations Report

In the early morning hours after brief artillery preparations, the enemy continued his attacks on the northern and northeastern fronts of the beachhead. After bitter fighting he was able to cross the Via Appia, 3 km northwest of Cisterna (G 0232) towards the northeast. Several attacks on Cisterna were turned back. In the afternoon and evening, the artillery batteries of the 362d Infantry Division were in close combat with enemy tanks and infantry.

In the sector of the 715th Infantry Division, the enemy penetrated between Cisterna and the Mussolini Canal in the morning. This penetration was stopped at the railroad; in the afternoon, the enemy succeeded in crossing the line.

With permission of the Commander in Chief Southwest, at dusk, the southern flank of the 715th Infantry Division was withdrawn to the Norma Line. The 29th Panzer Grenadier Division in the area north of Terracina, received orders to withdraw; it was to maintain contact with the 715th Infantry Division in the west, and with the Tenth Army in the east. The defense of Monte Calvilli was emphasized, since this point effects the supply line of the Tenth Army.

On the northern front of the beachhead, the penetration of the previous day in the 4th Parachute Division sector was eliminated by counterattacks. The old main line of resistance was reestablished, and heavy losses inflicted on the enemy.

The 3d Panzer Grenadier Division turned back several enemy attacks, especially near the highway Cle Carano (F 940309) – Spaccasassi (F 917330).

With consent of Army Group C, I Parachute Corps, during the night of 24 to 25 May, withdrew its main line of resistance to a secondary line in order to release troops. Preparations are to be made facilitating a further withdrawal to the B-line during the night of 25 to 26 May. Execution of the withdrawal is to take place on Army order only.

Army Group C orders that officers will be assigned to Velletri, Norma, Cori, and Sezze, to be personnally responsible for the defense of these towns. Emergency fortifications are to be erected. Civilian labor will be used. The rear positions will be manned by garrisons made up of rear echelon troops under the leadership of energetic officers.

In the quiet sectors of the front, raids will be executed to tie down enemy forces.

1060th Panzer Grenadier Regiment (92d Infantry Division) was attached to the LXXVI Panzer Corps. Fourteenth Army ordered the 92d Infantry Division to move a battalion, during the night of 25 to 26 May, from coastal defense into the area 8 km south of Rome. Furthermore, the 3d Battalion 192d Artillery Regiment (88 cm antiaircraft) will be moved forward for employment on the beachhead front.

Fourteenth Army orders the I Parachute Corps to transfer the following units to the LXXVI Panzer Corps: Regiment Staff of the Parachute Assault Regiment with one battalion, and the antitank company; 1st Tiger Company; Regiment Staff 145th Grenadier Regiment and 2d Battalion; and the 3d Battalion of the 8th Panzer Grenadier Regiment (less one company).

After the regrouping is completed, Fourteenth Army (excluding the coastal defense sector between Civitavecchia and the mouth of the Tiber) will be organized in the following manner.

Coastal Sector (between western flank of the I Parachute Corps and the mouth of the Tiber):

One battalion of the Parachute Assault Regiment.

Beachhead:

1st Parachute Corps, the bulk of the 4th Parachute Division, 65th Infantry Division (less 145th Grenadier Regiment and one assault gun company, Engineer Battalion, and the 3d Panzer Grenadier Division (less 8th Motorized Grenadier Regiment, two batteries of the 103d Assault Gun Battalion, and the 103d Reconnaissance Battalion).

LXXVI Panzer Corps:

In the sector of the 362d Infantry Division:
The remainder of the 362d Infantry Division, one
assault gun company (Ferdinands), one company of
the 103d Assault Gun Battalion, 65th Fusilier
Battalion, Parachute Assault Regiment (2 battalions),
165th Engineer Battalion (less one company), and the
129th Panzer Reconnaissance Battalion.

In the sector of the 715th Infantry Division:
the remainder of the 715th Infantry Division, one
Tiger company, one company of the 103rd Assault Gun
Battalion, one battalion of the 8th Panzer Grenadier
Regiment, and the 1060th Panzer Grenadier Regiment.

Combat Group "Fries": 29th Panzer Grenadier
Division, the remainder of the 94th Infantry Division, elements of the 103d Reconnaissance Battalion,
one battalion of the 8th Panzer Grenadier Regiment,
and one company of the 93d Panzer Engineer Battalion.

At 2245, the I Parachute Corps reported to the Fourteenth Army,
that the enemy was attacking since 2145; in the sector of the 3d Panzer Grenadier Division, on a 2 km front. This interferes with the
planned withdrawal. The question now arises whether the 3d Battalion
8th Panzer Grenadier Regiment will be available for the LXXVI Panzer
Corps.

B. Intelligence Report

An attack of the 1st Green Howards 15th Brigade of the 5th Infantry Division (Br) north of Moletta gorge (F 8031 - F 8231) was
supported by the Independent 3d Tank Battalion of the County of London
Yeomanry.

According to reports from agents and foreign radio broadcast,
a landing of the 36th Infantry Division (US) is probable.

C. Statistics

German losses (minus LXXVI Panzer Corps and 4th Parachute
Division): 12 killed, 81 wounded, and 8 missing.

German Artillery losses: 1 assault gun 7.5 cm (direct hit
by artillery). The following pieces were spiked: 3 howitzers
10.5 cm, 2 howitzers 15 cm, and 3 howitzers 22 cm (Mörser), (French).

Damaged: 1 gun 10 cm. Slightly damaged by artillery hits:
1 gun 17 cm, 2 field howitzers 10.5 cm, 1 field howitzer 10.5 cm
(Italian), and 1 field howitzer 15 cm.

Allied losses: 49 prisoners, 25 tanks destroyed, 6 tanks put out of commission, 1 tank captured, and 2 fighter-bombers downed.

LVIII.   25 MAY 1944

A.   Operations Report

After 0530, the enemy continued his attacks with heavy tank, artillery, and air support. The main effort was in the area northwest, north, and northeast of Cisterna (G 0232). He succeeded, in spite of heavy resistance on the part of our troops, in advancing to a line 3 km south of Velletri - 3 km east of Velletri-Giulianello. In Cisterna, a weak combat team of 80 men led by the commander of the 954th Grenadier Regiment of the 362d Infantry Division was surrounded and overcome by superior enemy forces.

During the night, the 3d Panzer Grenadier Division repulsed repeated heavy enemy attacks in the Spaccasassi area (F 917330) in hand-to-hand fighting.

On the left flank of the I Parachute Corps, beginning south of Cle Buon Riposo (F 859310), the main line of resistance was withdrawn to the secondary line. Strong outposts were maintained at the old line. Fourteenth Army ordered the immediate strengthening of the tank defenses at the boundary between the 362d Infantry Division and the 715th Infantry Division. To accomplish this one company of the 103d Assault Gun Battalion and 8 heavy antitank guns of the Antitank Battalion of the 4th Parachute Division were shifted from the I Parachute Corps to the LXXVI Panzer Corps.

In order to make the Velletri-Giulianello-Cori road usable, contact was to be made from east to west between the 362d Infantry Division and the 715th Infantry Division.

Telegraphic order by Field Marshal Kesselring to the Commanding General, Fourteenth Army read:

"The defensive battle has now reached its decisive stage. We must inflict such heavy casualties that the enemy's aggressive power is reduced. This will only be possible if the main lines of resistance are defended with the utmost courage and zeal. I therefore prohibit the withdrawal of divisions or the relinquishment of any key positions without my express orders."

During the evening, Field Marshal Kesselring informed the Commanding General Fourteenth Army that the Reconnaissance Battalion of the Panzer Division "Hermann Göring" is being moved to the breakthrough sector and will remain under Fourteenth Army orders. However, the bulk of the Division should be held back for possible commitment with the Tenth Army.

B.   Intelligence Report

From intercepted radio messages, it is believed that the 1st Armored Division (US) is employed in the Littoria-Cisterna-Lazzaria area.

Estimated enemy artillery ammunition expenditure: 108,000 rounds.

A. Operations Report

The enemy further developed his attacks. Around midday, armored forces succeeded in breaching the defensive position south of Velletri by advancing on both sides of the Appian way and from the east. Between the 362d Infantry Division and the mountain range the enemy pushed forward, as far as Artena.

In the evening 2d Panzer Grenadier Division "Hermann Göring" attacked from a line west of Labico, their objective being a line 2.5 km north of Giulianello.

In 3d Panzer Grenadier Division's sector enemy infantry and armored units attacked in force, along a broad front, at 1100. Except for a few minor penetrations the attack was repulsed after bitter fighting.

Commanding General, LXXVI Panzer Corps, reported to Commanding General, Fourteenth Army, that 715th Infantry Division had lost the greater part of its heavy weapons. Elements of the division were probably at Cori, Norma and Sezze. Moreover, as there was no signal equipment left, the division could not be employed for some time. Army Group C informed Fourteenth Army that Panzer Division "Hermann Göring" would be subordinated to LXXVI Panzer Corps. The Division is to be committed as a unit. In order to master the situation in the area south of Valmontone, Commander in Chief, South-west, ordered Tenth Army to transfer the following units to LXXVI Panzer Corps, during the night of 26 to 27 May: a regimental group, comprising two battalions, Staff, 5th Projector Brigade, with one regiment, and two heavy antiair craft artillery battalions. Apart from these reinforcements LXXVI Panzer Corps transferred two Grenadier battalions and two artillery battalions from the 29th Panzer Grenadier Division for commitment with the 715th Infantry Division.

In case of overwhelming enemy pressure, the 29th Panzer Grenadier Division was granted permission to withdraw to a line running along the crests from Rocca Massima, 6 km southeast of Cori, to 4 km southwest of Carpineto, to Roccagorga, south est of Prossedi. The following Fourteenth Army Order was issued.

During the night of 26 to 27 May, the elements of the I Parachute Corps, south of Aprilia between Cle Buon Riposo (F 859310) and the road intersection 2 km northwest of Tre Spaccasassi (F 917330), will fall back to the B-line, which is approximately 2 km behind the main line of resistance.

The elements to the east of this point will take up a flanking position along a line running east of Cle Mandria (F 902365) over Cle Pedica to a point 3 km southeast of Lanuvio, where it joins the C-line. Effective at 2200, the 362d Infantry Division will be subordinated to I Parachute Corps and will fall back to the C-line in its own sector. Its center of defense will be Velletri. The C-line, coming from the southwest, runs 1 km south of Lanuvio - 1 km south of Velletri - Labico.

At the earliest possible hour on 27 May, Panzer Division "Hermann Göring", under the command of the LXXVI Panzer Corps, will attack the enemy forces which have penetrated as far as Artena. They will drive the enemy back to the line: 4 km southeast of Velletri - 2 km south of Giulianello - Rocca Massima.

B. Intelligence Report

The 760th Tank Battalion was established as attached to the 34th Infantry Division (US). The commitment of the 36th Infantry Division (US) was established through prisoners of the 143d Infantry Regiment taken south of Velletri.

C. Statistics

German losses: Artillery losses inflicted by enemy artillery bombardments: All guns (6 Field Howitzers 15 cm) of 671st Artillery Regiment 715th Infantry Division, all guns (6 Field Howitzers 15 cm) 3d Battalion Artillery Demonstration Regiment, 3 field howitzers self-propelled (10.5 cm), 2 field howitzers self-propelled (15 cm), 1 gun (17 cm), 1 Russian gun (15.2 cm), 1 gun (21 cm).

Allied losses: 45 tanks destroyed, 6 planes downed by small arms.

LX. 27 May 1944

A. Operations Report

The enemy continued his attacks in the area south of Valmontone. He also extended the offensive to the sectors of the 65th Infantry and the 3d Panzer Grenadier Divisions. His main blows are on either side of the Aprilia - Anzio Highway, and on Highway 42E (F 877325 to F 917285) and east of Aprilia. After repeated attacks were repulsed by concentrated fire of all our artillery, the enemy succeeded in making several penetrations in the sector of the 3d Panzer Grenadier Division. Our last antitank guns, were destroyed. The weakened troops were forced to withdraw nearly 1.5 km to Spaccasassi Creek.

During the morning, the enemy advanced towards the new main line of resistance of the 362d Infantry Division. Repeated attacks were turned back.

Parts of the Panzer Division "Hermann Göring" counterattacking, from the area west of Valmontone, against a stubbornly fighting enemy reached the railroad line and the highway west of Artena. During the morning, the enemy succeeded in entering Artena by forcing the Panzer Reconnaissance Battalion "Hermann Göring" to withdraw to the north of the town.

Summarized Army orders for further operations follow.

The Army considers the following to be the intentions of the enemy: First, to make a breakthrough in the area between Aprilia and the Albanese Mountains, in a northwesterly direction; second, to make a breakthrough towards Valmontone with the bulk of its forces, in order to surround the southern flank of the Tenth Army, and to cut off their communications to the rear; and third, new landings on both sides of the mouth of the Tiber are within the realm of possibility.

The I Parachute Corps will hold its present position. In the sectors of the 4th Parachute Division, the 65th Infantry Division, and the 3d Panzer Grenadier Division, a gradual withdrawal to the C-line is probable, and must be prepared for. In the sector of the 362d Infantry Division, which is already in the C-line, the position will be held at all costs. The enemy must be brought to a final halt in front of the line. This order pertains to the entire C-line; it has been issued by Hitler.

It is the main mission of the LXXVI Panzer Corps drive the enemy back to the Velletri – Rocca Massima line, which he has penetrated in the direction of Valmontone. This is essential, in order to secure the western flank of the southern tip of the Tenth Army, and to insure once again its supply line over the Via Casilina, until the southern flank of the Tenth Army has reached the C-line. The Tenth Army has orders to transfer the 334th Infantry Division to the Fourteenth Army. The bulk of the 334th Infantry Division will be brought to the Tivoli sector, and elements of it, probably 2 Battaions to the sector 7 km southeast of Valmontone.

The Italian Parachute Regiment "Folgore" will be attached to the I Parachute Corps to fight a rearguard action.

B. Intelligence Report

The first Battalion 6th Armored Infantry Regiment of the 1st Armored Division (US) is west of Artena, according to prisoner of war statements. This Regiment, together with the 13th Armored Infantry Regiment 1st Armored Division (US), advanced from the Cisterna area toward Artena. The first objective was to be the Via Casilina; then the units were to push westward. Elements of the 36th Infantry Division (US) are to follow closely behind. The 1st Armored Regiment of the 1st Armored Division (US), was on the left flank of the 6th Armored Infantry Regiment. The 1st Armored Division (US) had on its left flank the 34th Infantry Division (US), and on its right, the 3d Infantry Division (US).

C. Statistics

German losses: (only the 4th Parachute Division and the 65th Infantry Division) 8 killed, 32 wounded, and 13 missing.

Allied losses: 32 prisoners, 17 tanks destroyed, and 3 tanks put out of commission.

A. Operations Report

The enemy attacks continued in the western and northern
sector of the Fourteenth Army with main effort at Stazione di
Campoleone (F 877384), and in the areas southeast and southwest of Lanuvio. Strong infantry and tank forces, part of
which had been just brought up, were employed in this attack.
All enemy attacks against the front of the 65th Infantry Division were repelled, but the enemy succeeded in making a
penetration at the boundary between the 65th Infantry Division
and the 3rd Panzer Grenadier Division. The penetration was
sealed and a front line reestablished.

Minor enemy attacks against the front of the 362d.
Infantry Division were repelled. The Panzer Division "Hermann
Göring", withstood a strong enemy counterattack west of
Stazione di Artena, and continued its attack gaining ground
towards Lariano, despite stubborn enemy resistance.

The Commander in Chief, Southwest issued this order.

At the expense of other sectors the enemy concentrates all available forces on his left flank. His
reserves which we believed to be located in the rear,
in Italy, are committed here almost exclusively. The
Commander in Chief, Southwest, will hold central Italy
and defend Rome under all circumstances. The right
flank of the Fourteenth Army will prevent the enemy
from breaking through the C-line. All available reserves will be concentrated in the area of Valmontone,
in order to stop the advancing enemy and to repel him
towards the south. The construction of the Campagna
switch position will be continued at all cost, even if
the population of Rome has to be employed.

Summarized Army orders for further operations:

In order to provide new reserves, the I Parachute
Corps will withdraw its western flank to the general
front line: Cle la Fossa (F 765332) - Ardea (F 787350) -
C-line east of Cle Piano di Frasso (F 816380). Strong
rear guards will remain in the present main line of
resistance. The following units will be transferred and
attached to the I Parachute Corps: 334th Infantry
Division from Tenth Army; 9th Air Force Field Battalion,
at present with 715th Infantry Division (Reinforced by
remnants of 7th Air Force Field Battalion it is to be
committed between the mouth of the Tiber and the main
line of resistance); Assault Battalion of the Service
School, Southwestern Theater; Füsilier Battalion of the
92d Infantry Division; and the 811th Panzer Engineer
Company (Goliath tanks) to be committed as infantry.

The task of the LXXVI Panzer Corps is to continue
the attacks on its western flank, in order to contact
the eastern flank of the I Parachute Corps. The
C-line is to be reached. In case of further withdrawal of the eastern flank of the Corps and the Tenth
Army, contact is to be established in the area 4 km
southeast of Sgurgola.

In addition to holding the C-line as the final main line of resistance, and to halting the major enemy attack, scouting and patrolling as well as defensive preparations in the area behind the C-line will be executed. The Italian Battalion "Barbarigo" will be attached to the I Parachute Corps for construction of field fortifications.

B. Intelligence Report

According to prisoner of war statements the 2d and 3d Battalion 147th Infantry Regiment of the 36th Infantry Division (US) are committed south of Velletri. General Ryder is said to be Commanding General of the 34th Infantry Division (US).

C. Statistics

German losses: not reported

Allied losses: 7 prisoners

LXII. 29 May 1944

A. Operations Report

The I Parachute Corps withdrew last night according to plan.

The 4th Parachute Division and 65th Infantry Division repelled several attacks, but the enemy succeeded in penetrating the line. This penetration occurred in the area east of the railroad, making a gap 2.5 km wide and 1.5 km deep in the center of the 3d Panzer Grenadier Division's sector.

During the night, Panzer Division "Hermann Göring" attacked and occupied Lariano and the road to the northeast. Enemy counterattacks were repulsed, and an enemy penetration west of Stazione di Artena was wiped out. During the evening, the right flank of the 29th Panzer Grenadier Division attacked in a southwesterly direction to make contact with Panzer Division "Hermann Göring".

At noon, Fourteenth Army informed Army Group C that the position of 65th Infantry Division was serious. For tank defense, the Division had at its disposal only 6 assault guns, 1 Tiger tank and several antitank guns. Field Marshall Kesselring ordered the antiaircraft artillery of the I Parachute Corps (approximately 14 batteries) be employed exclusively against tanks. Minefields were to be laid in the path of enemy tanks by all available engineers. A breakthrough must be avoided.

Army orders for further operations were:

After the unsuccessful attempt to break through at Via Casilina, the enemy transferred his point of main effort to the area between the Albanese mountains and the coast. According to radio intercepts, one armored regiment and elements of an armored infantry regiment of the 1st Armored Division (US) were transferred to that area. The Army expects the continuation of major enemy attacks in the I Parachute Corps sector southwest of the Albanese mountains to force a breakthrough towards Rome. At the same time, continuous attacks in the direction of Valmontone and stronger thrusts against the eastern flank of the LXXVI Parachute Corps can be expected.

The I Parachute Corps will defend the C-line, prevent an enemy breakthrough, and repel penetrations. The withdrawal of the western flank to the C-line is authorized. The following units and artillery are assigned to the Corps: 5 antitank guns of the 92d. Infantry Division, one engineer company of the 92d. Infantry Division, one engineer company of the 715th Infantry Division, the Panzer Battalion of the 29th Panzer Grenadier Division (less one company which is employed on the northern flank of the 29th Panzer Grenadier Division), and two antiaircraft battalions (to be transferred by the Commanding General of the Central Italian Airforce).

The penetration in the area of LXXVI Panzer Corps must be reduced as quickly as possible, by converging attacks of Panzer Division "Hermann Göring" and attacks by the northern flank of the 29th Panzer Grenadier Division. Army Group C ordered Battle Group " v Zangen", a reinforced Regimental Group of the 356th Infantry Division, presently employed for coastal defense on the Gulf of Genoa, to transfer to the area Grosseto - Orbetello, as Army Group Reserve.

B. Intelligence Report

According to reliable sources the three regiments of the 36th Infantry Division (US) are committed.

C. Statistics

German losses: no information

Allied losses: 65 prisoners, 3 airplanes downed, several damaged.

LXIII. 30 May 1944

A. Operations Report

The enemy continued his attack on a broad front with heavy artillery fire and strong armored forces. His main efforts were in the northern sector, on the eastern flank, and in the sector of the 65th Infantry Division. All attacks were repelled. On the right flank of the 3d. Panzer Grenadier Division, the enemy penetration could be considerably reduced by a counterattack.

The night raid of the Panzer Division "Hermann Göring" in the direction of Artena, encountered an enemy attack supported by tanks. The enemy penetration just west of Stazione di Artena was sealed off.

The right flank of the 29th Panzer Grenadier Division attacked during the night, and gained the line running from 2 km east of Artena to 5 km northwest of Segni.

The Fourteenth Army ordered the withdrawal of the "Ost" Battalion of the 362d Infantry Division from the front line, in order to employ this unit in the construction of fortifications.

During the night of 30 to 31 May, the 2d Battalion (less one company) 755th Grenadier Regiment of the 334th Infantry Division was transferred to the LXXVI Panzer Corps in the area south of Palestrina.

B. Intelligence Report

Prisoners of war revealed that the 108th Antiaircraft Battalion of the VI American Corps was employed northwest of Velletri. Two companies of the 1st Reconnaissance Battalion of the 1st Infantry Division (Br) were established near Cle Campoleone (F 870406). The 46th Tank Battalion (GHQ troops) of the 1st Infantry Division (Br) was identified through captured documents. General Walker has been identified as the Commander of the 36th Infantry Division (US).

C. Statistics

German losses: No reports

Allied losses: 106 prisoners, 28 tanks destroyed, and 1 airplane downed.

LXIV. 31 May 1944

A. Operations Report

The enemy continued his efforts to force a breakthrough in the center of the I Parachute Corps by employing strong infantry and armored units, supported by continuous barrage fire. In heavy fighting, the 65th Infantry Division succeeded in preventing the breakthrough along the railroad line Cisterna — Rome, and in holding a thinly-manned front, which blocked the enemy from northwest Cle Campoleone (F 860406) to a point 2 km northeast from Cle Campoleone. During the night, the right flank of the 3d Panzer Grenadier Division was able to regain the old main line of resistance at the Aprilia - Albano Highway, by counterattacking. In the morning hours, a few enemy tanks penetrated along the Aprilia - Albano Highway in the direction of Cecchina. An enemy breakthrough at the boundary line of the 65th Infantry Division and the 3d Panzer Grenadier Division was prevented.

The enemy managed to infiltrate two battalions at the boundary between the I Parachute Corps and the LXXVI Panzer Corps, and to advance on both sides of the mountain ridge, M. Artemisio, up to 3 km northwest of Velletri. An attack was launched by the Panzer Division "Hermann Göring" from Lariano in a southwesterly direction to close the gap between the two Corps.

The 29th Panzer Grenadier Division will be attached to Tenth Army as of midnight 1 June 1944.

The main mission of the Fourteenth Army for 1 June is: First, the repulsion of further enemy attacks; his main point of effort is assumed to be between the Albanese mountains and the coast. Second, the elimination of enemy penetrations between the I Parachute Corps and the LXXVI Panzer Corps at the earliest possible moment. The 334th Infantry Division, less Combat Group "Jänisch" will be assigned to the LXXVI Panzer Corps. It will be commited along and west of the boundary line between the Fourteenth and Tenth Armies. Combat Group "Jänisch" will remain under command of the I Parachute Corps, until further notice.

The 92d Infantry Division has received orders to transfer to the I Parachute Corps, during the night of 31 May to 1 June, the 3d Battalion 1059th Grenadier Regiment. It is also to prepare the 1st Battalion 1059th Grenadier Regiment, so that it can be attached to the I Parachute Corps in the evening of 1 June. I Parachute Corps will receive an armored combat team consisting of 10 Tiger tanks and 10 remote-controlled demolition vehicles from the 508th Panzer Battalion.

In the evening, an order by Field Marshal Kesselring emphasized the urgency of eliminating the enemy infiltration between the I Parachute Corps and LXXVI Panzer Corps. This was to be accomplished even though it might be necessary to use all the tanks of the Panzer Division "Hermann Göring", and to withdraw units from the northern flank of the 29th Panzer Grenadier Division.

Available tanks and assault guns on 31 May 1944:

Unit	Tanks	Assault Guns
Parachute Assault Gun Battalion, XI Air Force Corps	3	22 (Italian)
65th Infantry Division		1 (Italian)
3d Panzer Grenadier Division		15
Panzer Division "Hermann Göring"	20	7
508th Panzer Battalion	10 (Tiger)	
1st Company of the 653d Antitank Battalion		2 (Ferdinand)
Total	33 tanks	47 assault guns

B. Intelligence Report

The Fourteenth Army was now facing the following enemy division:

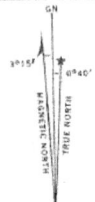

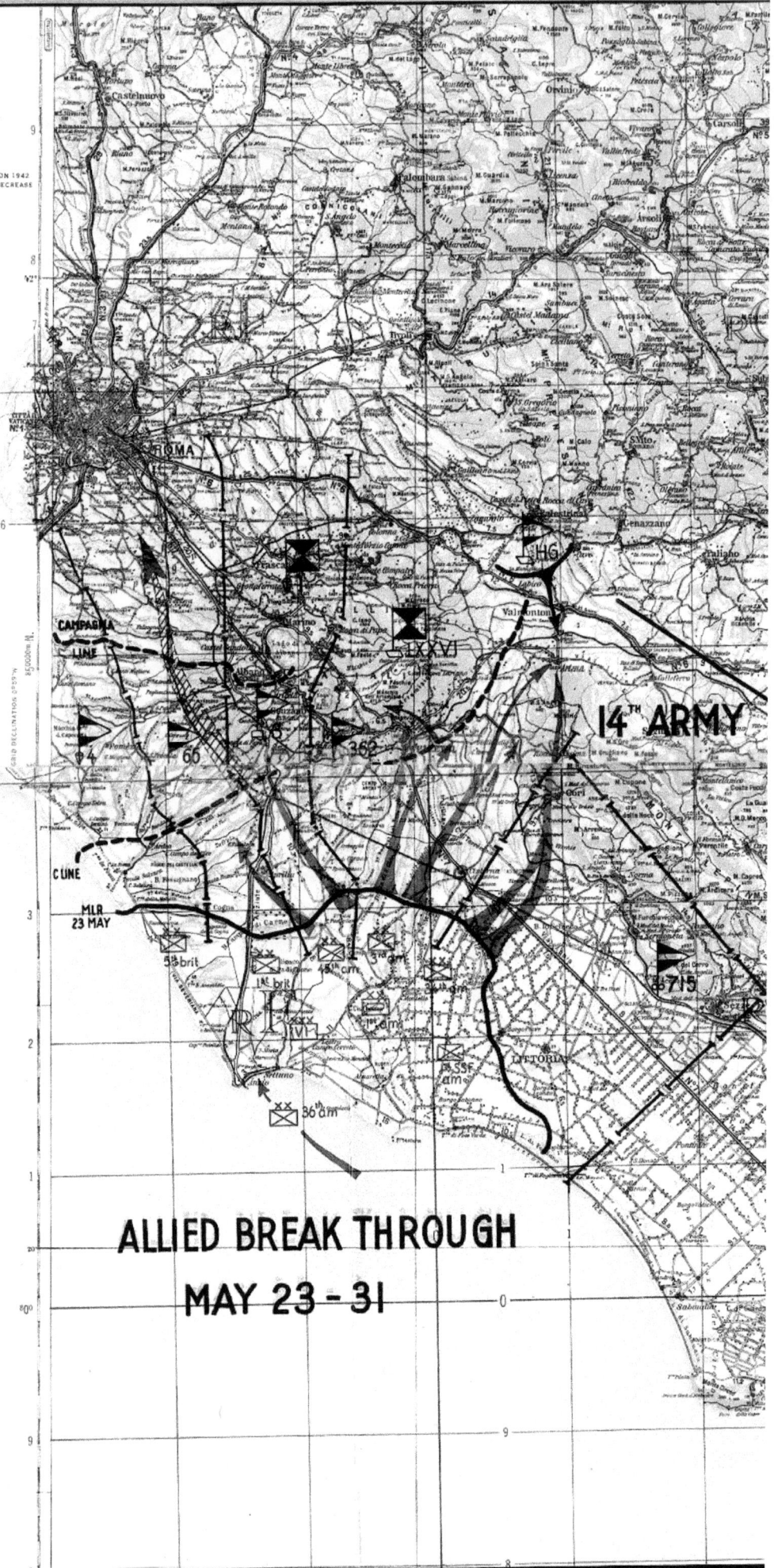

ALLIED BREAK THROUGH
MAY 23 - 31

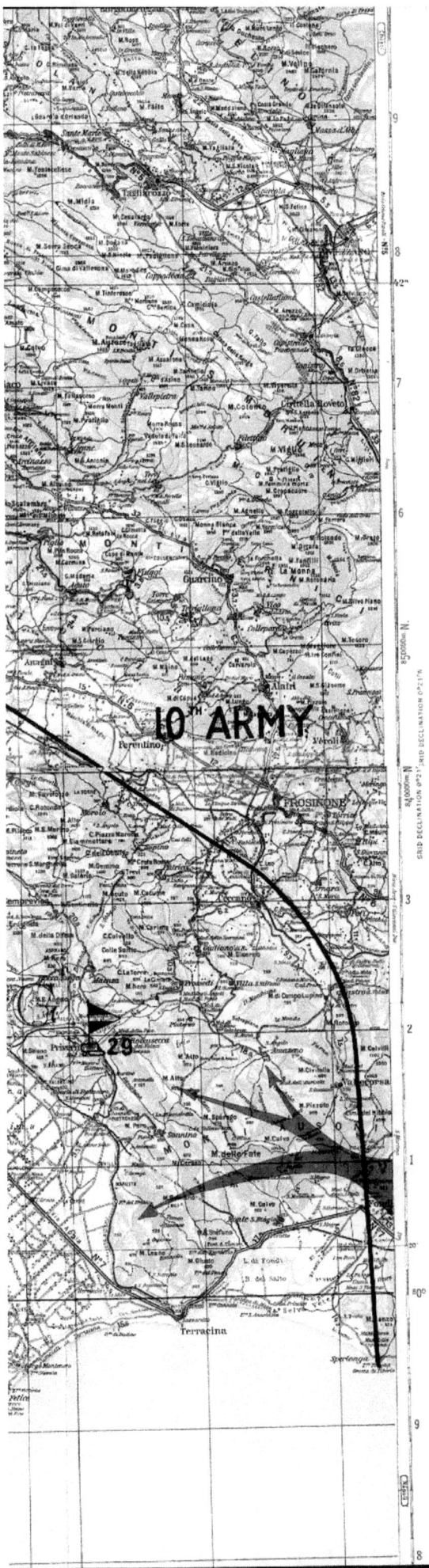

10TH ARMY

29

```
5th Infantry Division (Br)
1st Infantry Division (Br)
1st Armored Division (US)
34th Infantry Division (US)
36th Infantry Division (US)
85th Infantry Division (US)
3d  Infantry Division (US)
1st Special Service Force (US)
88th Infantry Division (US)
4th Moroccan Mountain Division (US)
```

Final estimate of enemy situation:

On 23 May, the enemy began his major attack, from
the beachhead, with a strong concentration of men and
materiel. The objective was to occupy the important
heights near Velletri, and then to thrust forward to
Valmontone. This would clear the way for a breakthrough
to Rome. His immediate objective was to cut the
important Tenth Army supply route to the Via Casilina
(Highway 6).

All available forces were concentrated in a spear-
head, viz the 1st Armored (US), 3.d. and 34th Infantry
Divisions (US), which succeeded in making a deep
penetration east of Velletri. Making use of this success,
the 36th Infantry Division (US) was brought up and
immediately commited at the point of main effort. The
attacking force was further strengthened by the 760th
Tank Battalion and 178th Artillery Regiment (US). The
1st Infantry Division (Br) was reinforced by the 3d
Tank Battalion, County of London Yeomanry.

The enemy changed his tactics from a slow advance
to a quick thrust. He attempted to achieve a strategical
success by driving a strong tank wedge forward. The
battle reached the climax when enemy units from the
main front and from the beachhead made contact. The
enemy now had a flanking position from which he could
attempt to roll up the front of the Tenth Army. At
the same time, the possibility existed that he would
capture Rome by attacking along the western slope of the
Albanese Mountains. Judging from the ships available
and the large reserves in North Africa, landings in
central and north Italy appeared possible.

C. Statistics

German losses: not reported. Guns destroyed:
1 field howitzer (15 cm) (by artillery fire), 4 assault guns
(by artillery fire).

Allied losses: 69 prisoners, 38 tanks put out of
commission, 2 airplanes downed; captured: 4 American command
and scout cars, 1 armored personnel carrier with equipment,
miscellaneous equipment.

SUMMARY

Prior to the landings, the first phase of the Anzio operation appeared pre-determined for the defender, by depleting the coastal area of Rome, while the first days after the landings were decisive for the Allies. All engagements thereafter, were the result of the above fact.

After the Allies had successfully invaded southern Italy, the main task of the German High Command was to prevent Allied advances by defending on a stabilized defensive front, since the German forces were not numerous enough to eliminate the Allies from the Italian mainland. This was accomplished, until the beginning of 1944, by means of the Gaeta - Ortona line (Bernhard or Gustav Position).

As continued attacks against this line promised little success for the Allies, the German High Command believed that Allied tactics would have to change and amphibious moves be planned. It was believed that these landings were intended to cut the supply lines of the German Tenth Army and neutralize the Bernhard position. Due to the small number of German troops in Italy, successful enemy landings, supported by intensified Allied attacks against the southern front, could have created a critical situation. The Allies had apparently recognized this and prepared for a landing, by attacks at the Garigliano River. It was believed that the immediate Allied intentions were to break through at the Garigliano, but to pin down German frontline units and draw German reserves forward. A break-through of the Bernhard position was only to be expected in conjunction with a successful amphibious operation against the weakened German rear areas.

This danger was recognized by the German High Command. Therefore, at the beginning of the Allied offensive on 18 January, Army Group C intended to reinforce the Garigliano front, without weakening the coastal defenses of central and upper Italy. Allied tactics simplified the task of Army Group. When only the US Fifth Army attacked in the sector south of Cassino on 18 January, the Germans were able to withdraw and transfer troops from the sector of the British Eighth Army, to reinforce the Cassino sector. The German High Command made the error of not transferring a maximum of forces at the outset of the offensive, but delayed until the situation became grave and the Allies threatened with a break-through on the Garigliano. To prevent this, all readily available German forces in the area of Rome and its coastal sector had to be committed.

As a result, the Allied success in the offensive south of Cassino was not only established, but increased in scope. Army Group C was compelled to commit all its troops along the defense line, including the reserves. It was also forced to relieve its units from the coast defenses west of Rome as reinforcements for the south. This created the favorable vacuum for successful Allied landings at Anzio.

The VI Army Corps (US) encountered no organized resistance, during the landings on 22 January, as there had been no leakage of the plans for the intended landing and, consequently, the German coastal defense forces were not alerted. The Allies landed during the night of the 21 to 22 January, and formed several small bridgeheads which were consolidated and expanded during the 22 January. The following two days, the beachhead forces did not attack, but concentrated on landing further reinforcements and securing the beachhead.

Due to this stand-still by the invading forces, the supply
lines of Tenth Army remained open, and neither the highways
leading south from Rome nor the Albanese Mountains were denied
to the Germans. It appeared to the German Command that Allied
plans did not contain a precise time-table for an assault against
these objectives, but made this attack dependent on the strength
of the German defending forces.

During the first two days after the landing, the Allies
appeared to make a critical error, in that they did not exploit
the weakness of the German defense by immediately extending the
beachhead on a strategic plane, even though this may have been
contrary to the original plans. The German Command realized that
the loss of the Albanese Mountains or the City of Rome would
have led to an Allied break-through on the southern front.

The fact that the Allies did not immediately exploit this
favorable situation on the beachhead determined the German course
for the entire operation and made it possible for Army Group C to
build a stabilized defensive line on the beachhead until 24 January. Later German reinforcements could be brought up as the
attacks of the US Fifth Army south of Cassino diminished. This
allowed for a release of reserves in this area to the Anzio
sector.

After conclusion of the first phase of the landings, the
German Command considered that neither the attacking Allied
forces nor the defending German forces obtained complete success.
The Allies did not reach their strategic objectives, and the
Germans did not succeed in preventing the landings or in eliminating the Allied Forces before they had established their
positions. By 25 January, both sides had built a stabilized
front line. Thus the beachhead became practically an extension
of the southern front. The battles of the following weeks and
months were fought in accordance with the original objectives
on both sides: the Allies to make a break-through from the
beachhead in a northernly and northeasternly direction, and the
Germans to eliminate the beachhead.

German operations depended on the condition of the terrain
and on the weather. For these reasons, German counterattacks
could only be made in the Aprilia sector, or from the area of
Cisterna, during a period of bad weather when the Allied airforce
and Naval artillery were less effective.

The opportunities for success, during this time, seemed
quite feasible, since the Allied forces on the beachhead appeared
not too strong. The German High Command did plan an attack for
28 January, from the area of Aprilia, to split the beachhead.
However, the concentration of German troops was delayed, because
reinforcements for the attack from upper Italy, France, and
Germany did not arrive in time, due to demolished railroads and
highways. The German High Command then had to postpone the attack
until 1 February. This plan was upset by the Allied attack on
30 January, which began in the area of Aprilia and resulted in a
deep penetration into the German defensive front. The German
High Command was forced to eliminate this penetration and gain
positions for a new counterattack. The penetration was eliminated by 9 February. During the following days, the Germans
prepared a new large-scale attack which, depending on weather
conditions, was scheduled for 15 February.

The attack, favored by good weather, began on 16 February.
On 17 February, Highway 82 across the beachhead was traversed
between Fta Campodi Carne and Cle Tre di Padigliones. It was the

opinion of the German High Command that the development of this
attack would create a crisis on the Allied side, this, if properly
exploited, could lead to a complete German success. Fourteenth
Army, however uncertain, whether sufficiently deep penetrations
in the Allied line had been made, by the evening of the second
day of the attack, did not commit its available reserves at that
time. In addition, the terrain was not suitable for tank employment as had been presumed. Fourteenth Army, having no faith in the
possible success of a break-through without supporting tanks, held
back its reserves. This decision brought the attack to a standstill
on 18 February, and the final success appeared to be in no proportion to the strength committed.

As a result of these experiences, Army Group C abandoned the
original plan of eliminating the Allied beachhead by an all-out,
large-scale attack. The revised intentions were to reduce the
beachhead by limited attacks against smaller objectives. The
German artillery, concentrated around the beachhead, was to interfere with Allied concentrations, which might be preparing for a
major attack. With these tactics, the German High Command hoped
that the Allies would evacuate the beachhead as soon as they realized
a further strategic extension could not be executed.

The first German offensive, under these plans, was made on
29 February, from the area of Cisterna with the Astura as
the primary objective. A secondary and more strategic action was
envisaged if the attack were successful. However, unfavorable
terrain for tanks due to weather, halted the assault. Later
German counterattacks of this type were of smaller scope, because
of the strong local reactions of the Allies, and the situation on
the Tenth Army front rarely permitted the concentration of strong
German assault forces in the Anzio sector.

As a result the Allies, in the months that followed, were
unable to enlarge the beachhead to any extent, while Fourteenth
Army was not able to eliminate it. Only in the latter part of May,
were the Allies able to break through the German defensive front
on the beachhead, and reach their original objectives. The German
High Command did not believe that this success resulted from
engagements on the beachhead, but rather from the effects of the
successful Allied offensive against the southern flank of Tenth
Army, causing a collapse of the German defensive front south of
Cassino.

ANNEX I

Order of Battle of German Divisions

Divisions	Type	Infantry* Regiments	Artillery Regiments	Fusilier or Rcn Battalions	(Panzer) Tank units	Antitank Battalions	Engineer Battalions	Antiaircraft units
1	Parachute	1, 3, 4	1	-	-	1	1	1
3	Pz. Gren.	8, 29	3	103 Rcn	103 Bn	3	3	-
4	Parachute	10, 11, 12	4	-	-	4	4	4
5	Mountain	85, 100	95	85 Rcn	-	95	95	-
8	Mountain	296, 297	1057	-	-	-	1057	-
15	Pz. Gren.	104, 115	33	115 Rcn	115 Rcn	33	33	315
16	SS-Pz. Gren.	35, 36	16	16 Rcn	16 Bn	16	16	16
26	Panzer	9, 67	93	26 Rcn	26 Regt	51	93	304
29	Pz. Gren.	15, 71	29	129 Rcn	129 Bn	29	29	313
44	Infantry	131, 132, 134	96	44 Füs	-	46	80	-
65	Infantry	145, 146, 147	165	65 Füs	165 Bn**	165	155	-
71	Infantry	191, 194, 211	171	71 Füs	-	171	171	171
90	Pz. Gren.	200, 361	190	190 Rcn	190 Bn**	90	190	293
92	Infantry	1059, 1060	192	92 Füs	-	192	192	-
94	Infantry	267, 274, 276	194	94 Füs	-	194	194	-
114**	Jäger	721, 741	661	114 Füs	-	114	114	-
162	Infantry	303, 314, 329	236	236 Füs	-	236	236	-
278	Infantry	992, 993, 994	278	278 Füs	-	278	278	-
305	Infantry	576, 577, 578	305	305 Füs	-	305	305	-
334	Infantry	754, 755, 756	334	334 Füs	-	334	334	-
356	Infantry	869, 870, 871	356	356 Füs	-	356	356	-
362	Infantry	954, 955, 956	362	362 Füs	-	362	362	-
715	Infantry	725, 735, 1028	671	715 Füs	-	715	715	-
"Hermann Göring"	Panzer	1, 2, "Hermann Göring"	1 "Hermann Göring"	1 Rcn	"Hermann Göring" Regt	1 "Hermann Göring"	1 "Hermann Göring"	-

The role that these divisions played during the Anzio campaign is defined in the preceding text. Since German Corps and Army units were constantly shifted in the course of the campaign, they are not included in this order of battle. The frequent regroupings are described in detail in the text.

* Under infantry regiments are included the parachute regiments of the parachute divisions, and the Panzer Grenadier regiments of the Panzer and Panzer Grenadier divisions.

** In these divisions the tank battalion has been replaced by an assault gun battalion.

*** This unit is composed mainly of "volunteers" from Soviet Central Asia. Its full designation is 162d Infantry Division (Turk).

Order of Battle of British Divisions

Inf Div	Inf Regt	Arty Regt	Engr Bn.	AT Bn	Rcn Bn	AAA Bn
1st	24 Gds, 2, 3	2, 19, 67	1	8	1	90
5th	13, 15, 17	9, 91, 156		53		
56th	167, 168, 169	64, 65, 113		67		100

British Units attached to Fifth Army:

24th, 78th, and 80th Artillery Regiments.
46th Royal Scots Greys (Armored Battalion)
6th Queen's Own Hussars (Armored Battalion)
6th Cheshire (Infantry Battalion)
2/VII Middlesex (Infantry Battalion)
1st Rifle Brigade
40th Marine Commando

Div	Regt	Arty Bn	Engr Bn	AT Bn	Rcn Bn
1st Armored	1, 13 (armd) 6	27, 68	16	701	81
3 d Inf	7, 15, 30	10,39,41,9	10	403	
34th Inf	133,135,168				
36th Inf					
45th Inf	157,179,180	159,160,171, 189		645	
82 d Airborne	325,326,504, 505, 509 (Parachute)				

US Units attached to Fifth Army:

1st Special Service Force Brigade
1st, 3 d, and 4th Ranger Battalions
36th Engineer Regiment
191st Armored Battalion
601st and 894th Antitank Battalion
751st Tank Battalion

ANNEX II

Germen tactical symbols

A. Unit symbols.

Army Group Headquarters

Army Headquarters

Corps Headquarters

Division Headquarters

Regimental Headquarters

Battalion

Company (infantry)

Company (Panzer)

Mountain (battalion)

Panzer or Armored (battalion)

Antitank (battalion)

Tank Destroyer (battalion)

Antiaircraft artillery (battalion)

Assault Gun (battalion)

Panzer Grenadier or armored infantry (division)

- 125 -

Engineer (battalion)

Artillery (battalion)

Reconnaissance (battalion)

Motorized (infantry battalion)

Parachute (battalion)

Air Force (battalion)

B. Tactical symbols

Main line of resistance

outposts

(battalion) in reserve

C. Symbols for tactical boundaries

Battalion boundary

Regimental boundary

Division boundary

Corps boundary

Army boundary

- 126

Description of German units

The following German units do not have corresponding Allied units. Therefore, the designation of these units has been left untranslated in the preceding text.

Jäger division: This type of division was originally designed for mountain and mobile warfare. It is equipped as a light infantry division, consisting of only two infantry regiments.

Panzer division: Consists of a Panzer (tank) regiment, two Panzer Grenadier regiments, a Panzer artillery regiment, a Panzer reconnaissance battalion, an antitank battalion which may be redesignated assault gun battalion, a Panzer engineer battalion, a Panzer signal battalion, an antiaircraft battalion, and services.

Panzer Grenadier division: Consists of two motorized infantry regiments to two battalions each, a motorized artillery regiment, a Panzer reconnaissance battalion, an engineer battalion, an antitank battalion, an antiaircraft battalion, a signal battalion, a tank battalion which is sometimes replaced by an assault gun battalion, and services.

Panzer Grenadier regiment: Consists of two battalions equipped with armored troop carriers, and two regimental support companies; the infantry howitzer company and the engineer company.

Füsilier battalion: Full designation: (Divisions-Füsilierbataillon). It performs both reconnaissance and infantry support functions in infantry divisions. Organization identical with that of infantry battalions, except that it has more mobility bicycles).

Description of German Armor

Type	Gun Armament		Weight short tons	Crew Men	Chassis	Remarks
Pz.III	5	cm	24.6	5		
Pz.IV	7.5	cm	26	5		
Pz.V "Panther"	7.5	cm	50	5		
Pz.VI "Tiger"	8.8	cm	62.75	5		
"Ferdinand" (later "Elephant")	8.8	cm	73	6	Tiger	tank destroyer
Assault Gun	7.5	cm	26.35	4	Pz.III	antitank as well as anti-personnel
Assault Howitzer	10.5	cm	25.8	4	Pz.III	antipersonnel
Assault Howitzer	15	cm	30.4	5	Pz.IV	"
"Hornet" (later "Rhinozeros")	8.8	cm	27	5	Pz.IV	tank destroyer

Remote Controlled Demolition Vehicles:

"Goliath" - line controlled demolition charge (length of wire 2000 yards); explosive charge 200 pounds, total weight 800 pounds; vehicle blows up when its demolition charge is set off.

"B IV" - radio controlled demolition vehicle; explosive charge 800 pounds; total weight 4.5 tons;

The B IV is driven under its own power to the line of departure near the target, usually an emplacement or pillbox. The control transmitter of the radio equipment, retained by the driver when he dismounts, is used to steer the vehicle to its destination. In contrast to the Goliath the B IV is not expendable, but deposits its load of explosive at the target and returns.